VIRGIN TERRITORY

The Story of Craig Virgin, America's Renaissance Runner

RANDY SHARER

Blackjack Road Publishing
Randy L. Sharer

Front cover photograph by Mark Shearman.

ISBN-13: 978-0-99650-651-9
LCCN: 2016915267

Distributed by Itasca Books

Printed in the United States of America

Contents

Introduction

"Everybody has a life cycle in sport."

— Craig Virgin

Did That Really Happen?

C raig Virgin is protective of his legacy as one of the greatest distance runners in American history. Even in his 60s, he's still feisty and competitive, but problematic knees, a surgically removed kidney and assorted detritus from a 1997 car crash and a 2004 fall on ice remind him he'll never break another record.

When he was breaking records, he did so at an astonishing rate. He became a high school legend in the early 1970s, winning his final 48 cross country races in a row, setting course records in 46. The two he failed to break, he already held. Many more records were to come, including the national high school record in the two-mile run, a mark previously held by the legendary Steve Prefontaine. Six years later, Craig broke Prefontaine's US record in the 10,000-meter run. In college, Craig won 29 of 33 cross country races, setting course records in 18. He remains the only US winner of the world cross country title, a crown he won twice. Among American-born runners, he became the first three-time Olympian in the 10K. Looking back, he views his career as if it happened to someone else.

"When I was in it, I was totally consumed by doing it," he said. "Years had to go by for me to appreciate what really happened."

What occurred was the result of talent and determination crossing paths with extreme optimism. Whether Craig's optimism reached the level of self-delusion will be for you to decide.

Even though Craig's exploits are fading from memory, he has some things working in his favor, namely the unforgettable times he left behind. As of 2016, he still holds the Illinois state meet cross country course record set in 1972, and no one has run the equivalent of his state track meet two-mile time from 1973.

Craig's career almost ended before it began. Born with a congenital urological disease, he was gravely ill as a child. Surgery corrected the problem . . . for a while.

Craig sidestepped death in 1997, five years after his retirement from elite racing, when his car collided with a wrong-way driver. He underwent 13 surgeries over the next 12 years. His fitness prior to the accident helped him survive, as did his penchant for withstanding pain.

Craig didn't die at the height of his success. That's a problem if you want to be remembered. As Craig said, "There are certain advantages when you die young and tragic. You are immortalized. Marilyn Monroe, James Dean, John Kennedy will never get old." The same goes for Steve Prefontaine, who died in a car crash at age 24.

As for Craig Virgin, he isn't getting any younger.

The last of Craig's four appearances on the cover of *Track & Field News* magazine was the June 1981 issue. (*Photo by Jeff Johnson*)

Chapter 1: Playing It Risky

*"There are moments of truth in every race . . .
sometimes several. How you react will determine
your destiny."*

— Craig Virgin

The cause seemed lost from the start. For one thing, Craig Virgin was a 24-year-old American in a footrace no American had ever won. For another, he'd suffered a leg injury a week earlier that had hampered his training. Great finishes, however, owe their memorability to the tension of adversity. Craig had been given a chance to be great—or instantly forgotten—in the March 9, 1980, International Association of Athletics Federations (IAAF) World Cross Country Championships in Paris. The race was the all-star game of distance running as it brought together the world's best from the mile to the marathon. Most entrants were older than Craig, but he'd been ahead of his time for years during a relentless march from 14-year-old prodigy to US Olympian.

Before the gun fired for the 7.2-mile (11,590-meter) event, the field of 190 antsy runners from 30 nations false started, negating Craig's excellent getaway. Officials controlled the runners with corralling ropes 150 meters out. When the gun went off again, Craig was facing the wrong way and fell. "I remember somebody grabbing me, and that kept me from going all the way down on my face," he said. "By the time I got my balance and took off, there was just a wall of humanity in front of me." It was enough to make Craig want to give up. He'd later describe his decision to forge ahead as the first of four "moments of truth" in that race.

The leaders passed the first uphill 800 meters at almost a four-minute-mile pace despite running on shaggy turf at the Longchamp Hippodrome, a famed horse-racing track. On the second of five laps, each of which measured 2,500 meters and included two sets of steeplechase barriers and a stack of wooden logs to hurdle, Nick Rose of Great Britain, the rival Craig respected more than any other, boldly set off to run away with the race. Craig, who began the second lap in 31st, swerved through traffic like a race car driver to climb into 25th. He could see the leader and recognized the loping stride of Rose, a Western Kentucky University alum who'd finished second to Craig in the 1975 NCAA (National Collegiate Athletic Association) cross country meet, but had beaten Craig in six other races since 1973.

If knowledge is power, then Craig's understanding of Rose as a man and a runner was indeed an asset. Craig knew Rose was a versatile tactician, who could win by setting the pace or by using his sub-four-minute-mile speed to finish with.

By the end of the second lap, Craig was ninth. At halfway, Rose still enjoyed a 70-meter lead over 1977 champion Leon Schots of Belgium. Even a collision with photographers on the second lap hadn't slowed Rose. Craig joined Schots and Aleksandr Antipov of the Soviet Union in the group chasing Rose on the third lap.

At that point, Craig had to weigh the pros and cons of drafting off others in the shelter of the chase pack versus setting off on his own to catch Rose. Craig's life to that point made the answer clear. He'd been inspired as a youngster by Frank Shorter's victory in the 1972 Olympic marathon, which didn't mean settling for second. Likewise, following in the footsteps and breaking the records of his hero, Steve Prefontaine, wouldn't allow Craig to play it safe. Ever since he'd begun running 11 years earlier and set his first national age-group record, Craig had been on a relentless path of improvement. While the careers of others were derailed by obstacles both physical and mental, Craig had survived to reach a second moment of truth. The rhetorical question he asked himself was, "Did I come 3,000 miles to run for second place or did I come 3,000 miles to try to win?"

Craig had to go.

On the fourth lap, he sliced Rose's lead from 40 meters to 20. With a lap left, Rose passed 10K in 29:25, but looked tired. He glanced over his shoulder and saw Craig's proximity. Rose reacted by surging, a discouraging sight for Craig. On the last backstretch, which featured a 400-meter incline that rose 10 meters, Craig was rejoined by Schots, Antipov and West German Hans-Jürgen Orthmann. "I forced myself to stay on their shoulder or a step ahead over the next half mile, and during that half mile, I was able to recover," Craig recalled of that third moment of truth.

Play-by-Play

With 900 to go, Rose dug deep, but the energy he sought had already been dispensed, a fact yet to be detected by the commentator on the British television broadcast. The transcript of his race descriptions should be read with a British accent as well as a gradually ascending vocal pitch and level of excitement.

Half a mile to go and the challenge is vanishing.

Virgin trying to get away. Orthmann trying to get away. Nick Rose will have none of it.

And the English that were here and were in the stands have gone down to the side of the track to cheer him on, the Bristol Boy.

And what a record it will be. American cross country champion. British cross country champion and, if he holds on to this lead, international and world cross country champion.

Look at that, it has closed once again. Virgin trying a burst. Nick Rose, head down. Orthmann leading the charge. The West German leading the charge now. Orthmann, who's got finishing speed.

This really is pulsating.

Orthmann of West Germany. Hans-Jürgen Orthmann, the 25-year-old, who beat us in indoor track and he's now closing the gap.

The commentary in Craig's mind told a different story. "When third and fourth place pulled up to me," he said, "I forced myself to run with them even though I wanted to give up and I was discouraged." He prayed for one more chance.

> And there is 500 meters to go and Nick Rose is getting tired.
> And Orthmann is coming on the charge and that is, Bobby, a tragedy for the man who has led so far. I can't remember West Germany ever winning this international race.
> Nick Rose, who's thrown down the gauntlet, cut out the pace, and Orthmann has closed on him and it's a tremendous finishing pace.
> And Virgin is closing, too.
> This is a magnificent finish.

Craig had run through his fatigue and recovered. He tried to gather himself for one last surge. The race had become a lung-blasting version of poker in which none of the players knew what hand the others held. "I knew I had to answer what they put down and then I had to lay down a card of my own and hopefully it was going to be the joker or the ace card, and that's how I played it," Craig said.

> Orthmann has got him in his sights. There is about 500 meters to go. Less than that, maybe 400 meters to go, and Orthmann is on his shoulder and Nick is looking tired.
> Oh, what a tragedy.
> And Orthmann, if he goes and continues to go, that will be the break point and Nick Rose has got to go with him. He must try and stay.
> Nick Rose, head rolling from side to side.
> The crowd absolutely lined with supporters here.
> Orthmann of West Germany with the finishing speed.
> Oh, and it's agony for Rose to watch this.
> They've got about 250 meters to go and a gap is growing and Virgin is closing on Nick Rose.

What a tragedy for the Bristol Boy.
Orthmann going away.
Virgin closing.
Orthmann of West Germany. Nick Rose. Craig
Virgin of America. The first three.
And there is not much between them now. This
could be the closest title.

Orthmann's attack on the last straightaway forced Craig to face a fourth and final "moment of truth." Should he answer the surge now or wait? Like all of his decisions that day, this one was made in a split second. "I just knew from my practice run the day before that it was just a touch too early and I let Orthmann do his thing," said Craig, who forced all negativity out of his mind. "I held off Antipov and Schots. None of us went with Orthmann when he made his move." Orthmann was no stranger to Craig, who'd lost to the West German in a 3K seven years earlier.

And Virgin is burning up and going past Nick Rose
and closing on Orthmann with 100 meters to go.
Orthmann has been overtaken on the inside.
Craig Virgin of America goes into the lead and
won't be overtaken. It's a unique American vic-
tory, I'm sure.
Nick Rose is third and it's America one, West
Germany two. Tragedy for Nick Rose of England.

The Double V

With 350 meters left, Orthmann, wearing a white cyclist's cap, had lifted his stride and taken the lead, but he'd moved too soon. "Whether it's sports, business or love, timing is everything," Craig said. "I timed that last half lap better than anybody else." As Orthmann glanced over his left shoulder, Craig passed on the right. He sprinted through the finish chute and lifted his hands to make a pair of peace signs. "It was not peace at all," he noted. "It was Winston Churchill's

V for victory. I had two Vs, one for Virgin and one for victory, and that became my signature salutation for many races to come."

Craig called his kick that day one of the best of his career. His time was 37 minutes, 1.1 seconds, which was 1.2 seconds better than Orthmann and 4.7 ahead of Rose. Those closest among the 25,000 spectators mobbed Craig, making him feel, at least for a moment, like a rock star. He'd helped the United States place second, one of five runner-up efforts he'd be part of. Rose's English squad won with 100 points, 63 ahead of the Americans.

The race reminded Rose of the 1973 NCAA meet when he'd lost an 80-yard lead to Steve Prefontaine. "People will say if I'd started slower I'd have won," Rose told Kenny Moore of *Sports Illustrated*, "but if I'd started slower it wouldn't be me." When contacted 29 years later, Rose maintained, "That's the way I ran. I just went out there without intention. I felt good and took it on. It's unfortunate it was a very, very long finishing straight. It seemed like, gosh, the end of a marathon. Craig hung back and his timing was spot on."

In a 2003 book, *The Toughest Race in the World—a Look at 30 Years of the IAAF World Cross Country Championships*, the account of the 1980 race notes Rose admitted "that he had lost count of the laps and thought there was only one lap remaining when in fact there were two." The same claim was made by Rose's former Western Kentucky University teammate, Swag Hartel, who said, "He got to the end of the fourth lap and he found out he had to go another lap. Nick is not the kind of guy to make excuses, but he thought he had the race won." When contacted in 2010, Rose insisted he hadn't miscounted. "I knew how many laps it was," he said. "I can't take anything away from Craig. He's a worthy champion and he won the race on the day and well done to him."

The bottom line was a 24-year-old farm boy from tiny Lebanon, Illinois, had proven American distance runners could beat the best in the world. History, however, has shown all he really proved was that *he* could. Through 2016, no other American man had become World Cross Country champion. To this day, while working as a professional speaker, Craig shows the video of that 1980 race. Each time, his sprint finish causes the audience to erupt in applause as if the race had just finished. "There are moments of truth in every race," he tells them. "I had several in that race where, thank God, I made the right decision rather than giving in to discouragement and frustration."

Craig timed his final sprint to perfection against West Germany's Hans-Jürgen Orthmann to win the 1980 World Cross Country Championships at Paris. (*Photo by Mark Shearman*)

Medical Detectives

Craig's victory in Paris cemented his position on the world stage. World-class athletes are thought to be perfect physical specimens. Yet, as previously noted, Craig was far from perfect when he came into the world on August 2, 1955. He was born with a congenitally enlarged ureter known as a megaloureter. The condition allowed urine to flush back into his kidneys, causing frequent infections. His condition was fairly rare. Out of every 500 births, one child has some congenital anomaly of the kidney and urinary tract. A doctor in 1982 described the appearance of Craig's kidneys as "very bizarre, but they have good function and he should be able to keep them."

Fortunately for Craig, medical science helped manage his condition long enough for him to become a world-class runner. It took some savvy detective work by doctors in 1960 to figure out what was wrong when a five-year-old Craig awoke from a kindergarten class nap seriously ill. The doctors' first guess was appendicitis. As Craig was prepared for an appendectomy, a doctor noticed blood in Craig's urine. The surgery was canceled as he underwent more testing, which pointed to a urological problem. Reconstructive surgery was scheduled just before Valentine's Day. His kindergarten classmates all sent valentines.

Within a year of that first surgery, it was clear it had failed to permanently stop the reflux and frequent kidney infections. Dr. Stuart Mauch was experienced, but he'd never seen a condition like Craig's. To the Virgins' shock, their family physician said that Craig's kidneys were so damaged by all the infections, it was unlikely Craig would live past age 18. That information—or exaggeration as it would later be determined—would appear in feature stories about Craig his entire career. The news rightfully caused his parents tearful anguish. Saving the day was Dr. William Mellick, a urologist at Cardinal Glennon Children's Hospital in St. Louis, who took over Craig's case and kept him alive for eight years with a sulfonamide antibiotic known as Gantrisin, which battled bacteria in the kidneys.

Craig took half a pill in the morning and half at night until he needed to have a second reconstructive surgery at age 13. In the meantime he dealt with chronic infections. On a good day, he would feel a "low ember burn." On a bad day, he'd have to be on the lookout for symptoms because he only had 24 to 48 hours to reach a hospital for intravenous antibiotic therapy before the burn turned "white hot." Between the first surgery and the second seven years later, he was hospitalized half a dozen times.

The second surgery in 1968 involved a new technique for reattaching the ureter, the tube that carries urine from the kidney to the bladder. The technique involved "sewing" the ureter through the bladder wall. Craig was sent home from the hospital and for the next 60 days had a bladder drain tube coming out of his abdomen. The tube funneled urine into a bag attached to his leg, not exactly the preferred accessory for a self-conscious eighth-grader.

Eleven years later, Craig's mother, Lorna Lee, told Amby Burfoot of *Runner's World* that "the teachers let him go to the bathroom alone when no one else was there, and lectured the other kids on how to react." The procedure restored 70 percent of the function to the damaged kidney. "He never really had to be sheltered," his mother told the *Belleville News-Democrat* in 1973. Doctors told Craig's family he was free to enjoy any activity except contact sports such as football.

Craig's second surgery around Thanksgiving of 1968 meant he went from being a member of the Lebanon Grade School basketball team to temporarily being its manager, but that job got interrupted. "In the middle of a Christmas Tournament game, suddenly I had this urge [to urinate]," he remembered. "I said, 'I'm not supposed to have this feeling.' The tube was plugged up." A doctor, without using anesthesia, replaced the tube with a new one. For the next month, Craig had to consume an inordinate amount of cranberry juice every day to regulate the acidity of his urine. The second operation came eight months before he began his running career on August 3, 1969, a day after his 14th birthday.

Pain Tolerance

Repairing the male urinary tract circa 1960 to 1969 was problematic and painful. In Craig's case, a trip to the hospital meant an intravenous pyelogram, or IVP, was in his near future. An IVP delivers dye so X-rays can be read. To receive an IVP meant you had to be catheterized. Craig used his mind to set aside the agony of painful procedures. Catheter pain was the worst. "When the infection would get out of control, I would only have a few hours before I was in a fever and then the shakes," he said. "If it went far enough, nausea would come in." As he said in Marc Bloom's book, *Run with the Champions*, "The discomforts I suffered as a youngster taught me to disassociate from pain."

It's a prerequisite that distance runners listen to their bodies. If they don't, a hot early pace can make for an agonizing finish. Likewise, a minor injury can turn into a major headache. By the time Craig's running career began, he was adept at listening to his body or, when necessary, disengaging from it.

"After the second operation," Craig recalled, "I thought things were under control and the problem would be all right." That was wishful thinking. A stone was discovered in Craig's right kidney in 1981 when he was 26. In August of 1983, the stone was removed. In 1994, his right kidney was removed, an event he blames—along with a 1997 auto accident—for short-circuiting what he hoped would be a successful age 40-and-over running career. One kidney couldn't quickly filter all the lactic acid produced by running.

Craig's surviving left kidney is more than three times the size of a normal kidney, giving him almost the same filtering capacity as those with two kidneys. He keeps an eye out for any symptoms of kidney trouble. As he said, "I now have no backup." If he has symptoms, he visits a urologist pronto. When he has annual blood tests, they check his creatine level, which could indicate a problem. Doctors don't anticipate further issues, but he must be monitored for life.

Some parents whose children have medical histories such as Craig's might have been leery about allowing them to participate in something as taxing as distance running. Craig's were not. He seemed healthy after the second operation so there was no reason to be overly protective. Looking back, he appreciates being treated like a normal kid.

Craig isn't convinced perfect kidneys would have made him a better runner. He admits they may have better filtered lactic acid and other waste from his bloodstream and thus boosted his performance. "On the other hand," he said, "had I not gone through that experience in my youth with infections and having to learn to monitor my body, and then having to learn to disassociate from the pain of medical procedures or the pain when I got really infected, would I have acquired the skills to run through the pain that I did later on in my athletic career? I don't know."

Meet the Parents

Craig's father, Vernon, grew up south of Lebanon, Illinois. (Craig was raised on a farm a few miles north of Lebanon.) Vernon's father, Charles Virgin, was a row crop and dairy farmer who also peddled eggs and garden vegetables. In 1915, the 21-year-old Charles married 19-year-old Grace Muck, who was born in the same farmhouse south of Lebanon where she'd die in 1972. Charles and Grace met at a dance back when it took a horse and buggy to get there.

Vernon would grow to match Charles's work ethic and take it to another level. As a young man, Vernon channeled his intensity into farming. Beginning in the 1960s, he also ran a livestock equipment distributorship while Lorna Lee handled the bookkeeping. She also worked as a school teacher.

Vernon was the youngest of five children and Lorna Lee was the oldest of five sisters. She was born in northeast Indiana near Fort Wayne. Her parents, Dwight and Rachel Putt, moved to Lebanon during World War II so her father could teach at nearby Scott Air Force Base where all Army Air Corps radio operators trained. Rachel was a homemaker, as was Grace. Both grandmothers kept a tinful of cookies on the counter for their grandchildren.

Lorna Lee was "book smart," graduating at age 19 from Washington University in St. Louis in just three years and one summer. If Craig got his intensity from "common-sense smart" Vernon, he got his knack for organizing disciplined training schedules from his mother. Both parents contributed to Craig's slender build. In their wedding photo, "they look like two toothpicks," according to Craig's brother, Brent. The 21-year-old Vernon appears to weigh about 125 pounds and 19-year-old Lorna Lee less than 100.

A popular story in Virgin family lore is that Lorna Lee met Vernon in a Lebanon High School typing class. For a lesson on correct posture, students had to balance a coin on the back of their hands as their fingers touched the keys. Lorna Lee didn't have any coins so Vernon loaned her some, an act that would alter the fabric of American distance running forever.

Chapter 2: Being Discovered

*"Nobody had quite figured out what was
ahead of me."*

— *Craig Virgin*

Kids growing up in Lebanon, an integrated community of 5,523, feel the social pull of St. Louis 30 miles to the west. They have the best of both worlds: the excitement of the big city and the everybody-knows-everybody support of a small town. Downtown Lebanon, all five blocks of it, sits atop a ridge three miles south of the farmhouse where Craig grew up. Illinois Route 4 separates the east side of town from the west while Route 50 jabs in from the east before glancing off toward O'Fallon, seven miles to the west.

Surrounded by farms, Lebanon is held together by a row of old Victorian buildings made of brick and still sporting mansard roofs. Several second-floor porches are decorated with iron grill-work. Wood awnings supported by poles look weary from their long task of protecting the sidewalks. It all appears like a Walt Disney replica of idyllic Americana. The town motto in the 1980s was "A Past to Remember—a Future to Mold." It could have been Craig's motto, too.

When Jack Shepard, the high school boys' statistician for *Track & Field News*, attended the 1997 National Junior Championships in Edwardsville, Illinois, he made a special side trip to Lebanon. "I slowed the car to well under the speed limit and still traversed Lebanon's main street from one end to the other in about a minute," Shepard recalled a dozen years later. "I still remember how the few buildings of the town hugged the top of a low ridge surrounded by relatively flat farmland. Without having done any research, I sometimes think it may be the smallest town to have had a national record holder in track and field."

The record-holder-to-be wasn't discovered on the track, but on the basketball court. He first went out for basketball in sixth grade, but a lack of height, weight, coordination and confidence were problematic. He often rode the bench until giving up the sport after his ninth-grade season. "I'm still finding splinters in my butt from those four years," laughed Craig decades later. He rode a lot of school buses in those grade school years, passing the time by reading sports novels. He remembered one involved a kid winning a scholarship to a state university. The idea stuck with him even though he couldn't tell if it would happen for him.

In eighth grade, Craig aspired to be the starting point guard for first-year coach Rich Neal, who noticed Craig's times sprinting a third-of-a-mile loop around the school's athletic field compared favorably to those of high school players. Those one-lap times weren't good by accident. Craig figured if he won every running drill, which he did, he'd be less likely to get cut from the team. Neal suggested to Craig's father that Craig give cross country a try when he got to high school. "What Coach Neal was kind enough not to say is that 'he's not very good in basketball,'" Craig said. "I owe him a lot."

Craig's childhood also included softball, baseball, trombone lessons and regular visits to the United Methodist Church in Lebanon. He was so pigeon toed he began wearing corrective shoes in third grade. He started wearing glasses in sixth grade. In seventh, he had four teeth removed and $1,000 worth of braces put on to push back two protruding upper front teeth. He played baseball for six years ending in eighth grade. "I loved baseball," Craig said. "It was my favorite sport." His baseball dreams orbited the idea of one day playing for the nearby St. Louis Cardinals. He'd listen to Cardinals games on his first transistor radio, a birthday gift from his aunt Charlene. He put the radio under his pillow at night and let legendary broadcasters Harry Caray and Jack Buck help him fight off sleep for as long as they could.

Craig's first trophy for running came from stealing bases. He was good enough in sixth grade to start for his junior high squad, which included seventh and eighth graders. A leadoff hitter, he led his team in stolen bases in seventh and eighth grades. His other strengths were fielding and throwing. The right-handed batter couldn't hit for power, but he could spray singles and doubles to all fields. If he had trouble hitting a certain pitcher, he would bunt. "I think he hit around .315," Neal told a newspaper years later. "But what I remember most about him was hitting infield practice with a fungo bat. I'd hit them hard, too hard I thought. But he'd just want me to hit them harder. I couldn't hit them hard enough to keep him happy."

Accepting the dangerous challenge of fielding wicked grounders was an act of bravery Craig duplicated in the batters' box. He wanted to get on base so badly he was willing to crowd the plate so he could get hit by a pitch. At the time, no one could've guessed how far his willingness to absorb pain would take him. He loved baseball, but distance running would love him more.

First Practice

The events of Craig's first high school cross country practice would appear in almost every newspaper and magazine story about him for the rest of his career. He arrived at practice wearing a junior high physical education T-shirt, shorts, knee socks and Chuck Taylor Converse All-Star high-top canvas basketball shoes. Coach Hank Feldt's workout that day consisted of 15 laps on a third-of-a-mile loop behind the school for a total of five miles. "I took off and the seniors probably laughed at me because I went to the front and I pushed the pace and quickly separated from everybody within a lap or two," Craig said. Teammates waited for him to die, but he didn't. Every time he lapped someone, Feldt's eyes grew wider. Craig eventually lapped the entire team.

Craig continued to beat the varsity runners for five days. On the sixth day, he awoke so stiff and sore he decided to quit and go out for fall baseball. Feldt's understated response was: "I would like to have you here, but if you want to play baseball, you go ahead and play baseball. Don't let me influence you. You're not going to make me mad or anything like that." When Craig saw he wasn't going to beat out a senior for the starting job at second base, he asked to return to cross country, at least for one season. The welcome mat was out and Craig's destiny was back on track.

Craig's first race in August of 1969 was a dual meet at Lebanon's Horner Park against Mascoutah. The prerace favorite was Mascoutah's Steve Watson. Craig's father, who'd been a miler in high school, suggested his son start slow and work his way to the front. A side stitch, the first and last of Craig's running career, frustrated him the first mile of the 2.75-mile race, but then he started passing people. He passed them all to win, but never saw Watson, who was forced to take a restroom break during the race behind a tree. That race taught Craig a lesson he never forgot: Mother Nature can't be fooled, so take care of business before the gun goes off.

As he would later, Craig combined running with other projects. That project in November of 1969 was an essay for a freshman English class. The essay, which received an A- from Mrs. Norris, was entitled "Running Cross-Country is Fun." Only two pages survive, but they provide a fascinating glimpse into the racing mind of a future champion:

> My essay is about what a cross-country runner feels and thinks about when he runs a race. I will now put you in his place.
>
> First of all when you step out of the bus and walk the course you feel a pride in your team and school. Then you begin feeling a slight uneasiness gnawing in the pit of your stomach.
>
> When you warm up and step up to the starting line you really get nervous; you wish the butterflies in your stomach would settle down. Then the starter asks if there are any questions and then gives a three-count start. It seems like he is torturing you with the long interval between "ready" and the sound of the gun. You feel like screaming out but then the gun goes off and you are caught in a mass of humanity streaking for the first pole [marking a turn].
>
> Your first instinct is to try to be up in front but usually you see some wise guy sprinting too hard for

the first quarter mile when in reality the course is 2.75 miles long. You look up and wonder if one of these boys is going to beat you today and the team will lose.

On the first mile the pace is awful. You begin to feel the first signs of physical exhaustion. After this first mile you can pretty well separate the "men from the boys" or the real contenders from the short sprinters. Your breath will start coming hard now and your legs start to feel a little heavy and you look and think that there must be a million miles to the finishing chute. You now wonder what made you come out for cross-country.

If you are not one of the faster starters, you will have to pass on the average of four to twelve men from the starting line to the finish to get first place. You must concentrate on your stride and try to keep up your original pace. You concentrate on one man at a time, always watching his feet until you pass him and start on the next man. Now is where you will need all the stamina, speed, and courage . . .

That's where the story ends.

That fall, Craig won seven of 20 races, but no invitationals, before placing fourth in the district meet to qualify for the Centralia Sectional, a race that in retrospect was pivotal to his future. Prior to Centralia, his tactic of starting conservatively and passing people had proven successful on courses where passing was easy. However, half of Centralia's Foundation Park course was on narrow paths through woods where passing was difficult. Craig got stuck in traffic and wound up 10th, three places from advancing to the state meet. As he remembered, "It was really devastating to me both physically and emotionally."

After that, Craig became a front runner.

Coach Feldt

Hank Feldt, whose specialties were baseball and basketball, had only been coaching cross country for two years when Craig Virgin came along. A cross country runner himself in high school, Feldt took an easygoing, yet no-nonsense approach that demanded things be done correctly. He became a construction worker after graduating from Mascoutah High School in 1951. Three years of military service followed before he enrolled at McKendree College in Lebanon to become an educator.

Despite being new to cross country coaching, Feldt knew more than a little about improving endurance, having taken two graduate courses from famed Indiana University swim coach Doc Counsilman, who coached nine-time Olympic gold medalist Mark Spitz among others. Counsilman's system touted interval and over-distance training. In workouts, Feldt demanded a lot, not as much as some coaches, but clearly enough to create a national record holder.

Craig came to believe whatever Feldt lacked in distance-running knowledge he made up for by being committed to Craig. "He helped me any way he could," Craig said. One important way was keeping the media apprised of Craig's exploits. For sportswriters, Feldt was a quote machine. Among his gems was this morsel to the *Belleville News-Democrat*: "If I'd ordered a runner and given them the specifications, I don't think I would have gotten a Craig Virgin because I would have forgotten something."

Feldt started the cross country program in 1967 and was head coach for six years. His teams won three conference and district titles, always aided by Craig's one-point contribution to the team score. Feldt served as Lebanon's athletic director for 30 years until he stepped down in 1992. He stayed on as girls' softball coach until 2013.

Feldt's influence on the cross country program lingered. Ira Price coached the 1975 cross country team to fifth in the state meet, the last year it was a single-class affair. In 1976, the first year of a two-class system, the Greyhounds won the small-school division. After the last of Feldt's former runners graduated, Lebanon qualified for eight more state meets, but never placed higher than seventh. His 13 years as track coach featured three conference and district titles to go with four top-10 state finishes.

When it came to coaching Craig, Feldt's philosophy was don't fix something that isn't broken. "Most coaches, when they get a little bit of success, they want to overcoach," Feldt said. "They really want to be a part of it." He just wanted to keep the train on the tracks. Craig was among the few runners Feldt had to rein in. Feldt was willing to collaborate with Craig in designing workouts, especially later in Craig's high school career. Such an athlete-coach relationship was unusual in those days when many coaches were dictators. The possibility a dictator could ignore feedback from a runner would always seem illogical to Craig.

Once Craig gained national prominence, Feldt marveled at how soon others considered him an expert. At one point he was invited to a California clinic where he expected to instruct junior high and high school coaches. He walked in to find college coaches such as Oregon's Bill Dellinger, Indiana's Sam Bell and Illinois' Gary Wieneke. "I'm thinking, 'You've got to be kidding me,'" Feldt said.

Track's Return

As the 1969–70 basketball season wound down, Feldt informed Craig the track program was being resurrected even though the school didn't have a track. Feldt told Craig he could be good. Craig said he'd give it a try.

After two weeks of training, the 5-foot-8, 130-pound Craig made his track debut on cinders at Mascoutah, placing second in the two-mile run in 10 minutes, 7 seconds. Later in the 1970 state meet at Champaign, his two-mile time of 9:31.9 was good enough to place seventh overall. It was the fastest an Illinois ninth-grader had ever run, but he missed the national freshman class record of 9:22.6 set by Mike Hann of Benson High in Portland, Oregon, in 1966. "That first record was my seed, my motivation," Craig told a reporter. "After that I didn't want to be mediocre at anything."

Other kids wanted success, too, and resented it being handed to Craig with what appeared such ease. "I felt in high school that there were some kids who just couldn't be around me without feeling competitive," Craig recalled. "They had to prove they could beat me, or try to beat me. This extended into the classroom. A lot of people talk about coping with defeat. Well, there are just as many problems in coping with success." Feldt remembered a senior who expected to be Lebanon's top cross country runner Craig's freshman year. He'd trained for years and felt it was his turn to get headlines. "He resents Craig to this very day," Feldt said. "In fact, he hates his guts."

Craig's freshman year, crowded as it was with accomplishments, drew recruiting letters from colleges in the fall of 1970. While athletic history is littered with prodigies who failed to improve, fans of Craig Virgin hadn't seen anything yet.

Chapter 3: The Meteoric Rise

"Once you realize what you can do, you shoot for everything."

— Craig Virgin

With his name on the national radar—at least within the confined world of high school distance running—Craig entered his sophomore cross country season determined to dominate and dedicated to the training that required. During the summer, he ran five miles every other day, a shockingly small amount considering what he was about to accomplish. After reading Illinois' top prep distance runner, Dave Merrick, did morning runs, Craig added daily three-mile morning runs to his workout routine on October 1, 1970. Craig believed blood circulated by morning runs cleansed tissues damaged by the previous workout.

As the miles passed, Craig appreciated the beauty of the rolling hills and lush pastures surrounding his family's farm. "I love the seasons, seeing the life cycles of living things," he told a writer. "That's when I can see God's plan." Each season came with distinctive smells. There was the earthy aroma of rain marching across plowed fields, the fragrance of newly mown hay, the moldy resolve of fallen leaves and the pungency of livestock, known to farmers as the "smell of money." The entire tableau was held together by a latticework of roads that had no rules about how far or fast they could be traversed on foot.

As Craig's mileage climbed, he continued a practice he'd come up with on his own based on trial and error the previous year of running negative splits in training. No matter what the workout interval, he ran each repetition slightly faster than the one before. At first his time would drop a second or a half second. Eventually it would only be by a tenth or two, but he liked getting faster. He always would.

Craig didn't improve on each repetition just by trying harder. If he was doing 12 440-yard intervals, he'd use the first three to loosen up. From there he'd try to get faster by altering his biomechanics. He'd constantly adjust his foot plant, ankle pop, knee position, pelvis tilt and arm carriage. He maintained a passive facial expression while keeping his neck and shoulders relaxed. With three intervals left, he'd dip into his energy reserves to *gut out* the remaining time drops.

Another training trick Craig came up with by accident was jogging during recovery intervals. Whoever actually invented it, Craig didn't copy them. (Emil Zátopek of Czechoslovakia, the 1952 Olympic 5K, 10K and marathon champion, came up with his golden rule in 1948: Run intervals fast and try to recover during the movement itself.)

Newspaper photos of Craig taken immediately after races routinely captured him on the verge of collapse. "I was so naïve, I just ran to total exhaustion in practices and in meets," he said. "That was how I felt you had to do it."

After the fourth race of his sophomore cross country season, his all-out philosophy nearly had tragic consequences. That September 13 race was the Columbia Invitational, a 2.75-mile affair that became the first invitational Craig won. He did so by 12 seconds, clocking 13:08, an effort that left him mentally "out to lunch" after the race. On the way back to Lebanon, Feldt, as he often did, let the team off the bus four miles from school so they could run back for additional training. As Craig reached the highway next to the school, he looked right first. At the instant he looked left, a car zoomed past so close its mirror nearly snagged the pocket of his hooded sweatshirt. As he leapt back, Craig saw the car's passenger wearing a startled expression. "Sometimes my life has been a matter of timing," he said. "A second or two either direction might have yielded different results."

Craig was undefeated that fall of 1970 heading into the Illinois state meet. Newspapers billed it as a showdown between Craig and the established veteran, Dave Merrick, the defending champion from New Lenox Lincoln-Way. When Craig placed seventh in the state two-mile the previous spring in 9:31.9, Merrick had run in another heat to win in 8:58.0, taking eight seconds off the state meet record. He'd also won the mile in 4:07.4.

The importance of Merrick on Craig's view of what was possible can't be overstated. Merrick's high school times rivaled those of Steve Prefontaine, who set the national high school two-mile record of 8:41.5 in 1969. Looking back, it's amazing runners of Craig and Merrick's stature had the opportunity to race each other in high school. They competed in the same heats of meets four times. Those meetings showed Craig what it took to be great.

Merrick the Mentor

David Allen Merrick was born September 21, 1953, in Oak Park, Illinois. As a teenager, he wore glasses. Craig perceived him to be studious and dedicated. He was respectful to Craig and in no way condescending. In fact, he encouraged Craig. "He didn't give me the cold shoulder, but I would not call him gregarious," Craig said. "He was a bit of an introvert."

By the end of Merrick's freshman year, he'd run a 4:51 mile and a 10:00.1 two-mile. Within a year he was down to 4:24.0 and 9:17.8. By age 16, he'd reached 4:07.4 indoors and clocked a national age and class record of 8:56.6 outdoors. Heading into the fall of 1970, the 5-foot-10, 130-pound Merrick was the nation's best schoolboy runner. Craig was naïve enough to think Merrick could be beaten.

Merrick's coaches told him who the other state cross country challengers were and then they mentioned one more contender. "There's a wildcard factor from down south and that's Craig Virgin," Merrick was told, "because he has no idea he's not that good."

The race—held for the first time at Peoria's Detweiller Park— measured 2.75 miles. The starting line was on the lower, north end of the loop course. The next year, to transition to a three-mile race, the starting line would move to the south end, 30 feet higher in elevation. There was only one class so small schools competed against big ones.

Merrick's accomplishments had elevated him to the status of demigod in the minds of many. No one had come within 18 seconds of him all season. Craig viewed the confrontation—in front of a crowd estimated at 5,000—as a chance to prove he wasn't intimidated by anyone. Bravely, or perhaps foolishly, he wanted to push the early pace to pressure Merrick. "I had every dream and aspiration that I could beat him," Craig said.

Forty years later, Craig remembered staying with Merrick for about a mile and a quarter. Craig had never before started a race that fast. "I wanted to run by myself and just run my own pace," recalled Merrick, who began a long surge at the mile mark. When Craig was slow to respond, Merrick threw in another 60-second burst and found himself alone. With a mile to go, Craig battled for second. "I remember in the final 600 yards everybody but their grandmother passed me," said Craig, who wound up sixth in 13:04. "The bottom line was, I staggered into the chute and threw up. I was emotionally beaten. I was physically beaten. I couldn't walk. I couldn't talk." Merrick won in 12:37.6, taking nearly 20 seconds off the course record.

Decades later, Craig felt he could've finished second if he hadn't tried to win. He also believed he could've won if Merrick hadn't been there. "I believe that I was both lucky and unlucky," Craig said. "I was lucky in that he set the bar of excellence for me." After that race, it took Craig several weeks to recover emotionally. The turning point came when the educational value of defeat sank in. "I prefer to look at it as a positive that even though he beat me and even though by going out with him in cross country, I paid a terrible price that last 600 meters," Craig said, "in the end it probably helped shape me to the point where I could go for Pre's record two years later." After the 1970 state cross country meet, Craig vowed he'd do everything possible to avoid a similar disaster. He never lost another high school cross country race, winning the final 48 of his prep career.

A Nice Deal

Craig's state meet loss caused him to give up basketball so he could train year round. With Feldt coaching basketball, Craig was on his own for the next four months. As fate would have it, he lived only a mile south of the neighboring St. Jacob Triad school district where Richard "Dick" Conley coached. Between the cross country and outdoor track seasons, Conley took his athletes to road races and all-comer indoor track meets. Craig was invited to tag along. "It seemed our guys really took to him," Conley said. "They supported him and cheered him on when we were competing against him. He got to be good friends with a lot of my runners. It was kind of a nice deal, you know?"

It was especially nice for Craig, who'd been running in Bata Bullets and Converse shoes, which were basically scaled-down basketball shoes. They were a heavy combination of stiff rubber and canvas. Conley had read about Onitsuka Tiger shoes from Japan. They were lightweight and had blue nylon uppers. Conley ordered them from Chicago-based Dick Pond Athletics for his team and made sure a pair found their way to Craig, who never forgot the favor.

If it takes a village to raise a child, it took a succession of benefactors such as Merrick and Conley to help Craig progress. Literature about distance running was scarce in the early 1970s. Craig developed his own training program from information he could scrounge from other runners and coaches. "You just learn so much by talking with the runners that it's unbelievable," he told Bob Emig of the *Metro-East Journal* based in East St. Louis, Illinois. Even though Emig was just beginning his career in sports journalism, his writing shows he quickly realized Craig was a once-in-a-lifetime topic. When Craig soared, so did Emig, who deftly took his readers along for the ride. Over the course of four years, Craig and Emig became friends.

During study halls, Craig planned his training for the next week or two. He'd make changes based on how the training was affecting him as well as weather conditions. It made sense to him that hard training needed to include recovery days. He tried to have at least two hard interval days per week along with one day of fartlek, a Swedish word meaning speed play. He'd bundle up for after-school workouts of six to 10 miles on country roads. For interval workouts, he usually used a grass field near the school or sometimes used the service road around the school. He didn't know exactly how far each interval was, but he timed each one so he could compare it to the others. If he wanted rolling hills, he headed north and west. If he wanted a flatter course, he went south and east. He timed his workouts with a regular wristwatch. He didn't get one with a stopwatch function until college.

Craig opened the 1971 indoor track season on February 21 against Merrick on the oversized, 262-yard, unbanked track at the University of Illinois Armory in Champaign. The 17-year-old Merrick blitzed two miles in 8:43.2, a time that trailed only the 1964 clocking of 8:40.0 by Gerry Lindgren of Spokane, Washington, in indoor prep history. Still only a sophomore, Craig was fifth in a personal best of 9:14.5.

Two weeks later, Craig improved in another indoor meet at Champaign with a 9:05.4 to place third. Such meets were his first chance to race collegians and postcollegians. Among the older runners was the University of Wisconsin–Parkside's 27-year-old Lucien Rosa, a 103-pound barefoot runner from Ceylon (now Sri Lanka). An Olympian in 1972, Rosa would place fourth in the 1974 Boston Marathon. He wasn't the first nor the last of Craig's opponents to become his friend. For Rosa, that friendship included a two-week training visit at Craig's home in 1974. Even when Craig was just 15, Rosa could tell he was special. "I thought, 'He's capable of winning a medal at the Olympics,'" Rosa remembered.

Wave Runner

Craig's first big test outdoors came in the April 3 Alton Relays where he faced a 49-man field the *St. Louis Post-Dispatch* called the finest ever assembled in the St. Louis area. Among the stars was Missouri cross country champion Don Overton. Despite an ailing left foot, Craig set a pace Overton matched until the final 330 yards when Craig slipped away for a 9:16.7 to 9:21.7 victory. "That caused a few waves in St. Louis where they finally started to take me seriously," recalled Craig, who would've been faster if not for the lapped runners in his path.

Merrick and Craig met twice more in 1971 and the gap shrank each time. Their only regular-season duel came in the April 24 Orphan Relays in Centralia. A crowd of 2,000 was on hand when the two-mile started at night. Craig led the first lap and Merrick took the lead midway through the second lap. He hit the mile mark in 4:21 with Craig at 4:30. Merrick went on to win in 8:51.6, the fourth-best prep time outdoors ever, with Craig second in a national age-15 record of 9:12.6. The previous best by a 15-year-old was 9:13.2 by Ralph Gamez of Hayward, California, in 1963.

Craig lowered the age-15 record three more times—clocking 9:11.6 on May 2, 9:11.4 on May 5 and 9:02.6 on May 23—before meeting Merrick again on May 29 in front of 15,544, the largest crowd to ever watch a state meet at Champaign's Memorial Stadium. Craig became ill five days before the meet and had to go on antibiotics. He felt well enough on race day to take the early lead, covering the first 880 yards in 2:10 and the first mile in 4:24. He led for more than five laps, countering three surges by Merrick. With three laps to go, Merrick passed and got a surprise. "[Craig] looks over and says, 'How do I break nine minutes?'" remembered Merrick, whose reply was, "'Just keep on going,' which he did."

Merrick created a gap that earned him the victory in a meet record 8:48.9 while Craig sped 8:57.3, breaking the national record for sophomores of 9:06.2 set by Kasto Lopez of Sanger, California, in 1969. Through 2016, 8:57.3 remained the national record for 15-year-olds. Merrick said of Craig after the race, "He is 'Little Mr. Gut of Illinois.' I've never seen anyone like him."

Years later, Merrick was still struck by Craig's tenacity. He saw in Craig a "nothing ventured, nothing gained" attitude that didn't permit him to try for second, only first. "He was naïvely tenacious about how good he wanted to be and that reflected his personality," Merrick said. "He approached every race to get the most out of it and do the best he could." Craig explained his philosophy in a feature story by Bob Emig—the writer who covered Craig's prep years more closely than any other: "Once you realize what you can do," Craig said, "you shoot for everything."

Merrick appeared destined for Olympic glory, but his injury-plagued college years—first at the University of Pennsylvania, then Alabama, and finally back at Penn—made that impossible. His failure to dominate in college showed Craig how easily a prodigy could get sidetracked.

Merrick looked back on Craig's career wistfully. "I'm envious of his legs and staying healthy," Merrick admitted. "I would have loved the chance to stay healthy."

Chapter 4: Learning on the Job

"I like to throw a challenge at a guy then try to kill him off."

— Craig Virgin

In the summer of 1971, prior to his junior year of high school, Craig committed himself to training five miles every day at a sub-seven-minute-per-mile pace or quicker—sometimes with two dogs as company. His family hosted a constant stream of stray dogs, whose longevity, sadly, ranged from three days to three years depending on how soon they adapted to the dangers of Route 4. His love for dogs was such that many workouts were interrupted so he could make friends with farm dogs coming out to the road as he passed. He never tried to sprint away from a dog. "That generally means 'chase me,'" he said.

Craig's workouts, which included a mix of intervals and fartlek as he saw fit, were preceded by a full day of farmwork such as baling hay or driving a tractor to pull a cultivator, disc or chisel plow. This was before his family had tractors with air-conditioned cabs. The only sunblock was dust stuck to sweat. Most of Craig's training was done after 8 p.m. when it was cooler. "If anything, during night workouts you have a tendency to push your body too hard," he told the *Champaign News-Gazette.* "I kind of float into automatic at night."

With Merrick now graduated along with the others who'd beaten Craig in the 1970 state cross country meet, no one stood between him and his first state title. The Illinois High School Association lengthened the official race distance to a maximum of three miles, which proved an advantage for Craig. "He can run the same speed forever,"

Feldt told the *Metro-East Journal*. The fact Craig had a big engine in a small chassis didn't hurt. He'd inherited his father's long torso and narrow hips. Craig's pulse had been recorded as low as 47 beats per minute. (The pulse of an average teen is between 60 and 100 beats.) "When I was really fit, I could lie in bed and the bed would shake because of my heart beating in my chest," he said.

Feldt marveled at Craig's ability to recover from a hard race in only four or five minutes while others were still panting. "He's nothing but skin and bones and muscle," Feldt was quoted as saying. "He's thin through the shoulders, but barrel-chested, and his endurance is just unbelievable. I think he can be one of the great ones."

Craig's season-opening race and the first three-miler of his career came on September 2, 1971, in a dual meet at Okawville. He established a course record of 14:15, the first of 33 consecutive course records that wouldn't end until the 11th race of his senior season. His junior cross country campaign featured 23 races, which is a lot by today's standards. Most top high school programs in the 21st century race once a week, twice on rare occasions during a mid-August to November season. In races where the runner-up's time is known, Craig's average margin of victory that season was 64 seconds.

Craig took a 17-race winning streak into the October 16 Mattoon Invitational where he'd get a rare opportunity to race Chicago area athletes. He'd attended the 42-team Mattoon meet the previous year to watch Merrick win. They met briefly. "He didn't know me from Adam," recalled Craig, who considered Mattoon the most important race of the regular season. Exuberant meet organizers also thought it was important, calling the seventh annual race "The Nation's Greatest Interscholastic Running Spectacle." The event typically drew 2,000 spectators.

Craig told the *Mattoon Journal Gazette*, "It will be my first chance at running against some of the good boys from Northern Illinois. We're not recognized as having real good cross country down here in Southern Illinois." On race day, Craig felt lucky because upon arrival, the odometer in the rented van that brought him read 77,777.7. The winner would receive a giant trophy and a kiss from each member of the Mattoon cheerleading squad. Craig derived more motivation from the latter than the former.

The Battle of Mattoon

Craig's primary competition at Mattoon was Chicago Lane Tech's Larry Gnapp, who'd finished seventh in the 1970 state cross country meet, one place behind Craig. Gnapp's attitude was "I'm not going to let this little squirt get away from me." Craig's attitude was "stay with me if you dare." Gnapp's coach convinced him he could outkick Craig near the finish. Thirty-eight years later, Gnapp recalled, "The trick was staying with the guy." The pair dashed stubbornly through the first mile of the mostly paved 2.8-mile course in 4:21, the fastest opening mile Gnapp had run in a race longer than two miles. "I let it kind of freak me out," he said, "and that's the point, when I heard that time, I made a decision to kind of let him go and see if I could get him later." But there was no chance of that.

Lebanon High School's 1971 state-qualifying cross country team included, front row from left, Greg Smith (40) and Mike Wertz (32), second row from left, John Wertz, Craig, Dana Frisby (26) and Robert McKee (28), back row from left, Greg MacMinn, Rich Youngs, Ken Fohne and Joe Hohrein. (*Photo courtesy of Lebanon High School*)

Craig passed the two-mile mark in 9:21 and finished in 12:41, 150 yards ahead of Gnapp, who hung on for second, but just barely. Opponents were rarely close enough at the end of three-mile races to outkick Craig, but in races of a mile or less, Craig was vulnerable, a fact Gnapp would prove the following indoor track season. Mattoon was a landmark for Craig in that he signed his first autographs there.

Craig continued his course-record-setting ways in the November 6, 1971, state cross country meet at Peoria's Detweiller Park where it was 38 degrees at race time, but felt 10 degrees cooler because of a 15-mph northwest wind. The crowd of 6,000 included 41 of Craig's relatives. He'd lifted the sport's image to the point it was broadcast for the first time by a radio station, Belleville's WIBV. "He's got all of Southern Illinois behind him," announcer Joe May told the *Peoria Journal Star*. May called the race from a deer stand after having the phone company string a line to the course.

Craig grabbed the early lead in the three-mile race, passing the mile mark in 4:29. An Associated Press photo showed him passing the two-mile mark in 9:20 with Gnapp his nearest challenger. Gnapp faded to 14th as Craig stretched his advantage to 29.3 seconds and nearly 200 yards by the finish, clocking 13:59.3 to lop 50 seconds off the course record. The runner-up was Lee Erickson of New Lenox Lincoln-Way, Merrick's alma mater. It was the closest anyone came all season to Craig, who became the first runner from south of Interstate 70 to win in the meet's 26-year history.

Another AP photo shows Craig leaping across the finish with a wide grin, his arms overhead. A handkerchief is in his hand because he had a cold. The awards ceremony was at Peoria Central High School where Craig received a three-minute standing ovation from a crowd of 3,500. He told the *Peoria Journal Star*, "I could have chopped maybe 10 seconds off the time if I really ran hard at the finish, but I was running smoothly and I just felt so good." As a parting shot, he added, "You can always push yourself a little harder."

Legendary Elmhurst York coach Joe Newton, whose team won the fourth of what would become a record 28 state titles, said of Craig, "He's the finest runner ever to have run."

Indoor Improvements

The 1972 indoor track season saw Craig continue his pattern of starting each campaign faster than he'd ended the previous. His season opener, a February 12 meet in Champaign's Armory, saw him lower his two-mile best from 8:57.3 to 8:55.0. He came back four hours later to run a career-best mile of 4:13.3.

In another Champaign meet on March 4, Craig won the two-mile in a personal best of 8:54.1 and managed third in the mile in 4:14.6 after being knocked down with more than a lap to go. His indoor season came to an inglorious end at the Oak Park Relays on March 26. The track, measuring nine laps to the mile, was more square than oval and challenged Craig in two ways. It left him unsure of the distance remaining, and the corners interrupted his momentum. Fans could watch from a balcony, but infield curtains intermittently blocked the view. Part of the track also disappeared underneath a section of bleachers. Craig's opponents drew inspiration from a *Chicago Sun-Times* article that said the nation's best distance runner was entered. Gnapp thought, "That's crap. I'm better than he is, particularly at the mile."

Gnapp quickly fell 15 yards behind, but somewhere during the second quarter, he realized Craig was no longer pulling away. Among the things sabotaging Craig that day was his suicidal 2:01 opening 880 yards. "I died a slow death the last two quarters," said Craig, who didn't know how fast he was running until he heard the 2:01 split, but he held out hope he could hold on. With 600 to go, hope was replaced by fast-approaching rigor mortis. On the homestretch before the last lap, Gnapp motored past and went on to win by four seconds in 4:13.7. Jubilant teammates carried Gnapp off the track. "One of the highlights of my high school career was beating him in that meet," Gnapp said. "A lot of things came my way after that. I got invitations to the big post-season meets."

Craig vomited after that race and later learned he had the flu. The setback left him reeling, but he bounced back quickly, as was his custom. "I was definitely damaged emotionally, psychologically," said Craig, who worked out his frustrations at the next race, the Alton

Relays two-mile. He overcame snow and wind along with Missouri cross country champion Mark Kimball to run 9:07.6.

Conditions changed for the May 2 O'Fallon Relays, which were run under the lights. The asphalt-and-rubber Grasstex surface was hard, forcing Craig into racing flats instead of spikes. He blitzed the first mile in 4:23 while pounding out an outdoor career best of 8:55.1 to break Merrick's age-16 world record of 8:56.6. "I learned to love track meets that were held at night under the lights," said Craig, noting wind, heat and humidity often diminished after dusk.

Bloom's Frank Flores (left), like others who tried to stay with Craig, achieved good results, but at a painful price. After winning the two-mile run in the 1972 Illinois state meet at Charleston, Craig helped carry Flores off the track. *(Photo by David K. Neesley)*

After Craig's career was long over, he'd cite over-racing as a pitfall. A classic example occurred the final eight days of his 1972 scholastic track season when he contested three distance doubles and another mile race. He went into that slog coming off a bronchial infection. The first two races, a 9:05.6 two-mile and a 4:16.5 mile, advanced him from the Highland district meet to Charleston, the site of the 1972 state meet. Instead of resting after the Friday district meet,

Craig won a distance double on Monday in the Meet of Champions at Carbondale, clocking meet records of 9:01.1 and 4:14.8. The latter race turned into an exhausting battle with Centralia's Stan Vannier, who led late in the race, forcing Craig to produce a career-best 58-second last lap to win by half a second. That may have contributed to Craig having a cold heading into the state meet for the second straight year. With the benefit of hindsight, he conceded he and Feldt simply didn't know that much racing could be detrimental.

In Friday's state preliminaries, Craig got a rare opportunity to run a mile fresh. He took advantage by clocking a personal best of 4:13.2. The next day in the two-mile final, despite oppressive heat, he won by 17.6 seconds in an age-16 world record of 8:51.9. He was miffed he'd missed Merrick's meet record of 8:48.9. "I think I blew it on the first mile," Craig told Bob Leavitt of the *Peoria Journal Star*, who described Craig as a "ball of cherub-faced energy." Runner-up Frank Flores from Chicago Heights Bloom got sick after the race. In an early sign of his compassion, Craig helped carry Flores off the track.

Craig almost didn't return 90 minutes later for the mile final because of foot blisters he'd developed during the two-mile. He shrugged off the pain to grab the lead in the first 220 yards. As the gun-lap began, Hillside Proviso West's Jim Hurt edged in front, but Craig held on to the idea he had another gear, a gear he'd discovered earlier against Vannier at Carbondale. Craig tucked behind Hurt on the final curve and made a slingshot move into the lead on the homestretch, winning by 1.7 seconds over Hurt in a personal record of 4:09.2.

The sun-drenched crowd of 7,300 gave Craig a standing ovation after his 58.2-second final lap. "I knew I had the speed to break 4:10," he told the *St. Louis Post-Dispatch*, "and I wanted to do it badly. When I began hitting 58 seconds in my last quarters in practices before the state meet, I knew I could make it. It was no fluke." As Craig recounted his double triumph to reporters, his father recorded it all on his movie camera. Many at that point would've called it a season, but Craig knew the Russians were coming.

Cold War Weapon

Among the weapons of choice during the Cold War between the Soviet Union and the United States were dual track and field meets. In the summer of 1972, the USSR sent its junior (age-19-and-under) team for the first time to battle the United States at Sacramento, California. Craig faced a two-step process to become one of two American qualifiers in the 5,000-meter run. The first step was a three-mile race at the Central Amateur Athletic Union (AAU) meet in Chicago. (The AAU was track's national governing body at that time.) In the longest track race he'd yet run, he pressed all the way to a world age-16 and junior class record of 13:49.2. That qualified him for his first national meet on June 24 at Lakewood, Colorado, nestled in the Rocky Mountains. It would be Craig's first time running at altitude.

The field for the three-mile race in Lakewood was worthy of its national status. Among the entrants were Tony Sandoval, Paul Geis and Pat Mandera. The 18-year-old Sandoval, destined to win the 1980 US Olympic Trials marathon, was from Los Alamos, New Mexico, where the 7,300-foot elevation exceeded that of mile-high Lakewood. The 19-year-old Geis, who was in the process of transferring from Rice University to Oregon, came in with a best of 13:32.6 followed by the 19-year-old Mandera of Indiana University at 13:40.2 and 16-year-old Craig at 13:49.2. Moving up to face national competition didn't worry Craig, who knew how he measured up statistically. What he didn't know was how he'd react to the altitude.

After the gun, Craig took the lead as usual. Having grown up at 500 feet of altitude, he held on for six laps of the cinder track before running side by side with Sandoval another four. The lack of oxygen caught up to Craig on the 11th lap as Sandoval went on to win by 2.4 seconds ahead of Craig's 14:10.8. Geis took third in 14:11.6. "I was seeing spots the whole last lap," remembered Craig, whose pulse was still 150 beats per minute an hour later. "For some reason, they didn't have tanks of oxygen. The sports medicine at those meets was primitive compared to what they have today." The fact he'd made his first national team proved the pain was worthwhile.

Craig warmed up for the Russians by contesting his first 5,000-meter run in an AAU meet at Florissant, Missouri, on July 8. An age-16 world record of 14:12.3 indicated he was ready. He raced the Russians on July 29 in handmade spikes with enough of a heel to make them suitable for distance running. Holes had been drilled in the spike plates to reduce their weight. The new company that made the shoes colored the soles green and adorned each white nylon upper with a black swoosh on each side. "I believe those were the first pair of Nike spikes ever worn in international track and field competition," said Craig, who never got rid of those shoes. They'd been given to him by Nike's first promotions man, Geoff Hollister.

Craig came to realize runners needed three types of shoes: a training flat, a racing flat and a racing spike. He even liked to have two kinds of training flats, a heavier supportive pair for high mileage and a lighter flexible pair for fartlek or track intervals. "I regarded my shoes as both a tool and a weapon," said Craig, who believed if James Bond needed a gun for every situation, he needed a shoe for every purpose. "There was a spike for every kind of condition or surface I was going to run on," he said. "Because they were the weapons of my trade, I took good care of them. I cleaned them after every race. I stuffed them with newspaper. I kept them in a dry place." Craig's shoe-care regimen paid off during his career and again 40 years later when a collector paid him more than $5,000 for a rare model.

Soviet Teachers

The dual meet against the Russians allowed each country two entrants in each event. The 5,000 pitted Craig and Sandoval against Vladimir Zatonsky and Andrey Ipatov. Commentator Bill Toomey, the 1968 Olympic decathlon gold medalist, told a national television audience that Craig was "perhaps the kid who finally gives our American runners some class in team distance competition." In the previous day's 10,000, Craig noticed the Russians tucked behind the Americans before kicking to a 1–2 finish. "I planned my tactics for Saturday and I was determined to make them take the lead," Craig told the *St. Louis Post-Dispatch*.

Craig found himself in the lead on the first lap, but waved his right arm in an attempt to get the Russians to pass. He slowed dramatically, but a trailing Russian gave him a push that nearly sent him sprawling. Sandoval lost contact in the second mile, leaving Craig alone with the Russians entering the final lap. Ipatov passed first and then slowed. As Craig tried to pass with 120 meters left, Zatonsky boxed him in. Craig hoped to slingshot back in front coming off the final curve, which might've worked against a single foe. Against two, however, he remained boxed through the final turn and most of the homestretch. Craig thought his only chance was to pass on the inside. He was almost through when the Russians cut him off. "The next thing I knew I caught an elbow in the chest, my spikes hit the curve and I stumbled," Craig said. "It happened right in front of a curve judge and he looked at us. We have slides of the exact moment." Craig studied the photos and wondered why the judge didn't rule interference.

Zatonsky's 59.1 last lap made him the winner in 14:13.6 with Ipatov second in 14:13.8 followed by Craig in 14:14.6 and Sandoval in 15:01.2. Afterward, Craig was ready to create an international incident. "I wanted to have a drag-out fight right there," said Craig, who found an interpreter to ask the Russians why they'd boxed him in. Their nonanswer was: "Well, you're a very fine runner and maybe we'll see you in Russia when the teams run next summer."

Decades later, Craig had cooled enough to admit "they executed just beautifully and I couldn't do a damn thing about it." He'd been handed a lesson in tactics as well as motivation for the 1973 US-USSR dual meet scheduled for Odessa in the Soviet Union. His effort was appreciated by the citizens of Lebanon, who gave him the key to the city upon his return.

Even though Craig's junior year ended on a loss, there was much to appreciate. "The thing that was different about my junior year wasn't just the fast times, but the fact that I won several races on a last-lap kick," he said. "I was beginning to see that I was going to have a full deck of cards to play with going into my senior year."

Chapter 5: A Senior Year to Remember

"The challenge was to set a record almost every time out."

— Craig Virgin

Despite his extended junior campaign, Craig allowed himself only 10 easy days before resuming full-scale training for what would prove to be an even longer senior year of running. He found visits to the world stage thrilling, but he was just as happy at home even though chores awaited his return. Farmwork kept him grounded. "When I fed cows in the morning, they didn't care whether I had broken a record or won a race," he said. "They just wanted to be fed."

As his teammates increased their summer training, they gauged their progress by entering three- to five-mile road races in Edwardsville every other week or so. Craig's father put a mattress in the back of his pickup truck to better transport the team. "We had a ball," remembered Craig, who especially enjoyed postrace trips to Dairy Queen.

Despite Lebanon's enrollment of about 400 students, Craig was the lone senior out for cross country. The fact his success didn't attract more to the sport puzzled some, but not Feldt, who told the *Metro-East Journal*, "Most of the kids see the runners working all summer, training an average of 12 to 15 miles per day, and they decide they just don't want to work that hard. Then, too, we've had two pretty successful seasons, including two trips to state in the last two years, so the guys we really need to come out figure they won't make the team this year, so they stay away."

After facing international competition, Craig never lacked motivation against domestic opponents. One perpetual opponent, his personal recordbook, kept him inspired. "I never lacked a challenge," said Craig, whose streak of course records, begun the previous autumn, ended at 33 on September 26 in the Cahokia Conference meet at Waterloo, Illinois, where his 13:32.6 for 2.8 miles narrowly missed his 1971 record of 13:32.0. "I was a little bummed out about it, but what was I going to do?" he said. "There were more important things to focus on like trying to win state again. At the time, I was just trying to win and set a record every time. It was kind of fun to keep it going." By the time Craig had run on a course two or three times, it had a record not easily broken. When he raced at Waterloo again 11 days later, he lowered the record to 13:25.7.

On October 7, Craig began documenting his training and racing results in a diary he maintained for most of his remaining career. His first entry was full of big dreams: "At this point, I am looking to a season of career bests. This whole year will be big. Some of my goals are: Illinois state cross country champion, mile champion, two-mile champion, best two-miler and miler in the nation. The Golden West and International Prep track meets will be something to look forward to . . . and the Russian tour. I have a lot of opportunities if everything goes all right." Notably, the diary lists goals of 8:40 for two miles, 4:00 for the mile, 3:41 for 1,500 meters, 13:44 for 5,000 meters, 13:20 for three miles, 28:23 for six miles and 29:17 for 10,000 meters.

Craig's diary reveals his ability to coach himself when necessary, a skill that would serve him well. Besides logging his mileage and interval times, he often critiqued his performance, whether it was a workout or a race. He usually mentioned the weather, the topography of the run, his health, diet and energy level. Admonitions to produce smoother running form and maintain mental toughness were common. He could also give himself a pep talk prior to a big race or a pat on the back after a good workout. Descriptions of Craig throughout his career mention the confidence he projected. The diary reveals moments of doubt and times when all he could do was hope for the best. More often than not over the next 12 years, his dreams would come true.

Not everyone handled Craig's growing fame well. High school teammate Rich Youngs said Craig tried to downplay his success "because a lot of kids outside of this (cross country) group kind of resented him because he was so good." When Craig made *Sports Illustrated's* Faces in the Crowd section on November 29, 1971, there was going to be a presentation for him at school. "He said, 'I don't want it there,'" Youngs recalled. "He didn't want to be in front like that."

School announcements included sports reports, and Craig could tell when classmates had reached a saturation point for news about him. "I didn't want to agitate the situation any more than it was," he said.

Craig's margins of victory in cross country as a senior were in the 25- to 60-second range, with one notable exception. He wanted to taper his training prior to the October 14 Mattoon Invitational, but the team had a home dual on October 12. He offered a deal to two of his fastest teammates, the Wertz brothers, Mike and John. He'd pace them before they'd all hold hands at the finish to tie. The race went as planned until the final 100 yards when John bolted in an attempt to steal the victory, a move that instantly angered Craig, who managed to reel in his teammate to win. In the chute, Craig punched John. "It created a divisive moment on the team," Craig admitted. "I'm not sure if we ever completely recovered 100 percent of the team harmony from that."

End Game

Heading into his final high school cross country race, the November 4, 1972, state meet in Peoria, Craig was impervious to the pressure that came with being the favorite. "I welcomed it," he said. "I did it because I put more pressure on myself than what anybody else could put on me." The weather was chilly and the course soggy, but there was little wind. Wearing a white turtleneck under his jersey, Craig broke to an early lead on the opening straightaway when he noticed the field was veering to the right ahead of the first turn. "So I went the 50 or so yards out there, too, just in case somebody had changed a flag on the course," he told the *Peoria Journal Star*. "I guess I should have had more confidence in myself."

Despite the extra distance, Craig passed the first mile in 4:25 and the second in 4:51. "I did slow down some to recover and then attacked the third mile," recalled Craig, who figured collapsing in the last mile was all that could stop him. "I wasn't going to collapse. I tried to enjoy the last 200 meters and, unlike the year before, I was too tired to leap through the finish line." His victory helped Lebanon place 14th in the single-class meet with 384 points, an improvement of five places and 54 points from 1971. His 4:35 last mile gave him a time of 13:50.6, which was 8.7 seconds under his 1971 record.

Craig thought his Detweiller Park record might last five years, 10 at the most. By the time it celebrated its 44th anniversary in 2016, it was the nation's oldest state cross country meet record. One reason for its age was that Illinois never changed its course length to 5,000 meters like most other states. The record had survived 92 races when you add up events from the single-class, two-class and three-class versions of the meet.

The Detweiller record became the Holy Grail for teenage hot-shots. To Craig, the record became an old friend. He admitted when it ultimately falls, he'll be sad—for a day—and then he'll get over it. "It's not like you can go out and race against the person trying to break your record," he said. "A record is what it is. It's static. It's out there and stands only to be broken."

Craig's Detweiller Park record has collected its share of controversy because the course's exact path was altered somewhat in 2003 and again in 2004. Claims that later versions were longer than the 1972 route drew the attention of an independent group of course-measurement experts. That group, led by Chicago Whitney Young coach Bob Geiger, was unable to conclude the course was significantly longer or shorter in 2007 than it was in 1972. What is certain is Craig did not take the shortest path possible in 1972 when he veered right in the opening quarter mile.

Craig finished his 95-race high school cross country career with 81 victories. He was 8–13 as a freshman, 25–1 as a sophomore, 23–0 as a junior and 25–0 as a senior. His final 48 consecutive victories included 46 course records. He later believed the absence of a teammate who could push him in practice was a good thing. "It allowed me to chase those records and run those paces because to go out and set those records, I had to literally, for the most part, run on my own almost from the gun," he said. "The only way to prepare myself physically and mentally for that was really to work out on my own at my own goal pace."

Cross Training

After the 1972 state meet, Craig added three weightlifting sessions a week to his training. Using his school's meager collection of equipment, he'd do repetitions of the military press, arm curls and other rudimentary lifts. Prior to then, his lifting consisted of farmwork such as baling hay or carrying sacks of feed or seed. "That kind of work gave me more strength than you'd imagine," he said. In college, he'd lift twice weekly using Nautilus brand equipment under the supervision of the football team's strength coach.

Craig's perpetual search for his limits led him to the AAU national cross country championships in Chicago on November 25. The race included collegians and postcollegians because there wouldn't be a national race for those 19-and-under until 1975, and the Foot Locker Cross Country Championships for preps weren't founded until 1979. Chicago was his first 10,000-meter race and his first race against recently crowned Olympic marathon champion Frank Shorter. Craig covered the muddy layout in 31:13 to finish 13th, 31 seconds behind Shorter. Craig beat four men from the 1972 NCAA cross country meet's top 15.

January and March of 1973 saw Craig make recruiting visits to Illinois, Missouri, Indiana, Kansas State and Florida, in that order. He enjoyed the recruiting process. As a junior and senior, his ritual after practice was to read recruiting letters stacked on the kitchen windowsill before supper. Contrary to rumors even Craig heard, no schools offered him illegal incentives.

Craig remembered his recruiting visit to the U of I—which offered a full scholarship covering room, board, books, tuition and tutoring—was done in strict accordance with NCAA rules. His parents dropped him off in Champaign and Coach Gary Wieneke later drove Craig to the Effingham Ramada Inn to return him. "My mom drove up with her mother to pick me up," Craig recalled. "I was hungry so he offered some food. He said, 'Mrs. Virgin, I'm sorry, but NCAA rules allow me to buy Craig some pie and coffee, allow me to buy you as his mother some pie and coffee, but I am terribly sorry they do not allow me to buy your mother a cup of coffee or some pie.' Illinois not only didn't buy me a car, but Coach Wieneke wouldn't even buy my grandmother a cup of coffee and a piece of pie. He was that much of a stickler for the rules."

Among Craig's regrets is that he didn't visit Oregon, whose coach, Bill Dellinger, traveled to Lebanon to invite Craig to Eugene. Prefontaine sent a letter encouraging Craig to consider the Ducks. "I should have gone out and spent three or four days there at Eugene and hung out with Prefontaine and the guys just for the experience," said Craig, who ruled out Oregon because it was so far from home his parents would've rarely seen him run.

Craig chose Illinois because it was close to Lebanon, and he considered Illinois to be the state's flagship university. No Illinois state champion distance runner had gone to the U of I since Morton's Al Carius transferred from Kansas in 1961. Craig wanted to prove a runner could successfully develop at the U of I. Once that decision was made, he came up with other reasons to support his choice. Chief among them was the fact he didn't want to lose his fan base. "I've gotten quite a bit of support from the people in the state and had to consider whether I wanted to give that up," he told the *Belleville News-Democrat*. Another reason to stay in Illinois was Pam McDonald, a blond junior who'd moved to Lebanon midway through Craig's senior year. They'd date off and on for the next five years.

After Craig chose Illinois, he called the "losing" coaches to inform them. Most wished him luck and said if he ever changed his mind, they'd still be interested. Indiana coach Sam Bell, upon hearing the news, slammed down the phone. "All I can tell you is when I raced against his top guys that next year and I beat them as a freshman in college, part of my motivation was him slamming that phone down on me," Craig admitted.

Call to Stardom

News of Craig's decision to join the Fighting Illini broke on April 19, 1973. Illinois' head track coach was Bob Wright, who said of Craig in a news release, "He's one of the most mature and articulate young men I've ever recruited and is an outstanding student. He has the ability and the mental toughness to be sensational as a college runner. We're just tickled he will become a Fighting Illini. He has the mental maturity of a college senior and that characteristic will be very much to his advantage as a college runner."

Ninety percent of Craig's recruitment was handled by Wieneke, Wright's assistant, who was in charge of the middle-distance and distance runners. As much as Wright was gregarious, Wieneke was equally reserved. Wieneke began his 36-year tenure as Illinois' head cross country coach in 1967 and his 28-year career as head track coach in 1974. Raised in East Moline, Illinois, he entered military service after high school before returning to enroll at Augustana College where he graduated in 1962. He clocked an Augustana record of 1:58.7 in the 880-yard run.

While working toward a master's degree in 1963, Wieneke helped coach Bowling Green's middle-distance and distance runners. He then coached one year of junior high track and also was a volunteer coach at Winnetka New Trier High School. Next came two years as an assistant and two more as head coach at Guilford High School in Rockford, Illinois. In his short time at Guilford, Wieneke coached 1966 state mile runner-up Greg Dykstra, 1967 state mile record setter Dave Calvert (4:11.7) and 1967 state mile runner-up Glen Town.

When it came time for Wright to hire a distance coach for Illinois, he turned down applicants from all over the country to call Wieneke. "When he called, I could've dropped dead," Wieneke later told David Woods of the *Champaign News-Gazette*.

Wieneke liked coaching far more than recruiting. His relationship with athletes was more father-son than buddy-buddy. What he enjoyed most was watching runners improve regardless of their talent level. In a telling remark to Woods, Wieneke said, "My adrenaline starts flowing about two o'clock when I start thinking about going to practice." His first cross country team at Illinois finished last in the Big 10, but by 1969, it had climbed to second.

Craig didn't realize until after he'd arrived on campus that Wieneke's expertise was in the half mile and mile. Illinois had an NCAA half-mile finalist every year from 1971 through 1974 both indoors and out. Wieneke knew enough about the longer distances to have made Rick Gross a cross country All-American in 1971. In 1972, Wieneke's two-mile relay team of Ron Phillips, Rob Mango, Lee LaBadie and Mike Durkin tied the world indoor record on the Houston Astrodome's oversized track. LaBadie became the Big 10's first sub-4:00 miler in 1971. Illinois won five Big 10 indoor track titles under Wieneke, along with six outdoor track titles and one cross country crown.

Wieneke was at the Drake Relays when Craig called in late April with the news he'd enroll at Illinois. "I knew he was going to make me a good coach," quipped Wieneke.

Art of the Sell

Mango and Durkin were the athletes who made Craig feel most comfortable about choosing the Illini. "He was a charming guy . . . a debonair kind of guy," Craig said of Mango, who became a prominent artist in New York City. Mango remembered meeting Craig's mother and "charming her to death" at his on-campus studio during Craig's visit. "That was the game right there," Mango said. "It was over. Craig is one of my favorite human beings. It was a great experience to be part of that part of his life. He was not just another kid coming along. There was always magic associated with his name. He backed it up all the way."

Mango could tell Craig approached running with passion and desire. "He had a killer instinct once the gun went off," Mango said.

Craig opened his 1973 indoor track season for Lebanon High as usual, faster than he'd left off, clocking a career-best two-mile of 8:50.8 at Champaign. His second win that day was a 4:12.0 mile. He needed to hit the ground running because he'd accepted an invitation to race three miles in the AAU national indoor meet at Madison Square Garden in New York City on February 23. Craig flew to New

York with his father. "It seemed like another world," Craig recalled of his first visit to the Big Apple. It would be his first chance to run on a banked, 160-yard board track.

It was a news-making race, but not for Craig, who repeatedly lost his balance and stumbled off the banked turns. He opened with a 4:20 mile, but a head cold left him struggling thereafter en route to a 10th-place finish of 13:50.0. Tracy Smith won in a world record of 13:07.2. Craig bounced back on March 3 with the best one-day double in prep history, clocking lifetime bests of 8:45.6 and 4:07.9 at Champaign.

Craig contested his first outdoor two-mile of 1973 in the April 7 Alton Relays. He'd battled flu all week. When the gun sounded, he dodged giant snowflakes through a 4:26.5 opening mile. He closed in 4:23.9 to notch an outdoor personal best of 8:50.4. He later brought the crowd to its feet when he rallied the Greyhounds to victory in the distance medley relay with a 4:17 mile. He didn't race again for 10 days, one of his longest breaks of the year, but it was hardly a vacation as he recovered from wisdom teeth removal.

Bob Emig of the *Metro-East Journal* wrote an April 24 story summarizing Craig's season and career. The piece had the wistful tone of a great high school career nearing its end. "It's closing out, isn't it?" Craig told Emig. "I just can't believe all the things that have happened over the last four years."

As brilliant as his senior season was, one of Craig's biggest memories is the only two-mile in which he failed to break 9:00. It was the May 2 O'Fallon Relays where 20-mph winds limited him to victory in 9:24.1. Decades later, he wished he hadn't run the two-mile that day so all his senior-year races would've been sub-9:00. "In those conditions, I wasn't going to break 9:00," he said. "I just decided to relax and enjoy it." His splits indicate he may have had a change of heart about relaxing. His first mile was 4:55 and his second 4:29.

Chasing Records

Craig's foot was back on the accelerator for the Orphan Relays on Centralia's cinder track, where he wanted to bolster his confidence before the state meet and produce a two-mile time close to his 8:45.6 best from the indoor season. He got both, clocking 8:46.5 for an age-17 national record that ranked second in US high school out-door track history behind Prefontaine's 8:41.5. At that point, Craig owned the nation's top four high school two-mile times of the year.

With time running out to break Prefontaine's national high school two-mile record, Craig's run-up to the state meet became a nightmare of over-racing, yet retained impeccable quality. His state meet mile heat included Glenbard West's Bill Fritz, who'd beaten Craig in an indoor mile. "I wasn't fixated on Bill in the prelims," said Craig, who won their heat, 4:10.5 to 4:12.3. Craig was struck by how easy that 4:10.5 felt.

Going for the national two-mile record in the 1973 Illinois state track meet left Craig drained prior to the mile. This photo appeared on the cover of the "1974 High School Track & Field Annual" published by *Track & Field News.* **(Photo by Gil Rocha)**

Craig considered and rejected a plan to run conservatively to ensure he'd win both the two-mile and mile. He was completely focused on breaking Prefontaine's April 25, 1969, record. The race-time temperature inside Champaign's Memorial Stadium was 88 degrees, well above the chilly nighttime conditions Pre had enjoyed during his 8:41.5. Craig's plan was to open with a 62-second lap, crank out six 66s and end with another 62 for 8:40.0. Conspicuously absent from the starting line was Fritz, who pulled out to save energy for the mile.

After the gun, East Peoria sophomore Jim Eicken beat Craig to the pole and forced him to run on the outside of lane one for a lap and a half. Even though Craig covered the first lap in 60.8, he'd soon regret the extra distance he was running. Eicken, who'd pulled out of the mile prelims the day before to save energy for the two-mile, had planned all along to challenge Craig. "My whole intent was I wasn't going to give ground to anybody," Eicken remembered.

Craig's second lap was 65.6, but his third was a disastrous 68.1 and the pacing plan never fully recovered. With 50 yards left, Bob Emig shouted, "He's got it." The crowd thought so too, until the time was announced as 8:42.6 — 1.1 seconds behind Pre's record. "Aw heck, aw heck," Craig repeated. His feet badly blistered, he was helped to the training room where he threw up and had diarrhea before being packed in ice. The mile would start in 80 minutes with or without him.

For 45 minutes, Craig wasn't sure he could report for the mile. "I decided to do it to show these fans who will be watching me here at Illinois the next four years that I had the guts to do it," Craig told the *Belleville News-Democrat*. His opening 880 of 2:07.7 was slower than he'd begun the two-mile, but he was still in front while Fritz was sixth. Fritz took the lead entering the final lap and held off Craig's late charge to win, 4:11.4 to 4:12.2.

After decades of analysis, Craig believed he could've won the mile if he'd only tried for a state record in the two-mile instead of a national record. He also believed he made the right decision to go for the national mark. "I'd been committed to that record all year," he said. "It would have been great if I could have broken it in the state meet. That was my last state meet and it was kind of a bittersweet experience not being able to defend the title in the mile as well." Softening the sting of disappointment was the fact Craig had several national-caliber postseason meets on his schedule where Pre's record could again be challenged.

Chapter 6: Surpassing Pre

"I have this rule I made for myself that I can't look back."

— Craig Virgin

S teve Roland "Pre" Prefontaine was born in Coos Bay, Oregon, on January 25, 1951, four years and seven months before Craig. Prefontaine's father, Ray, worked as a carpenter and welder while his German-born mother, Elfriede, was a seamstress. Coos Bay is a blue-collar town, the perfect breeding ground for a hardworking distance runner. Pre had shown an aptitude for running in junior high gym classes. Later, as a Marshfield High School freshman, he started out as the cross country team's seventh man, but moved up to second by season's end, finishing 53rd in the state meet. His 5:01 mile best in track as a freshman gave little hint of what was to come.

The following fall, Pre placed sixth in the state cross country meet. His sophomore track season featured bests of 4:29.1 in the mile and 9:42.1 in the two-mile, but he failed to qualify for the state track meet. Pre went undefeated in cross country as a junior and went on to lower the state two-mile record to 9:01.3. Another unbeaten cross country campaign preceded Pre's senior track season. His national high school record two-mile of 8:41.5 came in Corvallis on April 25, 1969.

Three years later, Prefontaine would place fourth in the 5,000-meter run at the 1972 Olympics while an impressionable Craig Virgin watched on television. "Watching Prefontaine and Shorter in Munich started the fire burning inside me and made me set the bar higher and think farther and faster," Craig said.

Craig's last tune-up before attempting to erase Prefontaine's record was the June 2 Top Ten meet at Dolton. On the Tuesday before the meet, Craig told *Star-Tribune Publications* he was going for the national scholastic mile record of 3:58.3 set by Jim Ryun of Wichita, Kansas, in 1965. (*Track & Field News* considered Ryun's "post-season" 3:55.3 in 1966 to be the national record.)

Crete-Monee's Craig Stanley paced Craig through opening laps of 59 and 64. Feeling quick and comfortable, Craig sped home in 63 and 58 for a career best of 4:05.5. "That restored the confidence that I had lost at the state meet," Craig told the *Chicago Sun-Times*. The only prep to run faster in 1973 was Matt Centrowitz of New York City's Power Memorial Academy at 4:02.7. Craig and Centrowitz would race each other often in the coming years. Craig's 4:05.5 ranked second in Illinois history behind Tom Sullivan's 4:03.5 from 1961. "I would have needed to change my training to be a little more specific for the mile to break 4:00," Craig said. "I didn't have the knowledge to train for speed back then and neither did my coach."

The second annual International Prep Invitational in Mount Prospect on June 9 drew the nation's top athletes and some from overseas. Elmhurst York's Joe Newton, the first high school coach to serve as a US Olympic coach in 1988, was the meet director. To heighten the drama for the crowd, Newton made the two-mile the last event at 3:30 p.m. The second-fastest entrant behind Craig (8:42.6) was Dave Taylor of Merced, California, who'd run 8:53.6. Also in the field were Robbie Perkins of Richmond, Virginia, at 8:57.8, Matt Centrowitz at 9:01.0 and Greg Meyer of Grand Rapids, Michigan, at 9:05.8.

The 86-degree weather at race time made it unlikely any two-miler would get a personal record, let alone a national one. The low 33 percent humidity and weak 5-mph wind helped, but the black rubberized asphalt track acted like a furnace. Centrowitz, who'd become a two-time Olympian, has colorful memories of the race. "It was the hottest fricking day," he said decades later. "It was a black track, hard as shit." Feldt stood opposite the starting line ready to read 220-yard splits and give a thumbs-up if Craig was on pace. Craig hoped to hear 32s and 33s. He'd hear nothing above 34.

The race quickly turned into one of Craig's many solo time trials in which no one would or could stay with him. "Craig took off and, after two laps, there was no more race," Centrowitz said. But Craig wasn't exactly alone as the crowd of 8,000 chanted "Go, Craig, go" through all eight laps. The crowd included Wieneke, who couldn't believe what he was seeing. "People literally dropped out of the competition," he recalled.

Afterward, Craig told Wieneke, "Yes, it was hot, but it's been a lot hotter on the tractor down at home." Craig blitzed the first lap in 62.5 and the second in 64.9. His feet began blistering inside his red, white and blue Nike Pre-Montreal spikes during a 65.6 third lap. A seventh lap of 65.9 left him needing a 64.2 to break Pre's record of 8:41.5. "Going into the final 100 yards, all I could think about was that I had just missed the record at the state meet and I just wanted to be sure that I didn't miss it again," Craig told the *Chicago Tribune*.

With the help of a standing ovation, Craig ground out a 63.5 last lap to complete an 8:40.9 masterpiece. "It's over! It's over! It's over!" he said as Feldt removed his spikes. It'd be 35 years before anyone in a race limited to high school runners would run faster. A straightaway behind, Centrowitz placed second in a personal best of 8:56.8 while Perkins was third in 9:01.1. "A good track on a cool night, he had another five or six seconds in him," said Perkins 36 years later. "These guys running fast today would have had a hard time beating Craig Virgin that day."

As Craig signed autographs, his immediate reaction wasn't joy. "Relief," he said, "relief that it was over now."

Craig's 8:40.9 nearly eclipsed Gerry Lindgren's 1964 national indoor record of 8:40.0 set against open competition that included older runners. Craig held the outdoor national record until 1979 when Jeff Nelson of Burbank, California, running against open competition at UCLA, placed third in 8:36.3. By 2016, Craig had slid to sixth in US history indoors and out.

Craig ended his high school career with a national record 17 sub-9:00 times for two miles (3,218.7 meters). The closest anyone came to matching him was Eric Hulst of Laguna Beach, California, who had 15 before graduating in 1976. Craig also ran two 3,000-meter races in the summer of 1973 that were the equivalent of sub-9:00 times (8:49.4 and 8:55.8).

Future Olympian Matt Centrowitz (second from left) tried to stay with Craig in the International Prep Invitational two-mile run, but after two laps Craig was alone on his journey to breaking Steve Prefontaine's national record. *(Photo by Gil Rocha)*

In the 1973 AAU national junior meet (limited to those 19 and under), Craig sped three miles in an age-17 world record of 13:36.8 at Gainesville, Florida. The old record of 13:38.2 had been set in 1971 by Dave Merrick. This effort qualified Craig for a rematch with the Russians at Odessa in the Soviet Union.

Before leaving for Europe, the US Junior National Team gathered in New York City. Craig flew into LaGuardia and took a limousine to the Royal Manhattan Hotel. Robbie Perkins remembered Craig made an unforgettable fashion statement in his plaid madras pants and jacket. "He showed up in New York ready to take over the city," Perkins said with a chuckle. "He really looked like something. We were all laughing at him." It wasn't the last time Craig would be the target of teasing by peers, who had no more success shaking his assurance than they did at beating him on the track. After going for a seven-mile run in Central Park with his teammates, Craig noted in his diary there were "weird people all over."

Prior to facing the USSR in a dual meet on July 27 and 28 at Odessa, the US team contested two other duals: July 14 at Heidenheim, Germany, and July 20 at Warsaw, Poland. After 31 hours of travel, Craig came down with a cold. That didn't stop him from taking the lead in the 3,000-meter race at Heidenheim where he and Bobby Grubbs faced two members of the West German Junior National Team. Craig could tell he wasn't 100 percent, but still hoped to break Prefontaine's national record of 8:08.0 set in 1969. The West Germans clung to Craig through a 4:21 first mile. "In the last 200 meters, they got me just like the Russians had the year before," said Craig, who took third in 8:10.2, the equivalent of an 8:49.5 two-mile. Hans-Jürgen Orthmann won in 8:08.8 followed by Michael Lederer in 8:09.2. Seven years later, the quality of that race became clearer when Craig and Orthmann went 1–2 in the World Cross Country Championships.

Collecting Memories

That night after the race, Craig took another step on his journey into adulthood by buying a beer stein. Beer was included in the stein's price of 3.50 marks and Craig didn't want to waste his money. While traveling on the top level of a double-decker bus back to the hotel, he chugged the liter of beer on an empty stomach. His only previous experience with alcohol had been a few sips of wine at family dinners. He developed such a buzz teammates had to help him off the bus. As for the stein, it broke before he got home.

The US team arrived in Warsaw, Poland, by bus two days earlier than their hosts expected. Polish officials informed the Americans they'd have to stay in "average" accommodations for two days before they could move into nicer digs. They wound up at the International Youth Hostel, which Craig described as "almost worse than primitive." The US coaches and their travel agents tried to find another hotel, but the Poles said that was impossible. Even a call to the US embassy didn't help. As Craig later related to Bob Emig, "There were no towels, bathrooms on every other floor, fungus in the showers, roaches all over the place, the food was bad and the waitresses had scabs all over their bodies." That night, Craig met an Australian and a Pole, who took him for a taxi tour of Warsaw. He returned with the impression "Poland is very depressing as you look at the conditions and the people."

By 4 a.m. the next day, Craig believed he had food poisoning on top of homesickness. His mood teeter-tottered between depression and encouragement as his body dealt with the fatigue of a long season. He did not find encouragement from US assistant coach Jerry Isom, who told Craig he was loafing and complaining too much about his health. The criticism made Craig appreciate Feldt's coaching style all the more. Craig noted in his diary that Isom "really doesn't know me."

The tumultuous week was enough to make Craig forsake his front-running style in a 3,000 against the Poles. He passed a mile in 4:30 and pulled away with two laps left to win in 8:16.0, the equivalent of an 8:55.6 two-mile. Craig and a few teammates blew off steam that night by meeting some American college girls for dinner at the Grand Hotel where Craig ate duck and apples washed down by tea and a screwdriver. The group moved on to a discotheque and Craig didn't get to sleep until 2:30 a.m.

On July 23, the Americans flew to Kiev for a passport check before flying on to Odessa. The Soviet versions of the Boy Scouts and Girl Scouts handed out flowers as the Americans got off their plane. By the time Craig disembarked, the flowers had run out. The next day the team visited the Black Sea, which was a mile from their hotel.

On one of the remaining off days, some Russians offered Craig 40 rubles for a pair of jeans. It was then he noticed secret police—at least a dozen wearing plain clothes yet distinguishable to his "alert eye"— around the hotel. That afternoon, an official AAU photographer was arrested for taking photos in downtown Odessa, but released 20 minutes later.

On a shopping outing, Craig got separated from his group. He walked "half-lost" two hours back to his hotel. "I thought the KGB was behind every building or tree," said Craig, who was so traumatized by the incident, it took several hours for his adrenaline to dissipate. Later that day he learned the Russians were bringing in "two fine 5,000-meter runners" to oppose him. He could accept the fact he was in for a tough race, but was ticked Isom didn't have much confidence in him.

Avenging a Loss

The top Russian in the 5,000 at Odessa was Enn Sellik, who'd later run in the 1976 and 1980 Olympics. Sellik's personal best was 20 seconds ahead of Craig's. "This was to some degree a revenge match, a grudge match for me because of the two Russians who had beaten me on American soil in Sacramento the year before," Craig said.

The meet was televised in the United States with Marty Liquori providing color commentary. Among his comments was:

> Virgin, of Lebanon, Illinois, will be attending the University of Illinois this fall and should be one of the greatest runners ever to come from the United States. He's a very talented boy. He really is dedicated and has a very cold and calculating approach to his training and racing. The complete runner, he's run a mile very quickly this year. He's run some great distance doubles. He seems to be very strong, and with age, he should improve greatly.

Centrowitz, who'd placed second in the 1,500 the day before, served as a rabbit, but did not figure in the team scoring. He paced Craig through opening laps of 63 and 67. Craig moved in front, but didn't gain separation until two laps remained. He remembered suffering the last half of the race. "I got to the bottom of the barrel of what I had," he recalled. "The only thing that got me through that race was the embarrassment that I felt from having let those two Russians beat me in the last 150 meters the year before in Sacramento." Craig won by 3.2 seconds over Sellik in 13:58.2, an age-17 national record that ranked third in national high school history behind Gerry Lindgren (13:44.0) and Prefontaine (13:52.8). Only eight Americans of any age ran faster in 1973 than Craig.

Craig's bold front-running earned him the Athlete of the Meet Award. "I ran the African way back in 1971, '72, '73," he said, "just go out hard and the last man standing wins." The Americans won the dual, 123–108.

At the postmeet banquet, a Russian gave Craig a gargoyle to ward off evil spirits. "It looked like an evil spirit itself," he said. The distance runners later congregated in Isom's suite to split five bottles of champagne and a bottle of vodka.

The next day the team flew to Moscow, which made an impression on Craig, whose diary notes: "Can't believe I'm in Moscow." He toured Lenin Stadium and Red Square on July 30 and shopped for gifts. The long list of gifts included five Cuban cigars, a bottle of vodka and some caviar. He also got a toy AK-47 rifle for his brother, Brent.

Craig had no way of knowing he'd never again be in Moscow, which in 1974 would win the right to host the 1980 Olympics. During the 30-hour journey to New York, Craig's suitcases were lost. In the confusion of trying to find his luggage (which he eventually received), he never got to say good-bye to his teammates.

Looking back across the decades, Craig believed he raced too much in high school yet maintained quality and consistency, especially his senior year. But it could be that what looks like over-racing was actually the perfect training for a national record setter. Dr. David Martin, who ran the Laboratory for Elite Athlete Performance at Georgia State University for 30 years and conducted scientific testing on Craig, studied the way Kenyans train compared with Americans. "They spend more time at race pace than we do so they are more specifically focused for training at speed and they do it more often," Martin said. So Craig may have been doing as much of his running at race pace as if he were a present-day Kenyan.

The quality of his last prep campaign led *Track & Field News* to name him its high school athlete of the year in 1973. All the magazine's 13 voters picked Craig No. 1, labeling him "one of prepdom's all-time greats." At that point, he owned 12 world age-group and national class records from two miles to 5,000 meters. He'd only lost four times his final three years, prompting the magazine to say, "His competitive record borders on the unbelievable."

Chapter 7: College Here He Comes

*"I knew one way to run . . . from the front, aggres-
sively, and to try to win."*

— Craig Virgin

C raig spent 10 days before college battling a urological infection.
He blamed dehydration brought on by his fear of drinking the
water in Europe. He was sick when a family photograph was taken
near the pond in their pasture. "It was all I could do to make it down
there to the pond and try to put on a happy face for the photographer,"
he recalled. "Whenever I see that picture, I think of how I was feeling
that day instead of the fact that was a landmark in our family life."

Loren Tate of the *News-Gazette* later wrote that Craig "was
recruited by the University of Illinois amid a storm of community
interest and media coverage. His arrival on campus was a happening."
That was true, but not as glamorous as it sounded. While Craig was
in Europe, the U of I had conducted its freshman orientation and
registration for classes. An associate athletic director was assigned
to register Craig for classes, but when Craig checked in, there was
no record of his enrollment. Over the next three days, with the help
of Wieneke's wife, June, Craig cobbled together 15 hours of classes.

Craig chose to live in Illini Towers, which he thought would be
more conducive to the disciplined lifestyle of a runner. Each four-
person unit had a kitchenette and a central living room flanked by
two bedrooms. While still in high school, Craig had chosen to room
at Illinois with fellow freshman Tom Bartsokas, a 9:15 two-miler
from New Athens, Illinois.

Even though he was a non-scholarship member of Illinois' cross country team, Bartsokas began the season as the No. 3 man. Within a month, he'd fallen out of the top seven. Craig remembered that Bartsokas became homesick and ran up hefty phone bills calling his hometown sweetheart. "Halfway through the semester, we ended up splitting off and he moved to another room," said Craig, noting Bartsokas left the team after two years. "I felt bad that we lost our friendship and I felt worse that he eventually gave up running."

A high pain threshold helped Craig hide how a urological infection made him feel while this family photo was taken in 1973. Pictured from left to right are Vernon, Lorna Lee, Brent, Craig, Sheree and Vicki. *(Photo courtesy of Craig Virgin)*

Craig had graduated from high school with a 4.3 grade point average on a 5.0 scale to rank seventh in a class of 97. The media had interviewed him so often he chose radio and television as his major. "I felt this would be kind of a neat thing to do for a living," said Craig, who estimated his career was chronicled in the print media twice as much as on radio and TV combined.

Over his last two years in high school, he faced two or three reporters after every major race. "I started to learn to be comfortable with the microphone," he said. "I enjoyed trying to explain what just happened in a way that would be good story material." He'd end up spending his first two years in college fulfilling general education requirements. It was only during his junior year that he realized "how weak the radio and TV department was at the University of Illinois."

From day one, Craig set the pace in practice. A fellow freshman, Les Myers, a walk-on from Stanford, Illinois, credited Craig for saving his best efforts for races. "I didn't see him just kill himself in workouts," Myers said. "He wouldn't waste that effort in a workout." Myers saw that when the championships phase of the season arrived, "all of a sudden [Craig was] in a different universe."

The first official race of Craig's college career was on the Illinois State University Golf Course 50 miles away in Normal. The team stayed in a hotel the night before the race. At breakfast, while Craig's teammates sipped tea and nibbled toast, they were shocked to see him wolf down a "farm breakfast" of pancakes, eggs, bacon and coffee. When a startled teammate asked Craig how he'd be able to race in two hours after such a breakfast, the reply was "I don't know. I've always been doing it this way."

Despite later getting lost on the wet five-mile course, Craig clocked 24:47.3 to take nearly 14 seconds off the course record. He remembered the ordeal as "a nightmare" on a "poorly marked" course. He estimated he ran an extra quarter mile.

Wieneke scheduled four dual meets and a triangular that season, which was five more minor races than most coaches schedule now. Craig set course records in four of those five. During an August time trial, he rolled his left ankle. Two days before a September 29 dual at Missouri, he twisted the ankle again. The injury, which would nag Craig the rest of his freshman year, was bad enough there was doubt he'd race at Missouri, which he considered an important opponent. He'd taken a recruiting visit to Missouri, which had Charlie McMullen, who'd placed 13th in the 1972 NCAA cross country meet.

Pain Threshold

After jogging three painful miles the day before the meet, Craig decided to race. It would be the first time his family would watch him run as a collegian. His former coaches, Hank Feldt and Rich Neal, also came. Rain turned Mizzou's hilly course into five miles of mud. McMullen and Craig broke away in the first half mile. By two miles, Craig had opened a gap and went on to win by 11.6 seconds in 25:14.4. As he crossed the finish, he collapsed. Later, he called it the most exhausting race of his life. "It was the first time I can remember falling down after the race," he told Gary Goldman of the *Missourian*, who labeled Craig a "master of hiding emotion and pain." Illinois track coach Bob Wright told Goldman that Craig "has the most ungodly threshold for pain I have ever seen."

Even as a college freshman, Craig (9) was a fixture at the front. Among those joining him in the lead pack of the 1973 Big 10 Conference cross country meet at Savoy, Illinois, were eventual runner-up Pat Mandera of Indiana (2) and eventual third-placer Mike Durkin (6). (*Photo courtesy of the University of Illinois*)

Craig returned to Normal on October 27 for the Illinois Intercollegiates as the Illini entered what they considered the "championships" phase of their season. Craig charged through cold rain with Durkin by his side until building a 15-second gap the final mile to win in a five-mile course record of 23:49. When asked how much he coached Craig, Wieneke said, "I just turn him on."

Anticipation for the November 3 Big 10 meet was such that the host Illini arranged to have the Champaign-Urbana Mass Transit District provide bus service to Savoy. Wieneke's course design was a cloverleaf of one-mile loops. Runners began near the clubhouse and returned to it on each loop, allowing fans to stand in one spot and see the entire race. In bad weather, fans could find shelter in the clubhouse. The start and finish were within 100 yards of each other. Craig rated it one of the best spectator courses he ever saw. The course was so flat a plane missing nearby Willard Airport could've safely landed on a fairway. However, flat didn't always mean fast due to many windy days and the absence of windbreaks. "It had the same resistance effect as running up a hill," Craig said of the wind. The Big 10 meet was the Illini's third home race of 1973, fourth if you count the Alumni meet. "We developed a real fan following," recalled Craig.

With a seven-meet unbeaten streak and six course records, Craig had created a buzz in Champaign-Urbana. "Craig's already an instant celebrity," wrote *Urbana Courier* sports editor Lon Eubanks. "He's a guy not limited by a season, running all year round. *Sports Illustrated* had a letter from a guy in California nominating him for athlete of the year." That letter noted, "Virgin's record as a runner borders on the unbelievable." The letter also said, "Craig Virgin is unsurpassed in the combination of dedication and quality. His dedication to the sport he loves is further exemplified by the fact that Lebanon High has no track. I urge SI to consider this athlete who has made it by himself without the help of sportswriters and media publicity."

On race day, Craig arrived 75 minutes before the gun and was "flabbergasted" to see 2,200 cars lining the winding road from Route 45 to the clubhouse and overflowing the parking lot onto the practice range. Officials estimated 5,000 to 7,000 fans stood six deep along snow fences marking the course. "People were coming out to see the phenom," said Durkin. Craig's principal challenger was Indiana's Pat Mandera, the 1972 Big 10 runner-up. Three-time champion Garry

Bjorklund of Minnesota, who'd set the meet record of 29:20.8 for six miles in 1971, was entered, but was injured and not considered a threat.

Indiana's Pat Mandera missed a turn in the final mile of the 1973 Big 10 Conference meet at Savoy, Illinois, where Craig won his first of four Big 10 cross country crowns. *(Photo by Gil Rocha)*

Craig taxed the field with a 4:37 opening mile with Durkin at his side and four Indiana Hoosiers stalking them. "The crowd was just going nuts having two Illini at the front of the race," recalled Craig, who tacked on miles of 4:46, 4:58, 4:47 and 4:42 until only Mandera remained. "The noise just built as the race went on."

In four Big 10 Conference cross country meets, no one caught Craig. Thankfully, his father did after the 1973 race in Savoy, Illinois. *(Photo courtesy of the University of Illinois)*

On a 180-degree turn entering the sixth mile, Mandera enjoyed a three-yard lead when he mistakenly went straight. Mandera couldn't see Craig trying to wave him back on course nor could he hear Craig yelling to stop. "The crowd just went bananas because they sensed blood in the water," remembered Craig. By the time Mandera reversed himself, Craig had a 20-yard lead. "I knew there was a turn, but I was just looking ahead and saw the flat [path to the finish]," Mandera told the *Urbana Courier*. "Everybody was just standing around, not saying anything. But I guess it was my fault."

Craig was hardly home free because he was in severe oxygen debt. When he reached the 600-yard finishing straight, he noticed, "There is a lot of room in there to think about how tired you are getting." He was so exhausted at the end he felt he bounced off the finish line tape instead of breaking it. He'd run the sixth mile in 4:40.8 to top Mandera by 4.2 seconds. Two steps into the chute, Craig collapsed and two officials drug him through. A photo after the finish caught Craig's face in contorted agony while his father attempted to hold him upright.

Unbeknownst to Craig, his course record effort of 28:30.8 would be the highlight of his freshman year.

Craig's pattern of running until he collapsed must have worried Wieneke. That much was hinted at in Loren Tate's column for the *Champaign News-Gazette* when he mentioned the November 10 NCAA District 4 meet at East Lansing, Michigan, where entrants would attempt to qualify for the NCAA national meet. "There may be an attempt to influence Virgin to ease off a bit and run 'just to qualify,' next weekend," Tate wrote. "But this is a style Craig doesn't understand." Tate was right.

Both Wieneke and Durkin told Craig he should simply try to be among the district's 10 individual qualifiers to save energy for the November 19 NCAA meet at Spokane, Washington. That philosophy had served Durkin well in track where he often did the minimum to qualify for finals, which he then won. "Everything Durkin told me made sense at the time," Craig said, "but [running to just qualify] did feel awkward and weird."

Temperatures were in the low 20s in hilly East Lansing where Craig would race in pantyhose for the first time to combat the chill.

He decided to eschew his front-running style and stay within the lead pack, which included Mandera and Eastern Michigan's Gordon Minty. An Englishman, Minty pushed the pace in the middle miles and went on to win the six-mile race in 29:08.4, nearly four seconds ahead of Mandera. Craig took third in 29:22, five seconds ahead of fourth-place qualifier Durkin. [Illinois' team did not advance in ninth.]

Doubts about tactics appear in Craig's diary, which reads, "I let Mandera and Minty go with about three-quarters of a mile [to go]. Whether I did the right thing or not is not settled. I felt bad about it and good at [the] same time." Decades later, Craig wished he'd gone for the win. "I knew one way to run," he said, "from the front, aggressively, and to try to win."

Qualifying for the NCAA meet meant Craig would finally face the stars he'd read about from other major conferences. "They were all going to be there, but most of all there was a guy named Steve Prefontaine. I knew he was going to be there," Craig said.

Prefontaine had already won two NCAA cross country titles when he redshirted the 1972 season to focus on the Olympics. The race at Hangman Valley Golf Course in Spokane, Washington, would be his final race in an Oregon uniform. During a tour of the beautiful, but hilly, six-mile course two days before the race, Craig spotted his US junior track teammate, Matt Centrowitz, who at that time ran for Manhattan College. Craig would later see another former prep rival, Terry Williams, who ran for Oregon. "It was exciting to be on the course and see the uniforms of these other schools that I had only read about," Craig said.

The sky was clear on race day with temperatures in the mid-30s. Wearing a long-sleeved shirt under his jersey, Craig trailed 30 runners after the first uphill quarter mile. " I elbowed and shoved to the outside of the crowd and passed a large group by swinging wide," he later told the *Metro-East Journal*. "I looked over my shoulder and there were Prefontaine and [East Tennessee State's Neil] Cusack, and I said to myself, 'Hey, these are the guys I want to run with.'"

Craig and Durkin reached the two-mile mark in 8:56. "I remember hearing the crowds chanting 'Pre,'" Craig recalled. Prefontaine needed support because Englishman Nick Rose, a sophomore from

Western Kentucky, had surged before the three-mile mark. Sporting a wild mane of rock-star hair, Rose had something to prove because the previous year he'd been running second when a calf injury knocked him back to ninth.

Midway through the 1973 six-miler, Rose had more than a 40-yard lead on Pre. Craig was in the top 10 along with Mandera and Minty. Pre began to move late in the third mile, but didn't reach Rose's heels until a mile and a half remained. With 1,000 yards left, Pre owned a slim lead that proved more than enough because Rose was spent. Rose later told Jon Hendershott of *Track & Field News*, "On that last fairway, I felt my chest get tight. The crowd [estimated at 4,000] really cheered for Pre and I had to let him go."

Pre went on to win in 28:14.8 followed by Rose (28:20.0) and Minty (28:22.0). Craig was 10th in 28:47.8. Pre, whose team won its second title in three years, thus joined Gerry Lindgren as a three-time champion. Pre's last title came by his smallest margin. As he told Hendershott, "I've never seen a guy that far ahead of me in a cross country race."

Meeting Pre

Even though Craig was the top freshman and fourth American, he scolded himself for not being aggressive enough the final two miles. That afternoon he'd speak to Prefontaine for the only time in their lives. The venue was a Spokane pool hall. "He was there at the pool table with a beer in one hand and a pool cue in the other," Craig recalled. "I remember he didn't put the beer down. He put the pool cue down to shake my hand. He said, 'Oh, so you're the guy who broke my record by just a second.'"

Craig would later wish he'd stayed longer and talked more. "It seemed like at the moment it was appropriate to leave," Craig said. "I figured I would see him again and, over time, we would get to know each other better. Little did I know what fate would have for both of us."

Placing 10th and losing to the sixth-place Mandera didn't sit well with Craig, who decided to enter the AAU national cross country meet just five days later in Gainesville, Florida. Wieneke told Craig the University of Illinois would pay his way, but it wouldn't pay Wieneke's way, so the 18-year-old went alone. "Somebody should have gone with me," said Craig, who warmed up three miles for the 10K race, far too much for the humid, 80-plus degree weather. He went out with the leaders, including Frank Shorter and Doug Brown, passing a mile in 4:27 and two miles in 9:21.

Late in the race, Shorter stopped to pull a stick off his spikes and Brown opened a 30-yard lead. Shorter responded with a steady drive and his kick in the final 300 yards made him the winner on the 10K course in 29:52.5. Brown took second in 29:55. With 300 yards left and still ahead of stars such as Marty Liquori and Jack Bacheler, Craig was sixth when he collapsed. Delirious from the heat, he'd rise and fall twice more before blacking out with 200 to go. "All I remember is waking up [15 minutes] after the race was over with an IV in my arm," said Craig, one of 93 runners in the field of 270 who failed to finish. "A doctor [Gatorade inventor Dr. Robert Cade] was standing over me and a crowd was standing around me."

Craig soon discovered heat exhaustion wasn't his worst problem. Somehow, either from falling or from being stepped on, ligaments in his right foot had been damaged. The injury would bother him the rest of the school year. Shorter's Florida Track Club, which had won the team title, took Craig to the home of club president Roy Benson and left him on a couch. "They were having a party in the next room and I was semiconscious on the couch," Craig recalled. "I should have been in the hospital."

Craig was in such a fog, he couldn't read his watch and kept asking what time it was because he had to fly home that night. "Eventually I got to the airport and I remember when I landed in Atlanta, I had to limp through the airport," he said. Dehydration caused another kidney infection, which doctors treated with a drug called Mandelamine. During the five years he'd been running, Craig had searched for his limits. He found them in Florida.

Chapter 8: Another Blue-Chipper Bombs?

*"I was going into minefields other people had
stepped into and didn't come out of."*

— Craig Virgin

After the fiasco in Florida, Craig didn't run for eight days. By the sixth, he could "feel the bug of running starting to nibble away again," but he knew he needed to heal his body and mind first. His recovery was slow and painful. It felt like his arch was strained.

After one limping five-mile run on December 9, Craig became frustrated with the care he was receiving. "Something is definitely worse than strained ligaments," he wrote. "[I] will have to raise a little hell and get things off the ground." X-rays on December 12 indicated stretched or torn ligaments on the front of his right ankle. There'd be no running the rest of the month.

Craig threw himself into alternative exercises with the same gusto he had for running. He went to the campus pool to swim and "run" in chest-deep water. He did push-ups. He did sit-ups. He worked out under the supervision of the U of I kinesiology clinic.

On January 2, 1974, Craig resumed running with three miles in the morning and three in the afternoon. The foot felt "okay," but his cardiovascular system was "real weak." By January 5, the ball of his left foot hurt from repeatedly striking the bottom of the pool during his pool runs. "What am I doing to deserve all these injuries?" he wondered. Five days later, he wrote, "[I] am getting slightly depressed as running is painful instead of fun."

While Craig struggled to get healthy on snow-covered roads that winter, he also volunteered to help recruit, a task for which he was a natural. "I realized early on that we needed more talent," said Craig, whose efforts landed six Illinois state champions including Dave Walters and Bill Fritz. "He's just such a great promoter," Fritz said. Walters wanted a training partner as great as fellow New Lenox Lincoln-Way High School star Dave Merrick. "If Craig hadn't been there," Walters admitted, "I doubt I would have gone."

Craig arrived at his first college track meet, the Illinois Indoor Invitational two-mile, filled with doubt. His reputation was such that when senior teammate Dave Brooks won in 8:54.7 while Craig took third in 8:59.0, the *News-Gazette* called it a "major surprise." Victories over Craig were so rare, those who did it never forgot. Brooks remembered trailing Craig by more than 30 yards with a half mile left. "I just started sprinting, which was crazy, but I somehow held on," he said. "I don't know how I did it, but boy it hurt."

Craig's foot still hurt the next week when he lost a two-mile at Purdue to teammate Rich Brooks, the brother of Dave Brooks, 9:03.1 to 9:04.8. "All my timing and rhythm is gone and I can't get up on my toes," Craig told Loren Tate.

The situation was so dire, Craig's father met with Wright and Wieneke two days after the Purdue meet, which wound up being Craig's last indoor race of 1974. (Vernon occasionally made business trips to Champaign to sell farm equipment to the U of I agriculture department.) They decided Craig would see a doctor on Wednesday. Impacting the decision-making process was the fact that NCAA rules at the time didn't allow freshmen to redshirt. Among those treating Craig was Durkin's father, Dr. John Durkin, who created a pad for Craig's foot and gave him an anti-inflammatory shot on February 9.

The foot felt fine the next day, until Craig sprained it again by stepping on a snow-covered section of broken concrete. He continued "light" training of seven or eight miles a day. He added orthotic insoles to his training shoes, which seemed to help, but were so stiff they caused blisters. The instability of his left ankle would lead to many twists that winter including one on February 26. Two days later the team left for the Big 10 indoor meet. Craig was left behind.

After March 3, Craig didn't run again for 28 days. Some days the pain was so bad he couldn't walk barefoot across his room. As Tate offered in a *News-Gazette* column, "The 18-year-old Lebanon athlete thrives on work. That, perhaps, is part of his problem. His mind is stronger than his body."

A foot injury made Craig's first college track season a long lesson in frustration.
(Photo courtesy of the University of Illinois)

On March 31, a St. Louis doctor told the exasperated Craig he had bursitis in the ball of his left foot, an ailment that eliminated the spring from his stride. Treatments included soaking the foot in hot water.

Craig missed Illinois' first two outdoor meets, but steadily increased the intensity of his training in hopes of running in the Kansas Relays. On April 18, he arrived in Lawrence, Kansas, where the team stayed in a fraternity house. While jogging downhill to the track, he stepped on a small stick and sprained his ankle again, forcing Illinois out of the four-mile relay. "I don't know when my luck is going to clear," he confided to his diary.

On April 24, Craig and Wieneke decided he'd skip the Drake Relays to train for a May 4 meet at Champaign. On May 1, he cranked his ankle once more, but decided to go ahead with his collegiate out-door debut in the six-mile run. His strategy was simple: "just gut it out." The plan worked as he won in 29:20.6, just 15 seconds shy of qualifying for the NCAA meet. "I'm on my way back," he wrote.

In the Big 10 six-mile run, Craig took second in 28:10.7, 9.3 seconds behind Mandera as both broke the meet record and qualified for the NCAA meet. "I tried to stay with Mandera," said Craig. "I was feeling more confident and my conditioning was starting to come back." He was ready for his first NCAA track meet in early June at Austin, Texas. His luck, alas, was not.

Miscounting

Craig arrived at the University of Texas hoping to break 28:00 in the six-mile run and finish in the top three. The start was moved back an hour to 8:45 p.m. because of dangerous heat, but it was still 90 when 29 entrants stepped to the line. Colorado's Ted Castaneda led midway in 14:14.9. Washington State's John Ngeno, a Kenyan, pulled away the second half to win in 28:14.6. Shortly after Ngeno won, Craig, running fourth at the time, sprinted the homestretch thinking his race was over, but he had another lap to go. "It was kind of pandemonium," he told *Track & Field News*. "I was passing guys that were ahead of me or being lapped."

Craig swore then and continued to believe he was shown the one-lap-to-go card. He remembered the stadium announcer saying, "Let's bring them on in." Southern Cal's Fred Ritcherson also sprinted in a lap early as nine starters failed to finish. When Craig crossed the finish line with a lap to go, he collapsed. Bystanders slid him into the steeplechase water pit to cool. As he revived, Craig overheard someone say, "Didn't he know he had one more lap to go?"

Upon realizing his error, he crawled under a TV broadcast trailer and cried for 10 minutes. "It seemed like the icing on the cake for a year that had been just a bunch of frustration and challenge," he said.

Craig thought he'd struck rock bottom, but not long after returning to Lebanon for the summer, he was diagnosed with mononucleosis. "That fear of failing in college after being a high school superstar stayed with me those four years," he admitted.

Craig didn't run for several weeks in the summer of 1974, but he worked on the farm and did exercises to strengthen his feet. Work boots proved therapeutic. His chest and shoulders grew stronger. He resumed running in July. Six weeks later, he reported to cross country practice in Champaign where 11 freshmen hotshots he'd helped recruit were eager to prove themselves. "That changed the whole dynamic of the team for the better and for the worse," Craig said.

Despite the disappointments of the previous nine months, pessimism didn't appear in Craig's diary, where his eight goals for 1974–75 included:

1. Becoming a Big 10 cross country champion
2. Becoming an NCAA cross country title contender
3. Becoming a Big 10 and an NCAA indoor champion at two or three miles
4. Achieving a sub-4:00 mile
5. Achieving a sub-13:00 three-mile
6. Becoming an NCAA outdoor champion in the three-mile or six-mile
7. Qualifying for the Pan-American Games
8. Being on a team that could win the Big 10 and contend for the NCAA title.

Craig made it through the first five days of two-a-day workouts in fine form. Never a slave to consecutive-day training streaks, he took the sixth day off. When the team's September 7 four-mile time trial at Savoy arrived, he was ready. The Craig Virgin of old returned as he ran 18:51, missing the school record by one second. The runner-up 39 seconds behind was Bill Fritz, one of four freshmen in the top 10.

Morning Burns

No freshman had a bigger impact on team chemistry than Dave Walters, a 5-foot-7, 127-pound go-getter, who'd won the 1973 Illinois state cross country title and the 1974 state track two-mile. "I sometimes felt that he was a little insecure about his speed and always tried to make up for it with extra-hard training and very aggressive racing," Craig said.

Walters believed he had to be competitive at all times, which played a role in the team's morning recovery jogs often turning into sub-5:00-per-mile battles. For a future world champion, the "morning burns" were not noticeably detrimental. That wasn't the case for the rest of the Fighting Illini. "What it did was peak us too early," Craig said.

As a sophomore, Craig deferred to Durkin, the team's senior captain. Craig would later blame himself for not talking to Durkin and Wieneke that fall about squelching the morning burns. "By the end of the season," Craig said, "the guys were all so tired they were leaving their best races in practice."

For Craig, the extra-hard training merely powered him through another unbeaten regular season. "Every two to three hard workouts, I was making progress on my fitness level," he said. "It was all of a sudden coming together."

Among the changes to Craig's lifestyle his sophomore year was the independence he gained by spending his life savings of $2,200 on a 1972 Pontiac Ventura Sprint. His parents gave him a birthday present of four Michelin mag tires. The car was blue with a white racing stripe. It had a three-speed automatic transmission with a two-barrel carburetor. Craig added an aggressive-sounding muffler. There was no AC, no power steering nor power brakes to rob the engine of boost. It was his pride and joy, which made it a target.

Getting home from college became easier after Craig bought a Pontiac Ventura Sprint. *(Photo courtesy of Craig Virgin)*

Walters thought it would be funny to drop a water balloon from the 13th floor of Illini Towers as Craig drove into the underground parking garage. Walters underestimated the tiny balloon's force at impact, which proved enough to shatter the windshield, showering Craig and two suitemates with glass. As half-mile star Charlie White recalled, "All these guys are like, 'Oh my goodness. We're in big trouble.' Craig comes in and he's just mad. He's wondering who did it, but he had a pretty good idea." Walters soon confessed and paid for the repairs. After Walters became an airline pilot, Craig joked he should've flown bombers. "We still laugh about that [balloon]," Walters said in 2009. "Craig never held that against me."

Craig found he could relax around Jeff Cox, his roommate for the next five semesters. "He was just so low key and easygoing that it was comfortable for me," Craig said. "I could be myself and there just wasn't any irritation. He was there as a steadying influence as somebody to talk to who understood my sport. It would have been very difficult for me to have a roommate who didn't understand my sport and didn't understand the constraints and pressures I had to live with."

Craig always focused more on breaking athletic records than societal rules, but he knew if he got in a bar fight or drove under the influence, it'd be front-page news. "I felt like if I let that happen, I would let my family down, I would let myself down and I would let the school and Coach Wieneke down," he said. "I never took big risks. I was a big fish in a small pond and when people put you up on a pedestal, there are a certain number who want to tear you down as fast as they can if you ever give them the opportunity."

Cox had a good relationship with Craig. "There were no big problems," Cox said, "or even minor ones." Craig wasn't usually the life of a party. "He was in and out of a party," Cox recalled. "He didn't stick around and consume alcohol or anything like that. He wasn't that type."

Walters found that Craig wasn't the easiest person to be around. "He and I came to several disagreements," Walters remembered, "but I think that was probably more a function of the individuals we were at that time. . . . We were at that stage in our life where we never wanted to back down from any challenge. That's why Craig and I couldn't live together very well, but I still loved him like a brother."

Affection between men often gets expressed with a humorous twist. That's the case with Craig's nickname among his teammates, who call him Burgie, a reference to his small, tight gluteus muscles that were shaped like hamburger buns. The intra-squad joke was that you could fit Craig's buns or "burgs" into the hands of the Allstate Insurance logo. "They can call me that, but I don't call myself that," said Craig, who always considered relationships with teammates among his most treasured.

Besides camaraderie, college brought Craig a few irritations. He discovered as a freshman that Champaign was "not a nirvana of distance running." The cityscape was flat and aesthetically uninteresting. Plus Craig missed his family. "I went home in college whenever I could," he said. "I missed the farm. I missed the country."

Craig's trips home had a positive effect on his running. "I would always go home and come back 5 percent stronger because I had a chance to run on hills," he said. "There was something reassuring and comforting, and it just put me in a positive frame of mind."

Messing with an opponent's mind was Craig's specialty. He routinely shook hands with foes, a practice Wieneke didn't encourage. "My coaching thing was, if I could keep my team away from everybody, I would," Wieneke said. "I don't want them shaking hands and all that stuff. . . . Craig would walk up and down the starting line and greet everybody with everybody knowing he was psyching them out big time."

Craig credits that strategy to Hank Feldt, who told him, "Don't ever pour coal on the fire." Feldt thought that runners acting "huffy" before races only inspired their opponents. He told Craig to be nice. So Craig chatted them up, often asking about their families. "It didn't work all the time, but a lot of times it took their edge off," he said. "It disarmed them just a little bit. I was an animal between the gun and the finish line, and after that I tried to be a nice guy."

Super Sophomores

The Big 10 meet was November 9 at Ann Arbor, Michigan, where an up-and-down six-mile course made finding a running rhythm difficult. After a 4:50 opening mile, Craig went on to win in 29:11.4, which put him 34.4 seconds in front of runner-up Greg Meyer of Michigan. The Illini, fourth in 1973, took third. Michigan State's Herb Lindsay ran 30:05.4 in third as sophomores swept the top three spots with times under Lindsay's old course record of 30:06.

The Big 10 opponents Craig dominated would become some of America's top distance runners. Besides Meyer, who went on to win the 1983 Boston Marathon, the Big 10 elite of Craig's era included: Lindsay, Michigan's Bill Donakowski, Minnesota's Steve Plasencia, Ohio State's Tom Byers, Wisconsin's Steve Lacy and Michigan State's Stan Mavis. "The Big 10 was tough," Meyer said years later.

"As good as we were in the Big 10 and as good as a lot of us ended up being after college, Craig owned us while in the Big 10. He was just better than us."

After Nick Rose, Lindsay was arguably Craig's most relevant rival. Lindsay grew up in rural northern Michigan. He was the youngest of six children until his widowed mother married a widower with six children. In a blended baby-booming family, Lindsay ultimately became the 12th youngest of 15 children. His parents called their hungry offspring for supper by ringing an old schoolhouse bell, whose sound gave him an appetite for speed he never lost. At Reed City High School, he won two state cross country titles and posted track bests of 9:22 in the two-mile and 4:24 in the mile. Reading about Craig and Merrick motivated Lindsay. "It helped inspire me to strive to run faster times in high school probably more than anything else," he said.

Craig's average margin of victory after seven cross country races in 1974 was 46 seconds. Such large gaps stemmed from the expectation he'd need to go all-out in the NCAA meet. "I can't slack off," he told Tate. "There have been times when I could have let up and still won. There are a lot of arguments that run through your mind when you're hurting, and it's hard to maintain your commitment. But I'm thinking ahead. I know you can't hold back and still be ready when you jump in with the top runners in the nationals."

Craig didn't hold back in the November 16 NCAA district meet at Madison, Wisconsin, where the field let him go after he opened with back-to-back 4:36 miles. He went on to produce a Yahara Hills course record of 28:42.8. "I wanted to get out in the first mile and when I saw the others weren't going to go with me, I relaxed and knew I could win," Craig told Don Kopriva of *Track & Field News*. Privately, Craig felt his last mile and a half wasn't good enough for NCAAs. The top five teams advanced, which left sixth-place Illinois 10 points from joining the club.

Craig then headed to Bloomington, Indiana, for the November 25 NCAA meet expecting the biggest challenge of the season. "I hope to cope with it psychologically," he told Reed Schreck of the *Urbana Courier*. "In high school the last two years, there really wasn't anybody who could stay with me. Monday, I'll find out if I either have it or I don't."

In a six-mile race that included 13 of the previous year's top 25, Craig expected Western Kentucky's Nick Rose to take the early lead, Washington State's John Ngeno to control the middle and Oregon's Paul Geis to finish strong. Ngeno had broken Prefontaine's district course record. "I'll just have to hope I can go out and stay with all of them," said Craig, who was bolder in his diary, writing that he'd "go for first place."

Nicholas Henry Rose

Rose grew up in Bristol, England. His father worked in a Rolls-Royce aircraft engine factory and his mother worked part-time in a bakery. He quit school at age 16 and spent the next three years working in a candy factory for $10 a week hauling coconut to the bon-bon makers. He trained after work and during lunch breaks, a routine that paid off with a world junior cross country title in 1971.

Rose was recruited to Western Kentucky in 1972 by assistant coach Alan Launder, also an Englishman. Around the hilltop campus in Bowling Green, Rose stood out as much for his shoulder-length blond locks, gold earring and overalls as he did for his running. The Western Kentucky media guide listed his hobbies as partying and music. Born on December 30, 1951, Rose was three years and eight months older than Craig. Rose was a cross country runner in the European tradition, which required a knack for running hills. If there was mud, too, all the better. Rose's philosophy on running was summed up in a 1978 *Track & Field News* story in which he said, "If I don't feel pain, I don't feel I've worked."

On NCAA race day, Rose followed his pattern of going out hard. Craig went along. Rain had made the course muddy so Craig chose to race in new Nike Waffle racers instead of spikes. He'd only had the shoes a week and had yet to test them in mud. "They looked like they would do okay," he said, but mud clumped onto the soles. His other mistake was wearing a hat that had earflaps and caused him to overheat. "It was like he was one of those guys that flew a World

War II bomber and had this strange thing on his head," Rose recalled. "That was my first memory of Craig."

Craig and Rose remained together through half of the two-lap course while 5,000 spectators scurried between vantage points. Craig and Rose passed the first mile in 4:47 and the second in 4:46, but Craig was always on the defensive, trying to counter what he estimated were seven surges. "Once I got the wind behind me, I took off," Rose told Schreck.

Craig remained in contention, reaching three miles in 14:29, three seconds behind Rose. Ngeno and Geis passed Craig, now struggling, before he reached the five-mile mark in 24:56. In the last quarter mile, six more passed, the last being Greg Meyer. Craig finished 12th overall, seventh among Americans and seventh among sophomores on the hilly course in 30:16. He was 54 seconds behind Rose, who'd taken 25 seconds off Craig's October 12 course record.

One of eight foreigners in the top 25, Rose told Kopriva of *Track & Field News*, "This is a strong man's course and suits European runners better because we have tougher courses over there."

Looking back, Craig saw the similarity between his sophomore state cross country meet in high school and his sophomore NCAA meet in that he probably could've finished second if he hadn't tried to win. "I went for the guy with the lead and died," he admitted. "I remember Greg Meyer looking over his shoulder as he ran by me the last 400 to 600 yards and I couldn't do a damn thing about it. I was out of gas and just lucky to finish the race." Wieneke told Schreck, "I think Craig could've finished significantly higher if he was just trying to place high instead of going for first place. But Craig did exactly what I try to teach all athletes to do in his situation. Heading for the lead right away was his only choice."

Feeling he should've handled himself better, Craig went home thinking: "I will never let this happen again." While he'd expected to feel tired late in the race, the fatigue he experienced was inexplicably acute. It would be another four months before doctors gave his problem a name.

Chapter 9: The Heartbreak Kid

*"He's the hard-training, clean-living All-American
boy and I'm the long-haired lay-about who likes
to stay up late every night and drink alcohol
at parties."*

— Nick Rose

C raig took six days off after the 1974 NCAA cross country meet. He'd run 900 miles in 93 days. Two months later he opened his 1975 indoor track season with an Illinois Invitational two-mile meet record of 8:42.0, missing his goal by five seconds. He felt chest tightness, which he attributed to a cold.

After he won the mile in 4:07.9 in a January 31 home dual against Northwestern, Craig felt a burning sensation in his chest. He followed with a two-day triple in the Illinois Intercollegiates, anchoring the distance medley relay to a meet and school record with a 4:08.8 mile on February 7 and setting meet records in the mile (4:08.2) and two-mile (8:48.6) the next day, his first double in two years. The next week he lowered the school two-mile record to 8:38.4. He'd motored through seven quarters in a lifetime best of 7:29, but tied up during a 68.9 final 440.

Craig faced Nick Rose for the first time on the track in the February 21 Illini Classic two-mile. On the eve of the race, Craig felt "awfully nervous and worked up." One thing that reassured him was the crowd support he knew he'd have. "I loved to run in those Friday night meets," he said. "It just felt special. I always got more jacked up for Friday night than I did for Saturday."

Craig raced a mile 27 times in college including 12 times on relays, but never ran faster than 4:01.6. After high school, he never ran the mile when he was most fit in May and June because his focus shifted to the 5K and 10K. *(Photo courtesy of the University of Illinois)*

The Armory reminded Craig of the twice-yearly visits he made his final three years of high school, always with brilliant results. In college, larger and larger crowds showed up. The oversized track, measuring 6¾ laps per mile, was fast. It had long straightaways, tight turns and no banking, but it was a magnet for teams seeking NCAA qualifying marks.

In 1975, Illinois hosted six indoor meets, which helped build a fan following. "There would be a crowd on both sides of the track because at that time they had bleachers on the backstretch, on the homestretch and on one of the turns," he said. "It was a real rocking atmosphere." But the night of the Illini Classic, Rose was the rock star as he won in 8:34.4 while Craig took second in 8:41.0. The next day Craig anchored his distance medley relay to a meet and school record of 9:41.2 with a 4:06.5 mile. That relay narrowly missed Pittsburgh's world record of 9:39.8. "I probably cost us that world record," admitted Craig, who couldn't tell if he was trying too hard or not trying hard enough. He knew for sure he was "in a physical slump."

Craig's indoor season came to an early end in the Big 10 meet at Bloomington, Indiana, where he roomed with Durkin because both were battling colds. In the mile prelims on March 7, Craig advanced with an exhausting 4:11.7. Three hours later, he built a 40-yard lead in the two-mile, passing halfway in 4:17. His suffering, however, had begun after only 880 yards. "The second half of the race was like a nightmare," said Craig, who began weaving between lanes one and two. His final 440s took 68 and 78 seconds. Three men passed him the final lap, leaving Craig fourth in 8:55.2, 10.4 seconds behind Michigan State winner Herb Lindsay.

In the next day's mile final, Craig took sixth in 4:10.3. It would be the worst Big 10 finish of his career. After that mile, he flopped on the high jump pit and fell asleep despite the commotion of the meet. The next day, he discussed all aspects of his running with Wieneke. "I just felt like God had taken my ability away from me somehow," Craig said.

When McKinley Hospital staff physician Dr. Robert Pace listened to Craig's heart, he heard the distinctive friction rub of pericarditis, an inflammation of the lining around the heart. Craig was immediately admitted and remained hospitalized for five days. Dr. Pace, who felt a virus may have caused the pericarditis, told the U of

I sports information department he was "amazed by Craig's competitiveness and the fact he was even able to finish the races in the Big 10 meet. The problem had a great deal of effect on his performance and only because he is a great physical specimen was he able to do what he did." What Craig couldn't do for the second straight year was compete in the NCAA indoor meet.

Craig's heart problems put his disappointing NCAA cross country showing in a new light. For the rest of his career, he'd look for medical reasons to explain unexpectedly poor showings, and he recommended other runners do the same. He resumed training April 7, jogging three miles in the morning and three in the afternoon with a 4:40 mile thrown into the latter workout. At the end of each workout that week, he visited the hospital to have his heart checked.

Craig sat out the team's first four outdoor meets, but returned for the Drake Relays where he contributed a 4:09.0 to the sixth-place four-mile relay on April 25 and a 4:13.5 to the third-place distance medley relay on April 26. The medley was especially humbling for Craig, who'd been handed a lead that Nick Rose and Kansas State's Jeff Schemmel quickly erased. Craig felt he'd been dumped in the deep end and had sunk. After competing in his first major relay carnival, he went for a cooldown outside the stadium. A water balloon launched from a passing car caught Craig in the stomach, knocking him to the ground and out of breath. If the world was trying to derail the ultimate optimist, it would need more than water balloons.

Craig made progress in the May 9 Illinois Intercollegiates at Charleston where he lowered the six-mile meet, stadium and school record to 28:10.0. Eight days later, he won his first Big 10 track title, touring three miles in a personal best of 13:34.7 to win by 130 yards and help Illinois capture the team title by 1.5 points over Indiana. "We had one of those meets where everything just went our way," Craig said.

Mourning News

Craig's last competition before the NCAA meet was a three-mile race at Wichita, Kansas, on May 31. When he arrived at breakfast, he was shown a mind-numbing headline.

Prefontaine was dead.

"That was all we talked about the rest of the day," said Craig, who suddenly felt the weight of America's distance-running future shift to his shoulders. He'd tell David Woods of the *News-Gazette*, "It was bad for American distance running as a whole."

Pre had run a 5,000-meter race the night before in 13:23.8 for his 25th consecutive victory in a race longer than a mile at Eugene, Oregon. His postrace activities included a trip to the Paddock Tavern for a few beers with his girlfriend. An hour later at 10 p.m., they arrived at a party at Nike promoter Geoff Hollister's home. According to Tom Jordan's book, *Pre*, guests estimated Prefontaine had four or five beers while at the party.

After leaving Hollister's party, Pre dropped off Frank Shorter at the home of *Sports Illustrated* writer Kenny Moore, where Shorter was staying as a guest. The last person to see Pre alive, Shorter put the number of beers Pre had at three or four, but neither he nor anyone at Hollister's party considered Pre drunk. Pre proceeded down Skyline Boulevard. When he reached the sharp curve near Birch Lane, his butterscotch 1973 MGB convertible crossed the center line, struck the natural rock wall and flipped on top of him. The car had a roll bar, but Pre wasn't wearing a seatbelt.

Bill Alvarado, who lived closest to the accident scene, heard the crash and went to investigate. He later told the *Eugene Register-Guard* Pre was still breathing when he arrived, but the car was too heavy to lift off Pre's chest. While Alvarado ran for help, police arrived, but Pre was already dead. Police instructed the mortician to draw a blood sample. Pre's blood registered an alcohol level of 0.16 percent. Oregon's legal limit was 0.10 percent.

Following a Hero

With one of his heroes gone, Craig was inspired as never before to follow in Pre's footsteps. Craig lowered the U of I three-mile record that day in Wichita to 13:22.6.

The 1975 NCAA track meet was 4,500 feet above sea level in Provo, Utah. The six-mile run on June 6 would be Craig's first race at altitude since the 1972 AAU junior meet near Denver. Washington

State's John Ngeno, who grew up at altitude in Kenya, took control midway while Craig led the chasers. Nevada's Domingo Tibaduiza, a Colombian, unleashed a 59-second final lap to drop Craig to third in 28:25.36. "I rarely vomited after a race. I vomited that night because of altitude sickness," said Craig, who finished 4.7 seconds behind Ngeno. Craig was the only American in the top seven and his time was under the stadium record of 28:44.0 set in the 1967 NCAA meet by Gerry Lindgren of Washington State. "It was one of my better races," Craig told Woods. "But I'm never fully satisfied unless I win."

Foreign athletes had won one or two NCAA titles each year from 1970 through 1973. A federal court then ruled it was unconstitutional for the NCAA to require foreign athletes to forfeit a year of eligibility for each year of post–high school competition they had run in their own countries. After that ruling, seven foreign athletes won NCAA titles in 1974 and nine in 1975.

A May 1975 story in *Track & Field News* addressed the issue and in it Craig told writer Tom Jordan, "I would like to see a system where foreign athletes would receive no athletic scholarship. However, this would not prohibit the athlete from coming over on his own, which is a basic freedom/right. But it would take a lot of ammo away from the heavy foreign-recruiting coach." Craig went on to note, "The runner hurt most is the one who in high school is not a real standout, yet who really blossoms in college running. These athletes are now getting passed over by power-hungry coaches who are dazzled by a Kenyan who has reportedly run 3:58. These runners are being cheated by coaches who want ready-made champions." Craig speculates even a runner as great as Prefontaine, who won seven NCAA titles, would've struggled to win that many after 1973 against the growing number of foreign stars.

Craig was still eager to race on June 14 when he accepted an invitation to the Meet of Champions in Berkeley, California. A crowd of 8,000 watched him win the six-mile run in a school record 27:48.8, breaking Frank Shorter's 1971 Edwards Stadium record of 27:50.0. That effort on a clay-and-cinder track slashed 21.2 seconds from Craig's previous best. "One of my biggest victories ever," he wrote in his diary. Only two Americans had run faster in 1975 — Prefontaine (27:18.6) and Wisconsin's three-time All-American Glenn Herold (27:33.6).

Craig's season came to an end June 20 in the AAU nationals at Eugene, Oregon, where he faced Marty Liquori on the track for the first time. This would be Craig's first race at hallowed Hayward Field where Prefontaine's funeral had been three weeks earlier. "I felt I had all this power again that I had been missing earlier," Craig said. "As bad as the indoor season ended, the outdoor season was ending on the plus side and I was literally feeling more powerful by the week."

Dream Believer

Craig opened the race with a 4:21 mile and reached two miles in 8:47. "I just kept thinking positive thoughts," he said. He weaved through traffic to reach three miles in a personal record of 13:08.6 before finishing fourth in 13:35.02. That still stood as the U of I record in 2016. Liquori sprinted away from Craig on the last lap to win in a meet record 13:29.0. Another record falling to Craig that day was the age-19 national mark that had belonged to Prefontaine.

Craig had borrowed money to travel to Eugene where he learned some athletes had had their way paid by their colleges even though that violated NCAA rules. Craig had been told before leaving the Midwest he couldn't affiliate with a club—such as the University of Chicago Track Club or the Florida Track club—and receive club funds for travel. When he arrived in Eugene, he was told he could affiliate with a club. All the rigmarole made him want to get involved in the AAU's decision making. He was even nominated to be one of 10 athlete representatives to the AAU, but wasn't elected.

Having ended his track season healthy, Craig took a week off before resuming training for his junior season of cross country. During that 14-week fall campaign he averaged 81 miles a week, twice topping out at 96. One factor boosting his mileage was the location of his two-bedroom apartment, which was above a garage off Springfield Avenue in Urbana. It was two miles from both the golf shanty where the team met for morning runs and from the track. Every morning and afternoon workout automatically included an extra four miles. On the first day of school, Craig followed an eight-mile morning with a 13-mile afternoon, the most miles he'd run in a single day.

As his roommate, Jeff Cox, recalled, "We made the mistake of moving to the north end of campus and then we'd have to be at the south end of campus by six in the morning. We usually did that on foot. For him, it was fine, but for me, I had to run two miles with Craig Virgin and then do the rest of the workout."

With Durkin gone, Craig assumed more of a leadership role on the team. Putting an end to the morning burns was his first order of business. "As captain, I put my foot down," he said. "I said, 'We're there to train for over-distance.'"

The team now included freshman Jim Eicken, national junior college mile champion Jeff Jirele and junior Gary Mumaw, who'd arrived the previous year but had to sit out after transferring from Indiana State. A high-mileage type, Mumaw often joined Craig on 15-mile Sunday runs. "I could tell the maturity of the team was increasing," Craig said. His talent had grown, too. On August 26, he was able to throw six surges into a 10-mile run. "A new weapon to use if I can get it down pat," he reported in his diary.

In his September 13 season opener at home against Southern Illinois, Craig surprised himself with a course and school record five-mile time of 23:47.0 despite windy conditions. This race exemplified Craig's advanced tactics. In the first two miles, he lured two SIU runners, John St. John and Kurt Leslie, away from the pack, hoping to draw them into early oxygen debt. Leslie faded from second to 12th, but St. John hung on for fourth as Illinois won, 18–43.

Craig set another course record in a dual at Missouri where he intended to leave a time that would say "Craig Virgin was here." He zipped over five hilly miles in 23:49.4, taking 31 seconds off the old mark owned by Oklahoma State's John Halberstadt. "It will be awhile before anyone touches that," said Wieneke.

On the way to Missouri, the Illini stopped for lunch at Craig's home in Lebanon. "His father and mother are just great people," said teammate Bill Fritz. Craig's parents watched him compete once or twice each season of cross country, indoor track and outdoor track. "While they didn't make every meet like some parents did, they had a busy life," Craig said. "I was just grateful when they could come up."

Gunning It

In the November 8 Big 10 meet at Madison, Wisconsin, Craig became the third three-time champion in the meet's 61-year history, joining the Minnesota duo of Garry Bjorklund (1969–71) and Fred Watson (1913–15). Craig swept across the five-mile Odana Hills Golf Course route in a course record 23:04.5 to finish 30 seconds ahead of Michigan State runner-up Herb Lindsay. Through 2016, no Big 10 winner had run faster, not even those who contested the 8K distance, which is 51 yards shorter.

A photo of Craig from that race put him on the cover of the December 1975 issue of *Track & Field News* for the first time. The headline read, "Virgin Runs Down Foreigners." The Illini placed a disappointing fourth, but were only nine points from second. Illinois matched that finish in the November 15 NCAA district meet at Bloomington, Indiana, where the top five teams and top 10 individuals not on those teams qualified for the national meet.

On the eve of the district meet, which included many momentum-robbing hills and turns, Craig viewed the course almost like a living thing. It had given him bad memories and now he'd make it pay. He won the windswept six-mile event in a course record 29:18.6, breaking the mark of 29:22 Rose had set while winning the 1974 NCAA meet. Lindsay, who'd finish second to Craig seven times in college, was second again in 30:06. Having gotten the confidence boost he needed, Craig told a reporter, "This is the hardest course I've ever been on. I hope I don't ever see it again in my college career. I was just so sick toward the end." In Craig's first 25 college races, he had 22 wins and 16 course records.

Craig's training leading into the November 24 NCAA meet at University Park, Pennsylvania, included frequent surges of 50 to 100 yards, moves he expected to need to escape challengers such as Nick Rose. His diary entry prior to the race illustrates his style of self-coaching: "I have visions of a good race. I must be cool and calculating. Must not burn out my first 2–3 miles. I must work on staying near the front and yet not blowing my wad. Must recognize real challengers and move accordingly! Most of all I must look at myself during the race and commit myself even when it hurts. You have to be the toughest SOB out there to win."

Craig's showdown with Rose offered a contrast in personalities. As Rose told Woods, "He's the hard-training, clean-living All-American boy and I'm the long-haired lay-about who likes to stay up late every night and drink alcohol at parties."

Run for the Rose

The six-mile course was on a 36-hole golf course. It was bone hard and wide with sweeping turns. Rose set the early pace on a windless, 40-degree day, passing one mile in 4:35. Wearing gloves and a long-sleeved turtleneck under his jersey, Craig was close behind in sixth. Rose and Penn's David Merrick reached two miles in 9:20 followed by Craig, Washington State's Joshua Kimeto and Penn State's George Malley. The first major hill was a quarter mile that rose 45 feet. Merrick was forced to slow by a side stitch. Rose, Craig, Kimeto and Washington State's John Ngeno passed three miles in 14:04. Rose and Craig opened a 20-yard gap before they reached the second major hill, a half-mile grind bookended by the lowest and highest points on the golf course. They motored past four miles in 18:38 and five in 23:37, all the while jostling each other at every opportunity. At one point, Rose tried to run Craig into a pole and Craig tried to push Rose into a tree. "It was just European-style tactics," Craig said. "There was nothing wrong with it. It was man against man and everything was legal as far as I was concerned."

Craig and Rose reached a 300-yard hill in the final mile together. Craig sensed Rose weakening and began to pull away 200 yards up that hill. "I was planning to go before the top of the hill," Rose said. "I didn't want it to come down to a final sprint. But it just happened that he was going on the hill and he pulled away."

From there, Craig ran scared. After stumbling through a dip in the course 120 yards from the finish, he regrouped to win in 28:23.3, leading 47 men under the course record. Rose finished 15.5 seconds behind in second. "He did everything he could to pull away," Craig told Woods. "I almost gave up. I thank God I didn't. I don't know how I hung on." The physical nature of the race wasn't reflected by the sportsman-like tone of the postrace interviews.

Craig said of Rose: "I've never seen a guttier runner."

Rose said it was "the smartest race I'd ever seen Craig run," adding, "he certainly deserved to win."

With only one senior in its lineup, Illinois finished 10th ahead of Big 10 champion Michigan in 22nd. The Africans from the University of Texas at El Paso (UTEP) edged Washington State's Africans for the title, 88–92, while the Irish-led Providence team took third. UTEP thus became the first school to sweep the NCAA indoor and outdoor track titles and the cross country crown in the same year. Merrick, the previously unbeaten IC4A champion from Penn, wound up ninth in 29:06.

While Craig was still in the finish chute, Wieneke came to him. "He is not a wildly demonstrative man, but I remember the grin on his face and his handshake," Craig said. "He grabbed my hand and then put his arm around me." That embrace almost became their last because, two days later, when Craig was driving near his Lebanon home, he tried to pass a semitrailer on snowy Route 4 and lost control. The car crossed the center line, spun 360 degrees and smashed into the left ditch. The impact was so great, it sprung the car's frame, but neither Craig nor his sister Sheree was hurt. Also surviving were the supplies they were transporting for Thanksgiving dinner, a meal that had taken on new meaning.

Chapter 10: 1976 Olympic Trials

"If you are a good one, you are alone."

— Craig Virgin

The specter of the Montreal Olympics loomed over every elite distance runner in 1976. For Craig, talk of him becoming an Olympian began not long after his rise to stardom. Such speculation gained credence when the November 1975 issue of *Track & Field News* listed contenders to make the US Olympic 10K team. The list included Craig, Frank Shorter, Glenn Herold, Greg Fredericks, Jeff Galloway, Garry Bjorklund, Dick Buerkle, Ted Castaneda, Jon Anderson, Gary Tuttle, Don Kardong, Jack Bacheler and preps Rudy Chapa and Eric Hulst, among others. The article noted Craig was "looking ahead to 1980, but any runner who overlooks him in 1976 may do so with regret. Virgin is only 20 and he has not done much long training. If his longer running pays off, he will be dangerous." Four months later, Garry Hill of *Track & Field News* picked Craig to finish third in the Olympic Trials 10K and contend for a spot in the 5K.

As he prepared for the June Olympic Trials, Craig also had other matters to tend to. Winning an NCAA title came with perks. One was a spot on the US team that would run in the World Cross Country Championships in Wales on February 28, a week prior to the Big 10 indoor meet and two weeks before the NCAA indoor meet. Out of loyalty to the U of I, he didn't go to Wales, but years later, he wished he had. "At the time, it seemed like the prudent thing to do was pass it by and consider it a compliment," he said. "I don't think I realized what the World Championships were all about yet."

Not long after his NCAA victory, Craig acquired contact lenses paid for by the U of I. During the cross country season, he'd gone off course several times, taking entire fields with him. His nearsightedness was especially troublesome in overcast conditions on courses that used flags instead of a chalk line to show the way. He wore glasses except when running because he didn't like them bouncing on his sweaty nose. He rated the contacts the biggest perk the school ever provided. "To be able to see perfectly in a track meet or cross country race and be able to see the lap cards well in advance," he said, "it just was wonderful."

Red-eye Racing

The NCAA title also brought Craig invitations from major US indoor meets. This proved good and bad because it usually meant competing on back-to-back days with a long flight in between. The first day would be a chance to face elite competition; the second would be to fulfill obligations he felt he had to his teammates. Wieneke said he never ordered Craig to run in home meets, but Craig felt an unspoken obligation to do so. In reality, Wieneke would've had trouble stopping Craig from running at home. "I like to run in front of the home crowd," he admitted to the *News-Gazette*.

Craig's first such double came January 24 when he placed third in the San Francisco Examiner Games two-mile in 8:42.6, finishing 2.2 seconds behind South Africa's Ewald Bonzet and 0.6 behind Frank Shorter. The banked 160-yard board track challenged Craig's balance as he twice fell off the track in the last half mile. Less than 24 hours later, and after two hours of sleep, Craig was back in Champaign winning the mile in the Illinois Invitational in 4:05.9. That ended the first of nine consecutive weekends of racing.

Craig faced the same kind of double the next weekend, which began with another tussle with Nick Rose in the Millrose Games 5K in front of a Madison Square Garden record crowd of 18,152 in New York City. The race was a rumble reminiscent of the physical tactics in the 1975 NCAA cross country meet, but this time Rose had a teammate, Tony Staynings, with him. "There were a lot of shenanigans between Rose and Staynings," Craig told David Woods of the

News-Gazette. "The official warned Rose twice about cutting in too close. I kind of lost a little bit of respect for those two boys. There was no call for that."

Craig led most of the final two miles of the 34-lap race. When Staynings passed, Craig thought it was Rose and followed, but the maneuver was a bluff as Staynings dropped out the next lap. Craig then borrowed Rose's tactic of increasing the pace every two or three laps. "I think that wore out Rose," Craig said. "I was just using his own stuff back on him." Rose wound up fourth, but Craig had to settle for second in 13:54.4 as Greg Fredericks sprinted by the last lap to win in 13:51.6. Craig had passed the three-mile point in a school-record 13:30-plus. He'd lost, but learned. "I'd never faced Fredericks before," he told Woods. "I need to face those guys before the Olympic Trials."

From 1975 on, Craig ran at least two races in most college meets. In the Illinois Intercollegiates, that meant a 4:05.9 distance medley relay leg followed by an open mile win in 4:04.0. In a February 4 dual at Wisconsin, it meant a 4:03.7 runner-up finish to Wisconsin's Steve Lacy in the mile and an 8:39.4 victory in the two-mile. Many of Craig's mile losses, including that one against Lacy, consisted of Craig leading until the final 100 yards. "I knew I got suckered in the mile and did all the work. [Lacy] let off the pace real early so I had to take it because I wanted it to be a decent time," Craig told the *Daily Illini.*

Craig's biggest showdown of February came in the Illini Classic at Champaign where he'd battle Rose over two miles. Afterward, Craig would call it the highest-quality indoor race of his college career as he sped a school record and an all-time Big 10 best of 8:32.4 to finish 0.8 behind Rose. Craig came back the next day to anchor his winning distance medley relay with a 4:03.7 mile.

Craig's double in the March 5 and 6 Big 10 meet was actually a triple because he also had to run a mile prelim. His 4:09.8 prelim didn't detract from his ability to win a tactical two-mile. In that race, Herb Lindsay tried drafting so Craig accelerated and then slammed on the brakes, forcing Lindsay into the lead in the second mile. The maneuver shook Lindsay, who finished 6.5 seconds behind Craig's winning 8:39.1. "He used strategies on me that he learned from the

Soviet athletes," said Lindsay with a laugh. "It's a pressure cooker to be in the lead. So how do you change that when someone is doing everything they can to hold on to push you as the leader? You stop and it completely disarms them. It completely disarmed me." It was the first time Craig used a stop-and-go tactic, but it wouldn't be the last.

Craig's long-awaited debut in the NCAA indoor meet was at Detroit's Cobo Hall, which had a banked, 165-yard board track requiring 11 laps for a mile. "It made hamburger of your feet," Craig remembered. The two-mile would be the last time Craig and Rose raced as collegians because Rose had no outdoor track eligibility left. It was expected to be a two-man battle between Craig and Rose, but Washington State's Joshua Kimeto of Kenya towed the field through the opening mile in 4:16.5. Rose began his kick with two laps to go. Craig reacted quickly, but couldn't pull back Rose's 2.8-second advantage and had to settle for second in 8:33.71 while Rose's 8:30.91 broke the meet record. "[Rose] had a higher gear than what I did when it came to closing the last 200 meters," said Craig, who helped Illinois score 13 points for fourth, the best finish in school history at that time.

Tumbling Times

Craig's early outdoor efforts in 1976 demonstrated improved speed. After a three-mile win in 13:39.2 on April 3 at home, he uncorked a career-best 4:02.8 mile the next week in a home dual (held at night under newly installed lights) in which he also purposely tied for first in the three-mile run with teammates Mark Avery and Dave Walters, who both notched personal records of 13:46.8.

Craig enjoyed meets like the Drake Relays, but never forgot he was trying to peak later in the season. "I purposely did not sharpen past a certain point for either Drake or Kansas, and that cost me a little bit in terms of ultimate performance, but it helped me because I still had room to grow come June instead of fading out," said Craig, who could see why college distance runners struggled to make Olympic teams. "Most of them had already run too hard in too many races." The tempo he used in his 10K training and racing didn't lend itself to fast times in the mile. The end of the relay circuit each season meant the end of his mile efforts as his focus turned to longer events. "That is one of my regrets now . . . that I didn't have a mile in there somewhere just to break 4:00 so I could say I did it once," admitted Craig, who never did break 4:00.

Forty days prior to the Olympic Trials, Craig had qualified to run the 5K, but not the 10K. He chose a low-key home meet May 8 to try for the 10K qualifying standard of 28:40.0. During his 25-lap quest, teammates were positioned around the track to shout encouragement. Wieneke let Craig know each lap how many seconds he was ahead or behind goal pace.

Craig and Bruce Fischer of the University of Chicago Track Club took turns in the lead, alternating every 800 meters through 5K. From there, Craig was on his own, but there was a problem. His chronic battle with blisters had caught the attention of U of I trainer Rod Cardinal, who used blister tape around the ball of Craig's right foot in an attempt to reduce friction. As the race progressed, the tape came off and wound itself into what felt like a cocklebur, creating the mother of all blisters. Craig tried to adjust his foot plant to get away from the pain. "I could feel it eating away for the last two miles and there wasn't a damn thing I could do about it," he told the *Chicago Sun-Times*.

After Craig finished and collapsed on the infield, Wieneke removed the shoe. "All this blood and body fluid came out of the shoe and Wieneke turned white," Craig recalled. "I remember he got sick on me." Craig would spend the next two days on crutches as a raw, three-square-inch section on his foot healed. Speeding his recovery was the fact he'd qualified for the Olympic Trials and the NCAA meet in 28:19.8, the fastest US time to that point in 1976.

The morning of the Big 10 meet in Champaign, Craig was able to walk pain free for the first time in a week. He went into the 5K undertrained and, as it turned out, overly worried about Herb Lindsay, who'd finish 15.9 seconds behind Craig's stadium record of 13:54.4. Craig might have run faster if he hadn't waved to the crowd several times in the closing laps. The *Urbana Courier* quoted him as saying, "I told Coach Wieneke that even if they'd cut my foot off, I'd have run today with that kind of crowd and in a meet like this."

The NCAA meet was at Franklin Field, home of the Penn Relays in Philadelphia. In the 10K, Craig quickly found himself in another high-contact race, but the combatant this time was two-time defending champion John Ngeno of Washington State. Both men repeatedly threw surges at the other after two miles, but neither could escape. Several coaches would tell Craig it was one of the most entertaining 10Ks they ever saw. It ended with Craig unleashing a 60.5-second last lap only to have Ngeno bolt to victory with a 57.6, clocking a meet-record 28:22.66. Craig's 28:25.52 in second also eclipsed the old meet record of 28:50.3 set by John Halberstadt in 1972.

Fast Farmer

Craig spent two weeks training in Lebanon prior to flying to Eugene for the Olympic Trials, where the top three in each event would qualify for the Olympics. He called Wieneke nearly every day to discuss workouts. Craig's routine was to sandwich eight hours of farmwork between a 6:30 a.m. run and an evening workout. Two or three times a week he visited Florissant Valley Community College in St. Louis to do speed work in spikes on a Tartan track. Sometimes he wouldn't get home for supper until 9:30 p.m.

The June issue of *Runner's World* magazine included a four-page feature on Craig. The piece notes he had "medium-length, brown, pageboy hair and the rugged good looks of an actor promoting radial tires on a television commercial." Craig didn't withhold his opinions, among them: "The Olympics are overemphasized. I wish they had a world championships every year instead." He wanted the best in the world to meet more often than once every four years, and he didn't see why such meetings had to include the political baggage of an Olympics.

Craig went to Eugene expecting to run both the 5K and 10K. The latter race came first with prelims on June 19 and finals on June 22. The top three in each of two 10K prelims along with the next three-fastest times and anyone running 28:45.0 or faster would advance. None of the 10K entrants had run faster in 1976 than Craig's 28:19.8.

Craig was excited to return to Eugene, where track ruled and distance runners were kings. "I found that I had to battle myself because I would get so excited and so pumped," he remembered. "I was really scared I was going to have an adrenaline overload." He stayed in a dorm near the track with former teammate Mike Durkin, who'd run a 3:56.7 mile in 1975 and would make the 1976 and 1980 Olympic teams in the 1,500-meter run. Craig took training runs on Pre's Trail. "Pre had only been dead for just over a year," Craig said. "His ghost was very much alive there at Hayward Field. I could still feel his presence."

Prior to the first 10K prelim of seven men, Frank Shorter and Craig agreed to run together and, if anyone was near, they'd surge in the middle of the race. They took turns leading and finished side by side, although Shorter was given the win by one hundredth of a second in 28:33.62. "Once there are just two of us, there's no use racing," Craig told Woods.

Performing on such a big stage suited Craig, who waved to the crowd. "The crowd was fun here," he told reporters. "If they're willing to clap, I'm willing to wave." At one point in the race, Craig was a few steps ahead of Shorter, who reached out as if to grab Craig's shirt to stop him from pulling away. "He even motioned to the crowd like he was pulling a ski boat rope behind me a couple times," Craig recalled. "The crowd started laughing."

It was a rare light moment in a meet known for do-or-die pressure. Other qualifiers for the nine-man final were Gary Tuttle (28:37.37) and Jeff Wells (28:40.81). Bill Rodgers, who'd made the marathon team earlier, won the second heat in a personal best of 28:32.79 followed by Bjorklund (28:44.4), Ted Castaneda (29:00.8) and Ed Mendoza (29:10.4).

Bjorklund, discussing the final three days away, told the *Eugene Register-Guard*, "Nobody has more guts than Virgin, and I like to think if I get through the first part of the race I've got a good chance at the end." Bjorklund had been living and training with Shorter in Boulder, Colorado, for several months. Rodgers, whose prelim was his second-ever 10K, said, "I look for Shorter and Virgin to go out hard, and I'll just try to go with them."

Craig tried, unsuccessfully, to arrange a pace-sharing strategy with Shorter prior to the final. "Frank is the hardest damn guy to talk to in the world," Craig told reporters. "Frank was noncommittal. He just winked at me." Shorter's assessment of Craig became evident when he told reporters, "Physically he's got all the equipment." On the morning of the final, Craig's mother told him their family had reserved hotel rooms in Montreal. In the cauldron of Olympic Trials pressure, that extra bit fit right in.

Stepping Softly

A crowd of 13,000—the biggest yet to see Craig run—attended the 10K final. Shorter—looking incredibly thin, almost dainty—laid down a relentless pace as the other eight finalists tried to cling to his 28-minute tempo. One by one they reluctantly fell back. The remaining four of Shorter, Bjorklund, Rodgers and Craig ran in such a bunch, three mini accidents nearly turned major.

On the 14th lap, Bjorklund lost his left shoe. Craig thought it was possible his foot removed Bjorklund's shoe. "I caught Frank's cleats a couple of times and Garry's a couple of times," Craig remembered. At any rate, Bjorklund stuck with the group. "For six years I've ate, slept and dreamed of having this chance," Bjorklund told the *Eugene Register-Guard*. "Losing a shoe wasn't going to stop me."

The leaders passed 5K in 14:02.4. "I did so much leading the first four miles that I tried to slow the fifth one down," said Shorter, who took off with Craig with two laps remaining. Craig yelled, "Don't move out yet, Frank. Let me hang on for a while."

Entering the last lap, the 20-year-old farm boy's deference to Shorter, the 28-year-old attorney, disappeared as Craig bolted to the front. "I don't know why in the world I took the lead on the last lap," he told Woods. Running so lightly his footsteps were inaudible, Shorter remained patient around the penultimate curve before taking the lead for good with 200 meters to go. His 60.3 last lap gave him a 15-yard margin of victory in 27:55.45. The only times faster in American history were Prefontaine's American record of 27:43.6 and Shorter's 27:51.4 for fifth in the 1972 Olympics.

The final 10 seconds of the race and the next 10 seconds took Craig on a surreal dash from anxiety to bottomless pain to infinite exultation. As he crossed second in a personal best of 27:59.43, he collapsed. "You don't know what a feeling it is to realize you're second in the Olympic Trials," he told Dave Dorr of the *St. Louis Post-Dispatch*. Now third best in US history, Craig had broken the collegiate record of 28:04.6 by Kenyan John Ngeno. Craig had also lowered Ngeno's collegiate six-mile record of 27:06.8 to 27:04.4, which broke the age-20 world record held by Great Britain's David Bedford. Craig's time was the world's sixth best to that point in 1976 and ranked 27th on the all-time world list. "I think when I crossed the finish line and I knew that I had made the team, it was just one of the happiest moments of my life," Craig recalled. "Suddenly all the pain went away."

Bjorklund took third in 28:03.74 as the top three became the first Olympians to wear Nike shoes. After taking a victory lap, Craig was greeted on the backstretch by legendary Oregon coach Bill Bowerman, who shook his hand and wrapped an arm around him. Bowerman asked if his parents were present. Upon learning they weren't, Bowerman said, "Come with me. I'll treat you to a phone call. Call them and tell them you made the Olympic team." Craig walked to a trackside phone booth to use Bowerman's credit card to call. It was an act of kindness Craig never forgot.

Craig returned to the starting line three days later for the 5K semifinals. He finished second in 13:43.10 behind Dick Buerkle's 13:41.76. With his calves growing sore after 62 laps of racing in a six-day span, Craig told Woods he might withdraw from the final. "I don't want to be foolish and throw away what I've already got," he said.

Craig's recollection is that US Olympic distance coach Sam Bell proposed to Wieneke that Craig not contest the 5K final. Bell didn't want Craig to get injured and miss the Olympics. Wieneke spent parts of two days discussing the issue with Craig, who eventually bought into the idea. "I felt really weird," Craig said years later. "Part of me was relieved because I was tired, but I know that I had one more race in me. I was running so much on adrenaline at that point in time that it didn't matter."

Loren Tate's June 30 column noted: "Wieneke is pleased Virgin withdrew of his own accord since it avoided a confrontation between the coach and athlete. Gary had absolutely made up his mind that Craig not compete after running the preliminary with sore legs. 'I didn't want to exercise my prerogative of pulling him out,' said Gary. 'But he just isn't ready for that kind of a double. He already won his spot in the 10,000. That doesn't mean he couldn't have finished third in the 5,000, but I didn't want him to hurt himself.'"

The lead pack in the 1976 US Olympic Trials 10K featured four of the biggest stars in American distance-running history in (from left) Bill Rodgers, Craig, Garry Bjorklund and Frank Shorter. *(Photo by Jeff Johnson)*

In the 5K final, Buerkle (13:26.6), Duncan Macdonald (13:29.6) and Paul Geis (13:38.6) made the Olympic team. The third-place time was more than three seconds slower than Craig's best. "I knew I could have [qualified in the 5K] and then I had this ominous feeling that I should have," Craig recalled. In Montreal 28 days later, he'd wish he had a second event.

Party Time

The Trials ended in a flurry of parties for the athletes, who were showered with free shoes and clothing from Nike, Puma and adidas. Craig felt on top of the world. When he stepped off the plane at Lambert Airport's Gate 10 in St. Louis, a group of 50 friends and family carrying homemade signs was there to greet him, including Pam McDonald of O'Fallon, the woman he dated the most between 1973 and 1978. After he was swarmed by a flurry of hugs and handshakes, Craig heard his father say, "This is for you. Savor it."

A motorcade escorted Craig to Lebanon where a parade ensued with Craig atop a fire truck. The parade, complete with the high school band, ended at City Hall where 500 people listened to speeches from the mayor, Coach Feldt and high school booster club president S. Gene Rhoden. "St. Louis has its Arch and Paris has the Eiffel Tower, but we want to leave the world the legend of Craig Virgin," Rhoden said as a Belleville radio station broadcasted the ceremony. Wearing a tan three-piece suit, Craig told the crowd, "The people here are my friends and I don't ever want to leave."

The way Lebanon felt about Craig was poetically summed up by Bob Emig, who wrote: "The Craig Virgin personality is such that it is of charismatic proportions. He can be in a crowd, but the crowd becomes one because the Virgin personality is pulling everyone into one. He is dominant, but not because he is over-bearing. Quite the opposite. He is unassuming. His broad smile is contagious. He's articulate. He's considerate. The all-American boy idea is not dead. Virgin is the all-American boy."

Chapter 11: 1976 Olympic Games

"In running, you never can rest on your laurels."

— Craig Virgin

As the second-youngest US Olympic team member, Craig had no delusions of possibly winning an Olympic medal in 1976, not against international veterans as much as 10 years older. "Your potential is greater as you get older because you gain strength," he told the *Courier & Press* of Evansville, Indiana. "A distance runner's peak years are 25 to 30." Among 1976 times, Craig's 27:59.43 ranked ninth in the world. Prior to 1972, the Olympic record had been 28:24.4.

Garry Bjorklund, 24, told the *Urbana Courier*, "Craig's chances of getting into the finals are good, but that's about it. I don't think we're in a position to look at medals." Craig agreed he could make the final. *Track & Field News* noted that Craig "trains lightly compared to most world class runners. Lacks finishing speed, but is smart for his age; aggressive. Improving by huge chunks, a minute in the last year alone."

The biggest incident leading up to the Olympics was a boycott by 28 African nations in protest of New Zealand allowing a South African rugby team to play exhibitions in New Zealand. South Africa had been banned from the Olympics since 1964 for its refusal to condemn apartheid. African nations wanted New Zealand banned, too. Only 92 nations competed at Montreal compared to 121 in Munich.

This affected Craig, who awoke two days prior to the opening ceremonies to see Africans, many in tears, gathering with their luggage in front of the Olympic Village. "It was just cruel," he said. "I just couldn't feel like the sacrifice was worth it. It was not going to overturn apartheid and I knew it." Craig told David Woods that "a lot of African athletes wanted to disobey their countries and run." Craig's college teammate, Charlton Ehizuelen, left when Nigeria withdrew. Ehizuelen had been staying in the same Olympic Village building as Craig and Mike Durkin. A medal threat in the long jump with a best of 27 feet, 1¼ inches, Ehizuelen left them a farewell note that read, "Sorry I can't jump. You and Mike have a good time. See you next fall."

Africa's departure radically changed the distance events in which Kenya and Ethiopia were major players. Things changed again when Shorter announced he'd only run the marathon, thus giving his 10K spot to Olympic Trials fifth-placer Ed Mendoza. Craig had hoped to work with Shorter in the 10K. "I think I learned a lot running with him at the Olympic Trials in Eugene and I think I would have learned even more if he'd run the 10,000 in Montreal," Craig told the *Urbana Courier*.

Team USA gathered for a few days in Plattsburg, New York, just over an hour's drive from Montreal, to train as well as get uniforms and freebies. "It was like Christmas," said Craig, recalling that official sponsor Montgomery Ward handed out leisure suits, pants, blazers, shirts and ties—all double-knit. There were warm-up suits for practice and others for more formal occasions, along with bags of toiletries.

The bounty included an official T-shirt, but Craig had brought samples of a shirt he'd helped design. "Suddenly I had eight or 10 people who wanted copies," said Craig, who placed an order for 120 red-white-and-blue shirts of two different designs. Printed on both designs were: USA XXIst OLYMPIAD. The shirts arrived while the team was still in Plattsburg, and Craig took leftovers into the Olympic Village. The shirts were so popular among US Olympians, Craig had to order more. His share of the profits with his partner, Durkin, was over $1,000, enough to buy Olympic tickets for family members. Durkin spent his share on an engagement ring.

When Craig arrived at the Olympic Village, he was shocked it was so far from finished. Even electrical outlets had yet to be covered. He was assigned to a three-bedroom apartment with bunk beds jammed into each room. His apartment housed 12 men including eventual decathlon gold medalist Bruce Jenner, 800 bronze medalist-to-be Rick

Wohlhuter and Durkin. At night, the unit produced more snoring than Craig had ever heard. Later he'd suspect the apartment also contained a 12-man stockpile of germs. "It was very crowded and very much like our old family reunions," said Craig, who rated the cafeteria the highlight of the Olympic Village, because it never closed and the food was exquisite. Of course, he partook in the trading of Olympic pins with fellow Olympians, but he preferred trading race jerseys and warm-ups.

High Security

The slaughter of 11 Israeli athletes and coaches by terrorists at the 1972 Olympics made security a priority in 1976. The Olympic Village was surrounded by a 10-foot fence topped by barbed wire. Policemen with dogs and submachine guns patrolled the perimeter. Helicopters buzzed overhead and visitors entered through metal detectors. "I had never been in a place with that much security," said Craig, who wound up moving out of the Olympic Village briefly at the invitation of Nike. The shoe company, still in its infancy, had a block of hotel rooms in suburban Montreal. Shorter also stayed there because Nike was courting him to wear its shoes in the marathon. He wound up wearing Onitsuka Tigers instead.

Craig contested two impromptu pre-Olympic races in Montreal. One was a 5K in which he placed third, 10.9 seconds behind Ethiopian winner Miruts Yifter, the 1972 Olympic 10K bronze medalist. Craig's 13:35.3 narrowly missed his personal best of 13:35.02 from 1975.

Optimistic by nature, Craig found himself surrounded by like-minded people during the opening ceremonies. When he later experienced the closing ceremonies, it was clear which he preferred. "The opening ceremonies are by far the happiest because everybody's dream is still alive," he said. "Everybody is optimistic. Nobody has had their dream dashed yet."

Athletes dressed in their national parade uniforms began staging a mile from the Olympic Stadium as they prepared to march in for the opening ceremonies. "It was just a wonderful experience," said Craig, who noticed Olympic veterans carrying programs. They informed him the programs would be used to shield their heads from the droppings of

500 doves that were scheduled to be released during the opening ceremonies. Within a half mile of the stadium, fans, many from the United States, lined the streets 20 deep as athletes marched past. "When the American contingent would go through, people would just go nuts and they were waving their little American flags," Craig recalled. "The noise was just deafening."

Inside the stadium, giant speakers were cranked to a bone-shaking volume. As adrenaline filled his body, Craig wished he could race immediately. The excitement made him recall watching the 1972 Olympics on television. He remembered thinking, "Man, what a change my life has undergone in just four short years."

On the eve of his July 23 10K prelim, Craig ate with his family. They had a French meal featuring rabbit at Nike's hotel base. Nothing was amiss until Craig awoke at 2 a.m. with stomach cramps. At first he suspected food poisoning, but it was later determined he'd contracted a flu virus that would also fell Paul Geis. Between vomiting and bouts of diarrhea, Craig was up and down the rest of the night. His race was scheduled for 5:40 p.m.

The decision to leave the Olympic Village now meant Craig didn't have immediate access to an infirmary. When he finally got help at 8 a.m., doctors were careful not to give him drugs that might test positive as performance enhancers. He was shocked to learn he'd lost five pounds in nine hours. The idea of withdrawing from his race wasn't considered. "I had come too far," he said. "I was going to make the best of the situation. At least I knew I was going to be as light on my feet as I was going to be."

Cooling Down

As his prelim approached, Craig went into self-coaching mode by thinking: "'Okay, you've got to suck it up and you've got to be mentally tough.' I tried to focus on the positive. I tried to focus on every confidence-enhancing technique or mantra that I could use." One such technique involved lying down to concentrate on relaxing each body part beginning with his toes. Then he'd run the race lap by lap in his mind as he'd learned to do from reading Maxwell Maltz' self-help book,

*Psycho-Cybernetics,*which asserts the mind-body connection is essential to reaching goals.

The routine for Craig's career had been to race soon after warming up. The 1976 Olympics didn't work that way. After warming up at the practice track, athletes still had to go through a lengthy check-in process. "That's a problem that most spectators and people who don't compete in the Olympics just don't understand," said Craig, who found it difficult to stay ready after a 20-minute walk to the staging area and 15 minutes of confinement in a small waiting room. "I really don't even know how you train for that."

Craig was in the second of three heats. The top four in each heat and the next three fastest would advance. Tension in the cramped waiting room in the bowels of the stadium grew as the 14 runners in the second heat killed time with tiny jogs back and forth. "You could almost taste the fear in the air," Craig recalled.

When Craig finally stepped on the track, he saw the biggest crowd of his career at more than 65,000. "My heart was ready to beat right out of my chest," he said. As he ran his final stride-outs, he was surprised he didn't feel bad considering his illness. "I tried to run smart," he said. "I tried to run efficient." That was enough to keep him in the hunt for a qualifying spot for 24 of the race's 25 laps. Craig passed a mile in 4:31.5 and three miles in 13:42. He led for parts of the 12th and 13th laps. He was part of a four-man surge that reached five miles in 22:49.9, but fizzled two laps later, allowing two others to regain contact.

In the stands, Craig's father videotaped the race with his new Sony Betamax while Craig's mother nervously sat next to a French-Canadian woman advising her, "Don't look. Don't look." On the 25th lap, those who'd qualify unleashed a 59- to 60-second final circuit while Craig managed only 66 to finish sixth in 28:30.22. His time ranked 20th among all three heats, all of which were won with times slower than his personal best. Looking back, he'd have preferred a steady, fast pace. "My lack of strength really took its toll in the last two miles," he told Woods.

As Craig walked back to the Olympic Village with his family and Gary Wieneke, US team coach Sam Bell came up and suggested Craig had spent too much time selling T-shirts to run well. "I just remember I didn't appreciate it very much," Craig said. "Later, he did have the gall to ask me to save a few of those T-shirts for him and his family, which of course I did, but I charged him a premium price." Craig's descriptions of Bell, first as a disappointed, phone-slamming recruiter, and later as a schemer to get Craig out of the Trials 5K, don't seem to mesh with the fact Craig never tossed a letter from Bell on US Olympic Team stationery dated August 26, 1976. It reads:

> My congratulations to you for the growth you have made as a runner since you decided to become one. I thought your growth in 1976 was phenomenal. I am still certain that you should have been in the 10,000 meter final and would have been a competitive factor in it had you not have run into the "Frenchman's revenge" in Montreal.
>
> I know that your best races are in front of you and even though I hope you won't bury those people from Indiana too much when you compete against them, I will be cheering for your improvement because I believe you can be competitive with the world.
>
> You have made a lot of growth in your approach to competition, training and your own limitations, and I know that the growth in those areas will continue. I will look forward to seeing you in the next year as you compete in your senior season for Illinois and will cheer with all the other Americans as you grow to the point where the world will be looking at you as they now look at the Virens, the Juantorenas, and others of that ability.

Wieneke hadn't known Craig was ill until the faltering final lap. In a phone interview with the *Urbana Courier*, Wieneke said, "I'm surprised that Craig ran as well as he did considering the physical problems he had. I was there to talk to him right after his race and you could tell he was really feeling the effects of his illness." Craig returned to the infirmary after his race. "I was really dizzy and I thought I'd better have the doctor check me again," he recalled.

Explaining Failure

The outcome left Craig crushed. He dreaded explaining what happened to his supporters. "It's going to be hard for me to go back home to people who had high expectations," he told Woods. "I hope people understand what it takes to run 10,000 meters, much less with the flu. I don't know how to face people and tell them, 'Well, I just got sick.' I don't want to do that. I just did the best I could under the circumstances." The day after his race, Craig's family had a picnic. He hoped they could accept his failure. "I'm sure there'll be more downfalls down the road," he told Woods. "There'll be a lot of happiness, too."

Craig watched Finland's Lasse Viren defend his title in the final in 27:40.38 followed by Portugal's Carlos Lopes (27:45.17) and Great Britain's Brendan Foster (27:54.92). Craig's best time would've put him fifth.

On July 30, Viren won the 5K in 13:24.8. The next day he contested the marathon, placing fifth in 2:13:10 behind East German Waldemar Cierpinski's winning 2:09:55. Shorter was second in 2:10:45. It was later revealed that East Germany provided performance-enhancing drugs to thousands of athletes over a 20-year period ending in 1988. Files found at Stasi headquarters in Leipzig in the 1990s implicated Cierpinski as a drug cheat.

The closing ceremonies took place on the eve of Craig's birthday. During the festivities and fireworks, he met a cute French-Canadian woman working as a liaison. They arranged to meet later at the Olympic Village. "I thought to myself, 'What a heck of a way to celebrate your 21st birthday,'" he recalled. "I remember I partied with every delegation that would allow me to party." The liaison arrived at 10 p.m. and took Craig out on the town. "I just know she helped me greet my birthday in grand fashion and I will always be grateful to her," said Craig, who later received a letter from her. "I don't even remember her name right now, but I will say this much—she did more for American-Canadian diplomacy that night than anybody ever did before or since with me. That's as far as I'll go on that topic."

Craig had planned to end his season at the Olympics, but ending on a bad note wasn't his style, so he accepted an invitation to race two miles at Philadelphia on August 4. The pace was torrid from the start, but Craig hung on for sixth in a Big 10 all-time best of 8:25.3, crushing his previous best of 8:32.4. Olympic 5K silver medalist Dick Quax of New Zealand won in 8:17.1 with Virin third in 8:21.5.

Under the Table

After the race a meet rep handed Craig $500, which he accepted even though he knew it violated the NCAA "pay for play" clause. "That was the first under-the-table money for running that I ever got in my life," he said. "I was barely getting by on my scholarship and my $100 allowance from my family." The illicit income helped him splurge for a $400 radio/cassette tape stereo system.

Craig didn't think it was fair that scholarship athletes were forbidden by the NCAA from holding jobs. His scholarship didn't cover all his expenses. "You were basically going to be impoverished for four years, which I resented," he said. Especially frustrating was the fact he was governed by three entities—the NCAA, USOC (United States Olympic Committee) and AAU—all of which wanted him to run for free. "When they disagree, the real person who gets hurt is the athlete," Craig told Don Pierson of the *Chicago Tribune*.

The US Olympic Committee had ruled that summer that Olympians could be compensated for lost wages. The NCAA told undergraduates on the Olympic team they couldn't accept subsidies from the USOC. "It'll be a challenge to see whether I can last for eight more years operating under the US system," Craig told Pierson. "I'm going to be doing a lot to try to help change it, to be a pioneer in making our system more equitable."

Craig ran his sixth and final track 10K of 1976—for free—in hot conditions and 95 percent humidity on August 6 in the US-USSR dual meet at College Park, Maryland. He broke away the final two miles to win in 28:35.2. "I was determined to make up for what had happened at the Olympics," Craig said. "That is a hard way to do it—by yourself."

Craig ended his long season with another two-mile for money in Philadelphia, a losing effort in the 8:48 range that earned him $500. "I knew by the second lap that I was dead meat and that I was past my peak and I was on the downhill slide," he said.

At any rate, he returned to Lebanon with a new image of himself. He was no longer just national class, he was world class. He returned to Champaign on August 23 for cross country practice, which Wieneke opened two weeks later than usual in an effort to keep his team mentally fresh.

The August issue of *Runner's World* included a three-page story written by Craig and illustrated by Rob Mango titled "Surviving Freshman Shock." It was about the obstacles that can sideline blue-chip distance-running recruits in college, a topic Craig knew well. "The incoming athlete must be capable of emotional stability and of adaptive ability in the presence of unfavorable conditions," he wrote. Another key point was, "A young runner soon finds that as the body gets older and faster it also becomes more susceptible to injuries."

Craig spoke to Wieneke about redshirting the 1976 cross country season. Craig decided not to because the team figured to be the best of his career. He also wanted to graduate the next spring. He lived slightly more comfortably that first semester of his senior year thanks to his $1,000 of under-the-table race earnings and a $1,000 gift from Grandpa Virgin.

Academically, Craig, carrying a 4.4 grade point average on a 5.0 scale, had realized that the U of I radio and television program was deficient. "I had to spend a day or two thinking, 'Do I want to go somewhere for a better education or finish out my degree at the U of I?'" Craig recalled. "Nowadays I probably would have had an offer to go professional." With the team outlook so bright, he chose to return and take as many business and advertising courses as possible. He knew he'd have a running career beyond college.

The *Track & Field News* cross country season preview noted: "In the individual race, Virgin is a good bet to repeat: defending champ, experienced, still hungry." UTEP's Wilson Waigwa was expected to challenge. There was no mention of a Washington State freshman from Kenya named Henry Rono.

The Secret Injury

Craig's fellow seniors were Jeff Jirele, Gary Mumaw and Les Myers. Dave Walters, Mark Avery and Bill Fritz were juniors and Jim Eicken a sophomore. Even though he was an Olympian, Craig didn't view a return to college competition as a letdown, especially not in the Big 10 where many future US stars were targeting him. As he approached the September 11 season opener against Southern Illinois at Carbondale's Midland Hills Golf Course, he felt impervious to injury. During premeet stretching, he felt a pull in the area of his right calf and Achilles tendon. He raced anyway, clocking a four-mile course record of 19:56. "Nineteen fifty-six on that thing is blazing," Wieneke said. "There isn't a flat place on that course."

Craig finished a step ahead of teammate Jim Eicken in a dual cross country meet against Missouri at Savoy in 1976. *(Photo courtesy of the University of Illinois)*

The terrain was especially hard on Craig's injured calf. "I don't even think that many of my teammates understood just how much pain I was in and how vulnerable I was," he said. The first media mention of the injury came in late October when Woods wrote: "He continues to be bothered by a sore Achilles tendon." Not wanting to give his rivals hope, Craig told Woods, "Once I start running, it's all right. It's just the acceleration."

The November 6 Big 10 meet in Glen Ellyn, Illinois, had special significance for Craig, who hoped to become the first four-time champion in the meet's 62-year history. Besides Craig, the race included five other Big 10 track champions: Herb Lindsay (1,500), Greg Meyer (steeplechase), Mark Johnson (10K), Steve Lacy (indoor mile) and Tom Byers (indoor 1,000). Joining that group was Minnesota's Steve Plasencia, who'd been fifth in the NCAA 5K outdoors.

Woods' preview focused on Wisconsin coach Dan McClimon's 1973 recruiting visit to Lebanon. "For one thing, I remember it was a long drive from Madison to Lebanon," McClimon said. "The other thing was that Craig told me, 'I want to be the first ever to win four Big 10 championships. That's why the Big 10 appeals to me.'"

The day before the race, Craig, as usual, made mental notes of the line he'd follow to maximize the best footing and the shortest path on the hilly, twisting course. An estimated 4,000 fans watched him open a lead on a 40-yard downhill section at the 1½-mile mark. "I could not take a chance of it being too tactical," said Craig, who made one other push before hammering the fourth mile in 4:32. A final mile of 4:41 made him the winner in 23:16.7. "There isn't anyone here that I talked to who can fathom running that fast," Wieneke told Woods. Lindsay grabbed second in 23:39 followed by Meyer (23:50), Plasencia (23:51) and Bill Donakowski (24:01). Michigan topped Illinois for the team title, 67–78, but if the race had been scored as a dual, the Illini would have won, 27–28. It was Illinois' best finish in seven years.

Craig's fourth Big 10 title didn't feel as expected. "I thought it would be an exuberant feeling, but it's a warm feeling to know that it's over with," he told the *Daily Illini*. Through 2016, no other man had won four consecutive Big 10 titles, although Indiana's Bob Kennedy and Michigan's Kevin Sullivan each won four in five years.

Craig's final home cross country meet in college was the NCAA District IV meet on November 13 where 3,000 fans gathered for what was largely a Big 10 rerun. A party was held for the runners the night before the race. Craig remembered his girlfriend, Pam McDonald, danced with Greg Meyer. "I think he was doing it in a joking manner," Craig said. "I let him go just so far. I gave him a lot of rope. I think he was looking over his shoulder just to see how much more I was going to give him." Meyer's recollection is that "Burgie liked to politic so he'd be walking around talking to everybody [and] left his girl sitting at the table. So I went out and danced with her and he got all upset. He was giving me grief for the first two miles of the race, hooting on me about it."

At 7 a.m. on race day, Craig visited Uncle John's Pancake House where he consumed his usual breakfast of two pancakes, two eggs, two cups of coffee and a glass of water. The Illini Striders booster club proclaimed it Craig Virgin Day, which lived up to its billing as Craig won in 29:04.4 with Lindsay second in 29:21. Meyer, fourth in 29:42, told the *Daily Illini*, "Virgin is running super right now. I don't think anyone is going to beat him the rest of the year."

The Illini made Wieneke's 39th birthday extra special by putting six men in the top 20 to secure the team title, 47–96, ahead of Michigan. It was the only NCAA district cross country title Wieneke would win and, as of 2016, Illinois hadn't won another. Next up was the November 22 NCAA meet in Denton, Texas, where a bevy of Kenyan, Irish and English stars awaited. Craig told Woods, "We're headed for the United Nations next weekend."

Chapter 12: Racing Rono

*"I realize we're getting to the end of our partic-
ular relationship, but I procrastinate thinking
about that."*

— Gary Wieneke

The NCAA cross country course at Denton, Texas, was relatively flat and featured one- and two-mile loops. For the first time in the meet's 38-year history, the course would stretch 10,000 meters [6.2 miles]. The one hill had to be climbed twice. Herb Lindsay said of the course, "It was just a baked clay surface. It was like running on a track. It was hard. It was really fast." On the Saturday prior to the Monday race, Craig toured the course and took time to joke with former high school rivals Matt Centrowitz and Terry Williams of Oregon.

At this point, Craig was aware Washington State freshman Henry Rono would contend. Rono's career included a 3,000-meter victory over Tanzania's Filbert Bayi, the world record holder in the 1,500. Other Kenyan contenders were Washington State's Joshua Kimeto, the NCAA 5K champion, teammate Samson Kimobwa, UTEP's James Munyala and Wilson Waigwa, along with Irishman John Treacy of Providence College. "In some ways, I have the best chance among Americans to beat the foreigners," Craig told Woods. "I've had some experience in different types of tactics. I know the type of race the Africans run."

Craig was less serious and less politically correct when *Track & Field News* quoted him as saying, "I think I'll announce that I ran against some New Zealand guys last week just to see if the Kenyans

One month after competing in the 1976 Montreal Olympics, Craig reported to Coach Gary Wieneke for cross country duty. *(Photo courtesy of the University of Illinois)*

will pull out!" That jab referred to Kenya's Olympic boycott because New Zealand allowed a South African rugby team to visit. Rono, Kimobwa and Kimeto, all Nandi tribesmen from a cattle-farming region of the Rift Valley, had been recommended to Washington State coach John Chapin by 1968 Olympic 1,500 gold medalist Kip Keino. Kimobwa was a diminutive loper with a high back kick while the muscular Rono was a glider with textbook form.

Wieneke and Craig both felt Illinois could finish in the top five, a level they hadn't reached since placing fifth in 1969. Craig roomed with Gary Mumaw on the eve of the race. Mumaw felt nervous and Craig didn't help matters. "I want to get to bed and here he's got all the pressure on him and he's just lackadaisical, lighthearted and I remember switching rooms that night because he wasn't going to bed and I wanted to go to bed," Mumaw said. "He came down pounding on the door. He said, 'Moo, Moo, I'm ready to go to bed now. You can come back.'"

A thousand spectators watched the race under cloudless, 50-degree conditions. The pace was ruthless as Rono, Kimobwa and Kimeto took a flamethrower to the first mile, splitting 4:17. They passed two miles in 8:47 and three in 13:27. "I gambled," Craig told *Track & Field News*. "I thought they were calling my bluff and would fade. But there was no way I could stay with them after the four-mile post. So I sat back and rested."

Craig began to recover during the fifth mile. He saw Rono grab his side and thought he saw both leaders sway. "It was then that I thought they were going to fold," Craig told the *Daily Illini*. "It was to their credit they didn't fold. Just one falter at that stage of the race would have been all I needed." Rono hustled past four miles in 18:00 and five in 22:37. "I knew that my goose was probably cooked with a mile to go, but I gave it the old college try," Craig said. "I did eat back into some of their distance, but it was a very discouraging experience for me."

Making NCAA History

Rono's winning 28:06.60 was so fast, no NCAA cross country champion had gone faster on any course as of 2016. He was only 7.2 seconds slower than Craig's collegiate record on the track. Kimobwa's runner-up time of 28:16.78 still ranked second in NCAA history in 2016. Craig's third-place 28:26.53 would've won any other year except 1979 when Rono sped 28:19.4.

The talent of those ahead of Craig became clear seven months after Denton when Kimobwa lowered David Bedford's world 10K record of 27:30.8 to 27:30.5. A year after that, Rono lowered it to 27:22.4. Lindsay, running an even pace throughout the NCAA meet, made a late charge to finish fourth in 28:30.69. It was the closest he ever came to Craig in cross country. Craig became the third in meet history to crack the top 12 four times, joining Steve Prefontaine and Nick Rose.

The hot pace stopped 22 in the field of 230 from finishing, including Oregon freshman Alberto Salazar. Only four of the top 12 were American. It was the first time foreigners had swept both the individual and team titles as UTEP, with four Kenyans in the top 15, defended its title in the 34-team field with 62 points. Illinois was fifth with 227. Through 2016, the Illini had yet to place that high again.

Denton was Craig's fourth loss and fastest time in 33 cross country races as a collegian, snapping a 15-race cross country winning streak. "I never dreamed a cross country race would go this fast," he told Woods. "If I'd known the race was going to be like this, I'd have been on a track the last three weeks." Craig blamed himself for not being more aggressive. "That's one thing United States runners in the future must learn to do," he said. "They must become more aggressive in racing the Africans and Europeans."

Losing to the 23-year-old Rono didn't sit well with Craig, who felt sorry for Americans deprived of scholarships by older foreigners. "I don't like to see all those foreigners come over here to reap the benefits of our education system at the expense of American youth," said Craig, who can't remember discussing the issue with 23-year-old Nigerian teammate Charlton Ehizuelen (born November 30, 1953). "He was age appropriate," said Craig, who was mailed a T-shirt by a college coach that read: *Don't be a xenophobe.* Craig shrugged off the jab—and some hate mail—because he believed the physical maturity enjoyed by older runners unfairly enhanced performance. Complicating the issue was the fact the NCAA had recently reduced the maximum number of track scholarships a school could offer to 14. The move sent some coaches overseas looking for athletes capable of scoring immediately in NCAA meets.

By being the top American in the NCAA meet, Craig qualified for the World Cross Country Championships at Düsseldorf, West Germany, on March 20, 1977. He chose not to go because the race fell one week after the NCAA indoor track meet and two weeks before the start of Illinois' outdoor season.

Craig continued to train the next several weeks at a reduced level, hoping his Achilles/calf problem would heal. Also in the mix of worries was his relationship with Pam McDonald, whom he sensed was ready to get married. "I could feel that pressure coming," said Craig, who was ready to explore the world. "She was very supportive of me during those four years that we were dating from a long distance. And even though I was occasionally dating other girls at school, I never had any relationship at school that lasted for any long period of time like it did with Pam."

Craig opened his 1977 indoor campaign with lackluster results. He was fifth in the Philadelphia Classic two-mile in 8:44.6 as Shorter won in 8:40.2. The next day, Craig won the mile in a home invitational in 4:08.0. In the January 28 Millrose Games, he ran 8:44.8 for third in a two-mile won by Western Kentucky's Tony Staynings of Great Britain in 8:41.4. "I was just struggling with my biomechanics," Craig said. "It was a period of frustration."

The Intimidator

During a stretch of nine consecutive weekends of racing, Craig contested the Big 10 indoor three-mile run at Ann Arbor, Michigan, where his reputation preceded him. "The intimidation I was able to do with the other runners basically broke them without me having to make a ton of moves," said Craig, who won in a school record 13:28.2. He returned to Michigan the next weekend hungry to win his first NCAA track title at Detroit's Cobo Hall. It didn't happen, though, as Brigham Young freshman Luis Hernandez, a 23-year-old Olympian from Mexico, won the three-mile in 13:20.6 followed by Kimobwa and Craig. "It was there for the taking," remembered Craig, who clocked a school record 13:23.0. "I could have been, should have been, 20 seconds faster had I been healthy."

Prior to Craig's final appearance in the Illinois Intercollegiates at Naperville, Loren Tate wrote about the fact Craig's collegiate career was nearing an end and how much he'd meant to the U of I. Tate noted: "The single most positive undergraduate force in Illini athletics over the past four years has entered the final month of his college career. The name is Craig Virgin and there is no way to measure the total influence of his presence."

While other U of I stars may have been more talented, Tate wrote, many also had disciplinary issues of one kind or another. All of his college career, Craig had been an inspiration to teammates and fans. While referring to the upcoming NCAA meet in Champaign, Craig told Tate, "I'd really like to win in front of the home fans. I remember two years ago when I first heard about the possibility of the NCAA coming here, I spent two hours encouraging Gary [Wieneke] to do it. . . . My first objective is to get my final exams out of the way—I'm real proud of graduating in four years—and then put all my concentration on track."

Craig's final grade point average of 4.4 on a 5.0 scale was a tenth higher than his high school GPA. The chronic fatigue of training had created an academic challenge for Craig, who had to battle drowsiness when sitting through afternoon classes. He made a point of sitting in the first three rows and engaging the instructor. "It kept my attention and kept me in the action," he said. His efforts earned him the Big 10 Medal of Honor, awarded to one student-athlete at each Big 10 school for academic and athletic success.

Stories about legendary runners sometimes take on mythical qualities as witnesses retell anecdotes again and again. Such an anecdote exists about University of Illinois–Chicago runner Jim Laubsted, whom Craig faced in a 10K at Naperville. Because of the large field, officials decided they'd pull lapped runners if they were 26th place or worse. Laubsted, known for running an even pace, was working his way up from 30th to 29th to 28th when his friends noticed Craig was moving even faster while lapping one runner after another.

Laubsted was 27th when Craig passed the 28th man. On personal record pace, Laubsted glanced back and immediately realized his predicament. He picked up his pace, moving into 26th with Craig on his shoulder. The mild-mannered Laubsted unleashed an all-out surge to stay in the race at the same time it appeared Craig was chiding him for having such audacity. At any rate, Laubsted remained ahead of Craig until passing the 25th man. Laubsted then eased up, but went on to pass several more runners en route to a personal best. His one-lap battle with Craig was his fastest lap by far.

Friends later asked Laubsted what possessed him to battle the Olympian. "Hey, it was his idea," Laubsted replied. As Craig had approached, he yelled for Laubsted to pick up his pace. That's when Laubsted looked back. While on Laubsted's shoulder, Craig said, "Come on, little brother." Craig continued to encourage Laubsted until he passed another runner. Craig lapped the entire field to win by 80.1 seconds in a meet record 28:32.6—the fastest time in the United States to that point in 1977. His time has been forgotten, but the story of his kindness lives on.

Looking Ahead

Most published stories about Craig in his final month of college focused on his running life after graduation when he'd need a job that allowed time to train. The stories often looked back at the highs and lows of his career. "The exposure I've gotten in the papers and the letters I've gotten from people around here . . . it gives me a good feeling," he told the *Daily Illini*. "I'm ready to move on, but I'm kind of sad that these four years have gone so fast."

Craig later told Bob Hammel of the *Bloomington* (Indiana) *Herald-Times*, "I have to prove to myself that I can run after college." In the same article, Wieneke lamented the impending end of Craig's career. "I realize we're getting to the end of our particular relationship, but I procrastinate thinking about that," Wieneke said. "I just enjoy what's happening now."

Illinois had two weeks off before the May 21 Big 10 meet at Bloomington, Indiana. Craig didn't have to contemplate doubling because Big 10 rules then forbade the 5K/10K double. He'd contest the 5K, but considered adding the steeplechase, going so far as to practice hurdling, a plan later nixed.

Craig's 14-day break included graduation as well as two days spent planting corn and soybeans in Lebanon so his family could come to the meet. The temperature soared to 90 on race day. Craig soaked himself with water and psyched himself with music, cranking the volume on his $400 Sony boom box as it played "Gonna Fly Now" from *Rocky*.

Five surges over the final mile helped Craig pull away from Minnesota's Steve Plasencia to capture his ninth Big 10 title. His 13:55.65 left him over 11 seconds ahead of Herb Lindsay, who nipped the broken Plasencia at the line. "Although I didn't get the time that I wanted, the tactics were sound," Craig told Woods. "I had one more surge under my belt if he hadn't let go." The team title went to Illinois by 19 points over Sam Bell's Hoosiers.

That meet was the last time Craig competed with his teammates, but it was far from the last time they'd be together. The team members, especially the distance runners, had gone through too much to pull the plug on their relationships. The centerpiece of their ongoing friendships was the alumni cross country race Wieneke continued to organize each fall. "It was such a unique group that you wanted to keep those friendships going," Wieneke said.

Craig, who'd later carve out space on his international racing schedule for the alumni race, remained an enthusiastic supporter of the reunions, but he wasn't alone. "We had good teams and I think that helps," said Mark Avery, explaining the group's lasting friendships. "When you have good teams, you have a lot of good memories and stuff. We were pretty tight."

Jirele suggested the continuing bond was forged in training to produce fitness. The fitness didn't last, but the bond did. "When running is done," he said, "it happens to everybody, all you have left are your memories, your friendships, your coaches. That's what we have and they are awful special."

Craig's teammate Les Myers likened what the former Illini shared to the bond created among soldiers. "What we went through together, it was something that really binds us in a way that goes beyond friendship or beyond common interest," he said. "It was a crucible. I guess it's sort of like war buddies. Somehow we all survived Coach Wieneke's workouts . . . and we'll always feel a bond because of that."

Craig chose to double in the NCAA meet at Champaign, which meant 50 laps of racing with a 5K heat on June 2, a 10K final on June

3 and a 5K final on June 4. "I decided to get my money's worth," he told Woods. In their 5K prelim, Kimobwa built a large lead over Craig. Feeling antsy with a mile to go, Craig set off in pursuit even though he only needed a top-six finish to advance. "That's when the crowd went crazy," he told Woods. "My adrenaline about shot out of my ears." Craig cut the gap to 1.4 seconds while finishing second in 13:53.18. "I wanted to put the throttle down a little bit to see what it felt like," he said.

Asking for Help

Prior to the next day's 38-man 10K final, Craig asked his countrymen to help set the early pace, but only Oregon freshman Alberto Salazar stepped forward. "Alberto did help some in the first mile, mile and a half of the race," Craig recalled. "That told me right there that Alberto Salazar had a lot of guts because here he was as a freshman and he was not scared or intimidated by those older foreign athletes."

At an Italian restaurant that night, Bruce Jenner—in town to provide color commentary for ABC's national telecast—stopped by Craig's table for a five-minute chat. "That was probably the longest one-on-one conversation I ever had with Bruce," Craig said. "He was very cordial."

After six laps in the 10K, Craig felt both surrounded and alone as the Kenyans conversed in Swahili. Sportswriters fell into two camps when it came to describing Craig's tactics that day. Tate said four Kenyans "boxed him, jostled him and took turns surging in a strategy to wear him down."

Joe Orris of the *Daily Illini* reported that Kimobwa complained that Craig had frequently bumped him early on, causing him to lose rhythm. "That's why I moved so fast to get away from him," the WSU runner explained. Craig admitted to Stan Hieronymus of the *Peoria Journal Star*, "I wanted to pressure him as much as I could physically. I wanted to bother him as much as I could legally." The tactic came at the cost of several spike wounds on Craig's legs.

The race broke open during a 64-second 15th lap when the lead group consisted of Craig, Rono and Kimobwa. Rono, who'd been ill, was shed by a 63-second 17th lap. The crowd stood and roared as Craig led briefly on the 20th lap before Kimobwa smoked lap 21. "He had been speeding up, then slowing down, and I thought he was going to do that again, but then he kept on going," Craig told the *Urbana Courier*. By lap 23, the Kenyan had a 50-yard cushion that was growing. The 5-foot-6, 119-pounder won in a meet record 28:10.27 while Craig clocked 28:22.48. Rono faded to 10th (29:22.6).

Bitterly disappointed, Craig told Tate, "I just couldn't do it. [Kimobwa] isn't inhuman, just awfully fit and terribly tough." Wieneke expressed pride in Craig's courage. "He is the only one who has challenged the Kenyans in recent years," Wieneke said. "That's an awfully lonely position." Craig's time would stand as the second fastest by an American in 1977.

Twenty-one hours later, Craig returned for his final college race, the 5K final, unsure if he could finish. Overnight he'd dealt with blisters, cramps and an inability to eat. "I was just exhausted," he told Tate. "Then I couldn't sleep." When Kimobwa and teammate Joshua Kimeto, the defending 5K champion, blitzed the first eight laps in 8:34, Craig let them go. "I definitely would have stayed with them if it hadn't been for Friday's race," Craig said. Kimeto went on to win in 13:38.14 with Kimobwa second (13:38.57). Craig ran 13:42.06 in fourth.

Showing Class

It was the eighth time in NCAA competition that Craig had been the top American. Kimeto's victory gave Kenya a sweep of events longer than 400 meters. Foreigners had won eight events and combined to score 185 points. Just seven years earlier, they'd won only two events and scored 76 points. As Craig jogged a final lap around Memorial Stadium, many in the crowd of 15,880 gave him a standing ovation. Setting aside his feelings about foreigners, Craig jogged to Kimeto and signaled to the crowd that it was Kimeto who deserved their applause. Walt Murphy of *Track & Field News* wrote that Craig "showed a lot of class by running a victory lap with Kimeto . . ." Kimeto told the media, "He's my friend. If you make enemies, who are you going to have to run against?"

Thirty years later, Kimeto's regard for Craig hadn't changed. In 2007, Kimeto traveled by bus for a day and a half to see Craig in Mombasa, Kenya, when Craig was the US junior team leader for the World Cross Country Championships. A photo of their reunion appeared in the May 2007 issue of *Track & Field News*.

Chapter 13: Athletics West

*"It's actually everything any club always wanted to
be but could not afford."*

— Craig Virgin

Eager as ever to test his limits, Craig showed up for the AAU national 10K at UCLA's Drake Stadium a week after his NCAA double. Physically, he felt fine during the race, but by the two-mile mark, he was fighting the urge to quit. He was still with the leaders at four miles when that urge became a demand he couldn't refuse. After two years with no significant rest, he stepped onto the infield and jogged to an exit. It was the first time he'd intentionally failed to finish a race. He told David Woods, "I was just out there going through the motions."

Craig returned to Lebanon "in kind of a small depression." He canceled the rest of his summer races, which included the Prefontaine Classic in Eugene. Wieneke told Tate, "Personally, I don't believe he ever fully recovered from the Olympics. He needed some time off then but we were right into cross country, and then to indoor and outdoor track."

The next three weeks, Craig worked at running camps in Champaign and Brevard, North Carolina, before resuming serious training. When not resting, running or farming, Craig contemplated his future. "The decision I make in the next few weeks may be even more important than my selection of a college four years ago," he told the *Urbana Courier*. One possibility was a standing employment offer from Nike, which flew him to Oregon to visit Nike headquarters.

The uncertainty was resolved August 5 when Craig accepted an offer to become the first member of a new Nike-sponsored club for elite postcollegians called Athletics West. It would be based in Eugene and pay athletes' travel, training and health expenses. Its goal was to find success on the European summer circuit while introducing Nike products to European consumers. "It's actually everything any club always wanted to be but could not afford," Craig told Woods. The *Urbana Courier* quoted Craig as saying, "The money is there, and we're in on the ground floor of what could be the most historic breakthrough in the history of track."

The club's coach, Harry Johnson, had led South Eugene High School to seven consecutive Oregon state track titles. He was chosen as coach by Nike cofounder Bill Bowerman. Helping put the club together was Nike's head of track and field promotions, Geoff Hollister, who'd given Craig his first pair of Nike spikes in 1972.

According to Hollister's 2008 book *Out of Nowhere: The Inside Story of How Nike Marketed the Culture of Running*, Johnson told Hollister, "We've got to get Virgin—he's a key. He's so good. And he'll push these guys." Having Craig gave the club instant credibility to attract other top athletes. The next four club members to arrive were former Penn State steeplechaser George Malley, 22, ex-Villanova miler Phil Kane, 22, ex-Oklahoma State miler Mike Manke, 25, and 30-year-old Jim Crawford, who'd done most of his running for the Army Track Team.

Distance men Doug Brown and Jeff Wells joined soon after followed by steeplechaser Henry Marsh, decathlete Craig Brigham and throwers Mac Wilkins and Al Feuerbach. A few nonmembers were allowed to train with the club. All the club members lived in Eugene except Brown, Wells, Marsh, Wilkins and Feuerbach. Brown and Marsh were finishing college while Wells was in the seminary. "Nike was going to pick up 100 percent of the trip to Europe including trying to book us into meets," Craig said. "What none of us really understood was that Nike had never done this before."

Even though Craig could see the club would allow American distance runners to develop as their European counterparts had for years, he didn't move West without regret. "It's really a tough decision to pack up and leave Illinois no matter how great it might sound," he told Woods.

Besides running for Athletics West, Craig would work 20 to 30 hours a week as an assistant manager in a Nike-owned store called the Athletic Department in Eugene. Each pay period, Craig would receive two paychecks, one for his actual work hours and another for whatever time he was short of 40 hours. His total reimbursement would be $14,000 per year, the equivalent of almost $57,000 in 2016. "We weren't getting rich, but we were more comfortable than a lot of runners who were trying to survive postcollegiately at that time," Craig said.

Heading West

Craig packed his car for the 2,500-mile drive to Eugene, but he didn't take everything. He left behind Pam McDonald. "Obviously, when I didn't marry her, when I left, that was making a statement," Craig said. "I just wasn't ready to get married yet." Neither was he ready to break up with Pam, who'd make two visits to Eugene during the next nine months. At the beginning of his three-day journey west, Craig stopped to say good-bye to Pam at the O'Fallon McDonald's restaurant where she worked. It took everything he had to remain composed. As O'Fallon disappeared in his rearview mirror, tears filled his eyes.

Craig found an apartment on the west side of Eugene with help from Harry Johnson. It wasn't long before Craig created a pseudo-family that included a neighbor couple and the couple who managed the housing complex.

Craig ended his six-race 1977 cross country campaign in the November 26 AAU nationals at Houston where he renewed his rivalry with Nick Rose. By two miles, Craig and Rose were side by side on a 10K course that skirted Buffalo Bayou. "It was just like old times," Craig said. With an earring in his left ear and his hair in a ponytail, Rose saw Craig take the lead on the homestretch. The Associated Press reported Craig made a tactical error when he ran into a gully, giving Rose the high ground and the path to a 30:14.3 to 30:22.8 victory.

Three weeks later at the Oregon Track Club's monthly 10K road race in Alton Baker Park, Craig won, beating his Athletics West teammates in the process. A race photo of Craig in his red, black and yellow Athletics West uniform was later sold as a poster in running magazines. "Nobody asked me my permission," Craig said years later. "Harry explained to me that it was public domain. I'm still not quite sure that was correct."

During an early Athletics West team meeting, Johnson told his charges they must buy into his training completely. It was the first of many omens that trouble lay ahead. Johnson's training formula echoed that of legendary coaches Arthur Lydiard of New Zealand and Bill Bowerman of Oregon—with some mathematical twists. The system featured bounding up and down hills on concrete pavement, long intervals and "steady state" or "tempo" runs. Among the bread-and-butter workouts was a 20K out-and-back run on Lorraine Highway where Johnson would yell mile splits. Craig, who viewed the 20Ks as races, often reached the turnaround under 31 minutes and came back faster, typically at sub-5:00-per-mile pace with the last few miles sub-4:40. It was a workout he never lost. Back East, Bill Rodgers was winning major road races slower than Craig's workout pace.

When Johnson was hired by Athletics West, he told the Associated Press, "We are looking for people with talent but also people willing to take direction and people who can make a contribution to our community." In a mid-November newspaper article, Johnson said of Craig, "He's strong-headed like Pre and he's been accustomed to telling his coaches when he's going to compete and how he's going to train. I'm not made that way and I'm going to provide him with an intelligent program which will be designed to have him run fast in the summer. It requires quite an adjustment from what he's used to doing in cross country and the indoor season. Once all these guys have been in the program a year, it will be easier because the guys from the East and Midwest are used to three seasons per year and we're only talking about one."

Quitting the Shoe Business

Working at the Athletic Department proved unfulfilling for Craig, who quit in January. He'd been selling shoes, clerking, processing credit card reports and stocking. "I wanted to go out and do community outreach stuff for the store," said Craig. "That's what interested me. Clerking at the store five days a week to talk running all the time was almost to the point of overkill for me. It was taking something that I really loved and [made it] work and drudgery."

The atmosphere among employees soured as those not in Athletics West wondered why they hadn't been chosen. "It created a certain amount of tension and friction," Craig said. "They poked fun — 'Well, it's three o'clock. You guys can leave now.'" Craig got word of his dissatisfaction to Bowerman, who agreed to find Craig another job. Craig wanted something in promotions, advertising or marketing.

After a Christmas trip to Lebanon, Craig began working for a Eugene-based company called Stretch & Sew, which was owned by Bowerman's neighbors, Herb and Ann Person. Stretch & Sew sold knit fabrics, along with sewing machines and other sewing accessories. Craig, who lived two miles from the business, enjoyed working in its advertising department from January until June when he left for Europe with Athletics West.

Athletics West members only trained together in the afternoons. Craig did a four- to six-mile run at 6:30 a.m. before going to work at Stretch & Sew, where he was treated as the resident celebrity athlete. Several employees were runners so they hit him up for advice, which he happily provided. "I made new friends outside the athletic world, which was good for me," Craig said.

Craig's first race of 1978 was bad, as he twisted an ankle during the US Cross Country Trials on January 28 in Atlanta and didn't finish. "I didn't try to gut it out because I knew I was already on the team," said Craig, who had qualified by being the first American in the AAU nationals. Jeff Wells, third in the trials, was the only other Athletics West member to qualify. "By January and February there started to be an underlying negative current on the team where guys started to lose their respect for Harry," Craig said.

Craig's indoor track season consisted of a single two-mile race in the Illini Classic at Champaign on February 24. "Damned if I didn't lead the whole blasted thing and I got outkicked by Niall O'Shaughnessy on the last lap," said Craig, who lost by a second and a half in 8:37.1.

February saw Pam McDonald make her second trip to Eugene. She stayed five days. "It was at the end of that visit that I finally had to verbalize the fact that I just wasn't ready to get married, and I wasn't 100 percent sure that if I was to get married, that she was the right person," Craig said. "We had dated for almost five years and she felt that if I didn't know well enough by that time, I'd never know." Before March ended, Pam had eloped with someone else. That was jolting news for Craig, who nevertheless knew he couldn't ask her to wait.

As Craig trained for the March 25 World Cross Country Championships, some Athletics West members began to break down from mileage that was both high and intense. "The criticism of Harry started to become more rampant and they would talk behind his back," Craig recalled. "They would make sarcastic fun of him behind his back. I had never been around that." Johnson handed out workouts without explaining how they'd benefit the runners. "He was ahead of his time with the Nike slogan of 'Just Do It,'" Craig quipped.

Johnson dismissed suggestions that a workout be altered. Malley described the workouts as an "exercise in numerology." For example, if the 1,500-meter guys were supposed to run a 600, an 800, a 600, a 400 and a 200, then the 3,000-meter guys would run an 800, a 1,200, a 1,000 and a 400. "I had never been in a coaching relationship that was that totalitarian and where I didn't have at least some input," Craig said.

World Cross Country Debut

Craig's debut in the World Cross Country Championships, which many considered distance running's showcase, came in 1978 at Glasgow, Scotland, where several days of rain made hilly Bellahouston Park a quagmire. In spots, the 12K course consisted of shin-deep mud. "A ton of guys put their foot down into mud and came up and the shoe was gone," Craig said. "It just sucked it right off and they never found them again."

Having run over plowed fields as a kid, Craig found the muddy terrain in Glasgow, Scotland, to his liking at the 1978 World Cross Country Championships where he finished sixth. Chasing him were England's Mike McLeod (65) and Scotland's Nat Muir (left). *(Photo by Mark Shearman)*

Despite limping on an injured heel, Craig finished sixth in 39:54, which was 29 seconds behind winner John Treacy of Ireland. Competitors referred to Treacy as the "mud lark" because he could run so lightly over mud. The US team's second-place finish, five points behind France, was the best in US history and the closest Craig ever got to a team title. A photo of him, splattered in mud, appeared in the July 1978 issue of *Runner's World*.

Back in Eugene, as Johnson introduced more track workouts to the club's training, the runners most often found themselves at South Eugene High School or Lane Community College, but never at Hayward Field. Johnson and Oregon coach Bill Dellinger didn't get along and Craig never knew why. Johnson didn't want his athletes to socialize with the Ducks, let alone train with them. "Only twice in the whole year did I ever get together with Alberto [Salazar] and Rudy [Chapa] and go for a run," recalled Craig, who raced only twice as a member of Athletics West at Hayward Field. The first time was May 6 in a 10K he won in 28:19.4.

Over the ensuing two months, Craig would set nine personal records, but not in the May 31 Prefontaine Classic at Hayward Field, where he contested the 5K against Marty Liquori, the American record holder at 13:15.1. Woods wrote that Craig was popular in Eugene judging by the response to his prerace introduction. "Could you believe the crowd?" Craig asked Woods. After the race opened with two 68-second laps, Craig thought, "This is no race for Eugene, for the Pre Classic. It's like the Big 10 meet . . . same old tactics. No one wants to take it." No one except Craig, who surged in the rabbit-less race, but couldn't escape as Liquori won, 13:37.7 to 13:40.7. It was Craig's fastest 5K in two years.

Craig confided to Woods that he thought he could develop a fan following in Eugene like Prefontaine had. "I think when I first came out here, if I ran well, something like that could develop," said Craig, who could see there'd be no chance to build rapport with fans without racing more in Eugene. Johnson's program, however, was aimed at success overseas. "He wanted to have us ready for Europe, which to some degree is correct," Craig said, "but we needed to do a little bit more PR stuff in Eugene than what we did."

Craig returned to Los Angeles on June 10 for the AAU national 10K seeking redemption for dropping out in 1977. With 7¾ laps left, he blasted away with laps of 64 and 67 before soloing the rest of the way to secure his first national title in 28:15.0. "It was satisfying because it was a good tactical race and that's the way I'll have to run in Europe," Craig told Woods. "I'm glad I was able to handle the surges and then put in one of my own."

After an all-night packing session before leaving Eugene for a three-month track tour, Craig drove his Fiat atop a nearby butte to watch the sun rise. The future looked bright.

Chapter 14: 1978 European Tour

*"The type of training I've used is different from
what they're accustomed to."*

— Harry Johnson

On the day Athletics West arrived in Europe, Henry Rono lowered
the 10K world record to 27:22.4. The time impressed Craig and
his teammates, who moved into rooms at a sports complex near a track
stadium and a lake in a small town outside Helsinki, Finland. Nike had
Pre to thank for forming connections in Finland.

Craig roomed with fellow Olympian Henry Marsh, who along with
Jeff Wells became Craig's closest friends during the tour. Craig was
so tidy his teammates called him "Felix," the neat roommate in *The
Odd Couple* TV series. After renting a van, the group went shopping
in Helsinki. Craig had his eye on a reindeer or wolf hide to hang on his
wall. The athletes filled their spare time playing ping-pong, basketball,
darts and poker, along with discussing the moral aspect of accepting
under-the-table payments for competing in Europe.

The first of Craig's 16 European races in 65 days was the Helsinki
Games 5K on June 15. Lasse Viren, the double gold medalist from
both the Munich and Montreal Olympics, led the first lap as the crowd
chanted, "Lasse, Lasse." Craig wound up fifth in a personal best
of 13:34.09.

On June 16, Athletics West drove to Lappeenranta, Finland, located
near a lake 20 miles from the Russian border. The team stayed in a youth
hostel and slept on narrow bunk beds. The athletes placed blankets over
the windows to block out the long hours of Scandinavian sunshine. At
night, they went to a disco for supper and dancing.

On race day, Craig had a fever and congestion bad enough to warrant a trip to the hospital, where he received medicine for a viral infection. The treatment allowed him to win that night's 3K in a personal best and stadium record 7:57.6, the equivalent of an 8:35.8 two-mile. The race reinforced the idea that in the future, Craig needed to force himself into a long drive to sap competitors' kicks. The race also taught him that "V" is pronounced like "W" and vice versa in Finland, where the track announcer had proclaimed "Craig Wirgin" the winner.

At a postmeet dinner reception, it was ladies' night so women could ask men to dance. All of the Athletics West gang drew frequent dance requests. "The Finnish are rough dancers and, on a tiny dance floor, it was like bumper cars," Craig wrote.

On June 27, Craig learned Rono had set his fourth world record within an 81-day span with a 7:32.1 3K in Oslo, Norway. The next day Craig had tea with Samson Kimobwa and discussed Kimobwa's 1977 10K world record at Helsinki. "He feels Rono is an animal," Craig reported in his diary. Craig viewed Rono's success as a tool to broaden his own dreams.

Marsh flew home on June 29 to take part in the US-USSR dual, a departure that left Craig with mixed feelings. "In some ways, I'd like to go back also, but I'm also driven by a desire to see how fast I can run and to see countries, people and things unfamiliar to me," wrote Craig, who often crossed paths with other track stars that summer. They included Holland's Jos Hermans and Americans Steve Scott, Bill Rodgers, Craig Masback, Larry Jessee and Marty Liquori. A frequent topic was how to build a career on the European track circuit.

In the June 29 World Games in Helsinki, Craig won his first international 10K in 27:57.2, the fourth-best time in US history. He won by a tenth of a second over Hermans, who'd ranked fifth in the world in 1977. The finish was so close, Hermans took a victory lap, which he later felt embarrassed about on the awards stand as the results were announced. "We had a good laugh about it," Craig wrote.

The team then took an overnight ferry to Stockholm, Sweden. As the athletes disembarked, they were greeted by a billboard displaying bare female breasts. "I'm saying, 'My God. What is that? What a country!'" Craig recalled. "I felt like I was in a more liberal environment in Helsinki, but when I got to Sweden, literally there was nudity or seminudity around us all the time. I remember the culture shock. I started to feel that America was very Victorian compared to the enlightened Scandinavians to whom breasts were just part of the body and people often bathed topless and sometimes bottomless at the parks and nobody said a thing about it."

Rabbiting

Craig didn't say no when the meet director offered him $300 to serve as rabbit for the DN Galen 10K in Stockholm on July 3. He was asked to run 66 seconds a lap for six laps, but he only averaged 69.5. In that race, Doug Brown of Athletics West supplanted Craig at No. 4 in US history by running 27:54.2. "It would have been a good race for me to be in, drat," wrote Craig.

Craig knew Brown's time could impact his bonus from the club. As part of a hush-hush financial deal, athletes got an extra $2,500 for being the club leader in a particular event, and also if they won a national title. Harry Johnson had been sure to collect the athletes' signed contracts. "Back then, they did things under the table a lot where there weren't any hard, concrete records kept," Craig said. Brown had likely just cost Craig $2,500 by being 2.9 seconds faster in the 10K.

Craig celebrated the Fourth of July by notching a 5K personal record of 13:25.7 to place seventh on day two of the DN Galen meet. His time ranked sixth in US history, but didn't threaten Liquori, who won in 13:16.2. New Zealander Rod Dixon was second in 13:17.4. Other notables were Portugal's Fernando Mamede in third (13:17.8) and Japan's Toshihiko Seko in 11th (13:40.5). "I had the satisfaction of knowing I belonged there," Craig said.

The Americans and New Zealanders saw they couldn't reach the top competing inside their own countries. "We realized there is no point in running against the clock and running against each other," Dixon said. "We had to get to Europe and we had to run against the best in the world and then gauge our success or failure from those trips. I think Craig realized—of course coming on the heels of Prefontaine, who made those European campaigns and traveled—to go to another level, he had to, too."

Personal records didn't prevent Craig from criticizing his performances. "My major problem," he wrote, "seems to be that I'm just not willing to compete when the going gets tough over the last 800 meters. No amount of training can help. I just have to be committed to racing over the last fourth of the race and not just the first three-fourths of the race. It seems that if I'm convinced I can't win the race, I just don't compete hard. This is a problem that only I can face and conquer. No coach, friend or family can do it for me."

During a 12-day break between races, Craig discussed his training with Harry Johnson and felt they came to a better understanding. As much as Craig loved seeing the world, Lebanon was never far from his thoughts. He spent about $2 a day mailing letters. His goal was to write to everyone in his address book at least once. He treasured mail from family and friends at the club's base camp in Växjö, Sweden.

No Pain, No Gain

At several points during the tour, Craig and other Athletics West members received treatments from Finnish masseur Ilpo Nikkila, whose methods were frequently painful, but always therapeutic. The 54-year-old Nikkila, a bald 250-pounder, didn't speak English, but made quite an impression on Craig. When the team left Finland on a nine-hour ferry ride to Stockholm on July 28, Craig noted in his diary, "I wished Ilpo the best and said goodbye. I will miss him. He helped me greatly."

For 30 years, Craig forgot about the ferry trip until it was mentioned in Geoff Hollister's book *Out of Nowhere: The Inside Story of How Nike Marketed the Culture of Running*. According to the diary, Athletics West made two ferry trips from Helsinki to Stockholm that summer, the first on June 30 and the second on July 28. In the book, Hollister, the head of Nike track and field promotions, wrote after the World Games in Helsinki on June 29:

The next morning, Harry and the rest of us were waiting for Craig Virgin to show at the gangway of the ferry that would steam overnight to Stockholm. Craig never went anywhere unless his hair was perfectly blow dried, and this could take some time. The ferry left without him.

Harry and I talked about the progress of the club. The training program, which was basically Bowerman's Oregon program, was beginning to show results. A train ride to Växjö returned us to our base camp with nice trail runs around the lake. Virgin would show up hours later in disbelief that we had left him behind. He was in time for dinner, and Jody, Harry's wife, had prepared a big bowl of local strawberries and passed them around the table. Everyone took a reasonable portion, with Virgin and Jim Crawford being the last. The bowl came to Craig and he heaped his bowl and passed it on to "Craw." Jim looked over the edge of the porcelain bowl to spot four small strawberries at the bottom. "Gee Craig, thanks. That was big of you."

Virgin, totally oblivious, said "No problem."

Ferry Tale

Decades later, Craig didn't remember missing a ferry. "We never left anybody behind because there was too much of a risk that something bad could happen," he said. "We looked out for each other a lot more than Geoff talked about in that book."

Malley, who agreed Craig never missed a ferry in 1978, said vignettes about Craig in Hollister's book were meant to be nasty because Hollister was angry about Craig leaving the club later in 1978. As Malley saw it, even if Craig took too many strawberries once upon a time, who'd make a fuss about it 30 years later? Craig conceded the strawberry mistake happened. "I took too many strawberries and didn't realize there was another guy yet to go that hadn't gotten any," confessed Craig, still embarrassed by the faux pas decades later. To make amends, he bought Crawford a few beers that night, a gesture that didn't make it into the book. At Hollister's book signing during the 2008 Olympic Trials, Craig presented him a bowl of strawberries.

Craig's last personal record of 1978 came on August 3 in a 3K against John Treacy at Malmö, Sweden. With three laps to go, Craig surged for a lap, but couldn't unhinge Treacy, who went on to win by 3.4 seconds as Craig wound up fourth in 7:51.96.

In an August 9 1,500 at Reykjavik, Iceland, Craig finished a tired sixth in 4:47.0. His peak had passed, but his tour still had stops in Copenhagen, Warsaw and Brussels. His homesickness became so acute during the 65-day tour's final two weeks he had to force himself to walk past airport gates with homebound flights. The adventure of professional running in Europe had become a job.

The August 10 edition of the *Eugene Register-Guard* carried a feature story by John Henderson about the Athletics West tour. Johnson's seven runners had produced 20 personal bests by the time of Henderson's interview. "I've been very satisfied with the performances," Johnson said. "But they all realize there will be more results in another year. The type of training I've used is different from what they're accustomed to. I told the 1,500 guys from day one not to expect anything exciting this year. We work on a two-year success program. I think Craig will go gangbusters next year, and by 1980 he'll really be ready."

Craig had hoped to take a crack at Steve Prefontaine's American 10K record in Copenhagen on August 11, but since he had to travel from Iceland beginning at 5 a.m. that day, a record assault was impossible. During one 13-day stretch, he'd slept in 10 different beds in six different countries. A crowd of 50,000 in Brussels watched Craig's final tour stop, a 15th-place 13:49.5 in the 5K. "I struggled to even finish that race," he said. "I knew that I just was shot. I never again wanted to be racing in Europe for two and a half months straight."

While Craig was abroad, he was invited to one of America's premier road races, a 7.1-miler at Falmouth, Massachusetts, on August 20. He arrived at Falmouth the day before the race after 16 hours of travel from Belgium. Awaiting him was a field of 3,400 including nine Olympians, 16 AAU national champions and 13 sub-four-minute milers. After two miles, it was a four-man race featuring Bill Rodgers, Mike Roche, Alberto Salazar and Craig. The 80-degree heat and 70 percent humidity peeled away Roche and Craig and ultimately zapped Salazar so badly he couldn't recall fading to 10th. "I woke up in a bathtub full of ice," Salazar told the *Boston Globe*. Salazar's temperature soared to 108 as he became one of 20 runners hospitalized because of heat problems. His condition was so serious, last rites were administered.

The Roady

Rodgers was credited with a course-record 32:03 while Roche grabbed second in 32:21. By placing third in 32:55, Craig earned $500 on top of his $500 appearance fee. He told the *Cape Cod Times*, "I was very tired today and surprised I did so well. I'd love to come back and try it again when I've had time to run the course and I'm better rested." Beating all but two of America's best road runners while race weary and jet lagged told Craig he had reached a new level. Even better, he'd found a new world to conquer.

Johnson gave his athletes two weeks off after the tour. Craig went to Lebanon and spoke to his parents about leaving Athletics West. At the end of his 10-day visit, he decided to leave the club. The satisfaction he had from clocking nine personal bests with Athletics West was outweighed by four things: Johnson's unwillingness to alter workouts based on athletes' input, the mutinous attitudes of teammates toward Johnson, Craig's wish to run cross country and road races, and his desire to live near family and friends. To not be involved in planning his training was especially galling. "It [Athletics West] isn't the utopia that many think it is," Craig told Tom Jordan of *Track & Field News*. "You pay a penalty in your loss of freedom."

After the first few weeks in Europe, "a virus of bad morale" had infected Athletics West. "It was a virus of attitude," Craig said. "Here I am getting PRs and I'm not in a happy environment and people around me weren't happy. They were complaining constantly. They were talking bad about Harry and about the training." After returning to Eugene, Craig met with Johnson. "I could tell he pretty much knew what was coming when I walked in the office," Craig said. Johnson told Craig that Nike wouldn't subsidize his training unless he stayed in Eugene with the team. Johnson then told Craig to turn in his uniforms and forget about receiving the $5,000 bonus Craig was owed for being a national champion and having the club's top 5K time.

Craig drove to Nike headquarters in Portland the next day to meet with Nike marketing director Rob Strasser, who said, "We appreciate all you have done for the team." Strasser also told Craig that Johnson had threatened to quit if Nike did anything beyond giving Craig shoes and clothing. Nike had invested so much in the club by that time, it couldn't risk losing Johnson. Strasser told Craig his market value to another sponsor was at least $20,000 a year. "This was a crushing moment for me after all those years of loyalty to Nike," said Craig, who'd worn Nikes in the 1976 Olympics without being paid. He'd worn them to break Prefontaine's national high school two-mile record. He'd worn them in 1972 against the Soviets. He felt part of the Nike family, only to discover family ties could easily be severed.

Leaving Athletics West came with consequences, which Craig read about later that week while sitting at Herb Person's kitchen table. In the *Eugene Register-Guard*, John Conrad quoted Johnson as saying, "I'm tired of talking about my differences with Virgin. But I don't believe Craig can be effective in any group situation except his family. He doesn't really want a coach. He just wants somebody around to pat him on the back. I still say he's the most talented distance running prospect in the country. But his 13:25 and 27:57 aren't that great except in this country."

The story went on to note how Craig's desire to do more road racing was opposed by Johnson, who believed road racing compromised one's ability in outdoor track. "I see no value in road racing or indoor track if your goal is to be competitive on the track," Johnson said. "I don't think a guy can do both and be world class. I guess there were two mistakes in the beginning. I thought Craig was completely devoted to reaching his potential on the track and he seems to have thought he could get me to change my thinking."

Bitter Ending

Conrad's story took a nasty twist when it referred to Craig having conflicts with teammates. Doug Brown told Conrad, "Virgin's very I-oriented and doesn't care much about anyone else. He's a fish out of water working with a group, and he refused to accept coaching. I think everyone else conceded the fact they were going to be coached when they came here." Conrad then noted, "Virgin dismisses any problems he might have had with teammates, but admits he and Johnson could never adapt to each other."

"I have no desire to slander Athletics West, Harry Johnson or Eugene," Craig told Conrad. "I'm grateful to Nike for starting the club and to the people in Eugene who were so good to me. I don't know if I'm uncoachable, but if I'm going to have one, there has to be a better relationship than I had with Harry. We don't agree on the coach-athlete relationship or about the emphasis on track to the exclusion of road running and cross country. I do believe giving athletes a pat on the back is part of coaching. At least I don't think a successful coach can completely ignore it. I thought there should have been some respect for what a particular athlete responds to, what has worked for him in the past and what he feels he can't do without. I think there should be equal input, and Harry disagrees."

Craig later told the Kankakee (Illinois) *Daily Journal*, "I feel I'm coachable, but that's not the point. It's a question of whether you want a dictatorial situation or an equal partnership relationship. The whole time I was there, I didn't have one weekend to myself because there were mandatory workouts at least one of the two days every weekend. He didn't think a guy was mature enough to do what was necessary by himself."

As soon as Craig left Athletics West, Malley left, too. "If I would have been the only one, I don't think I would have quit," said Malley, who dismissed Brown's complaint that Craig wasn't a team player. "Doug Brown was in Tennessee while we were in Eugene," Malley said.

While racing in Europe in the summer of 1977, Malley, the American record holder at that time in the 3,000 steeplechase at 8:22.5, had been recruited by Hollister and Johnson to join Athletics

After leaving Athletics West in August of 1978, Craig was asked by Coach Harry Johnson to turn in his uniform. Craig battled Jeff Wells (left) in a 5K at College Park, Maryland, on May 14, 1978. *(Photo by Jeff Johnson)*

West. When he finally met them in Eugene, red flags popped up. "My first impression was these guys really talked about themselves," Malley said. "It seemed to me they had no interest in the sport other than how either of those two fit into it. All we heard about Johnson was 'He's the best coach in the world and you're lucky to have this opportunity to be coached by the best coach in the world.'" Malley set aside his concerns because he knew he'd have to retire from track without Nike's financial support. "The fact of the matter was we were lucky because nothing like that had ever existed before [in the United States]," Malley said.

In a surprise move prior to the 1980 Olympic Trials, Nike replaced Johnson as Athletics West coach with New Zealander Dick Quax, a former 5K world record holder. A five-paragraph story buried on page 52 of the August 1980 issue of *Track & Field News* noted: "Johnson's coaching and training methods for distance runners were strictly controlled by Johnson and not the athletes, and have been yielding diminishing returns for the club. Athletes' dissatisfaction apparently led Nike leaders to choose a coach with a more casual and individual-oriented manner." The story went on to say Nike made the change when it did to present a new image of the club to help recruit prospective athletes attending the Olympic Trials in Eugene. Quax subsequently allowed athletes more control of their training and racing.

"I actually felt sorry for him," Craig said of Johnson. "I want to make it perfectly clear that I respected Harry as a man, as a hard worker and as a coach. I thought he took some misinterpretations of the Lydiard training program. He jumped all the way from high school to the international level and he needed some grounding in between to really understand what was going on. [He needed to] figure out how to change his tactics when it came to training post-collegiate athletes differently than he would train 14- to 18-year-olds at South Eugene High School."

Chapter 15: A New Beginning

*"Either I was going to be proven the biggest damn
fool in America for having left that situation or I
was going to be a success."*

— Craig Virgin

In his first month back in Lebanon, the emotional center of
Craig's universe, he lived in a remodeled room in his parents' basement, worked for his parents' livestock equipment distributorship and typed a 15-page plan for his running career. "I
wanted to put my training philosophy on paper if I was going to
coach myself," said Craig, who arranged to consult weekly with
Gary Wieneke.

Craig's plan divided the year into quarters with October
through December used for base building, January through March
for injecting quality into the base and April through June for speed
work on the track before peaking in July and August. The second
quarter culminated with the World Cross Country Championships
and the Crescent City Classic 10K in New Orleans. The third
quarter ended with the national track championships and the fourth
concluded with races in Europe. September was meant to be a
recovery month, but a review of Craig's race results show it rarely
was. Luring him back were offers of $1,000 to $3,000 per event
from road race directors. By 1980, he was getting $5,000 a race.

Moving back in with his parents was no problem for Craig,
who had a good relationship with them. He appreciated returning
from a workout to microwave suppers made by his mother. He
traveled so much between 1979 and 1981 he felt no constraints

about living at home. His sisters, Sheree and Vicki, had moved out by then, but his brother, Brent, 11 years younger, still lived at home. "That gave me a chance to get to know Brent a little bit better because I had been gone for five years when Brent was just getting big enough to relate to," Craig said.

Craig loved visiting major cities, but hated traffic and feeling overcrowded. He was perfectly comfortable in Lebanon. "I loved coming back," he said. "I was like a lion who would return to his cave to lick his wounds before the next battle."

Craig left his lair for four races in September of 1978, which saw him win his sixth consecutive alumni cross country four-miler at Savoy in 18:56.2, missing his 1975 course record by 10 seconds. "This is like a high school reunion," he told Woods while surveying the gathering of ex-teammates. "I'm really happy to see some of them still running." Craig also informed Woods of his interest in trying a marathon.

The next big goal was the AAU national cross country meet in Seattle on November 25. As Craig prepared, he felt in the best shape he'd ever been in at the start of an intensive training program. He was starting to feel the strength of all the years of running.

Craig knew trouble was afoot in Seattle when he inspected the course the day before the race and found it unlined. On race day, Alberto Salazar, who'd won the previous week's NCAA cross country title, broke away from the pack at the two-mile mark along with Greg Meyer. The line marking the route zigzagged across the course numerous times in multiple directions. When Salazar and Meyer came to a fork, a course marshal accidentally sent them on a loop they weren't supposed to run until the end. Craig saw the mistake and yelled, but Salazar and Meyer didn't hear. "I didn't know how they were going to correct it," Craig said. "I basically quit racing."

The race director shuffled the order in which the course's loops were to be run so runners wound up covering the prescribed 10K, but the mile markers were useless. Craig considered dropping out. "I was at several American major cross country meets that were loosely organized," he said. "That was one of them."

Salazar and Meyer stopped attacking each other for fear of taking a wrong turn. When they reached the final 50 yards, it was each man for himself and Meyer won, 29:35.9 to 29:36.3. Craig coasted home third in 29:57. Placing third meant Craig would have to run a later qualifying race to earn a berth on the eight-man US roster for the World Championships. That became unnecessary when Salazar, who wanted to focus on track, dropped off the team and was replaced by Craig.

In terms of footwear, Craig was a free agent for two months after leaving Athletics West. He considered signing with Onitsuka, Brooks and adidas. The race in Seattle was the first public sign that adidas would henceforth have its three-stripe logo on Craig's feet. He accepted a $12,000, one-year contract to wear adidas gear because of the company's connections in Europe. "I knew if I wanted to advance in track and field," he said, "I had to go to Europe."

Virgin Stories

Craig's departure from Athletics West was still a sore subject for Nike promotions man Geoff Hollister, who wrote in his book that after the Seattle race he "took the Colorado Track Club to dinner and Virgin stories filled the air. Now that Craig was no longer with Nike, no one held back. It softened the blow of the switch." The content of the stories isn't disclosed, but the way Hollister felt was clear.

Craig inched up his December mileage to prepare for his marathon debut January 14 in San Diego. After one 20-mile workout, he wrote, "I'm finding that you have to attack these long runs psychologically different than my other training runs. You can't let yourself think about how far you're running or how long you've been out. You have to really concentrate on pace, relaxation and efficiency."

Craig ended 1978 with one of the most dramatic races of his career, the Runner's World Invitational Five-Mile Road Race in Los Altos, California, on New Year's Eve. Salazar and Oregon teammate Rudy Chapa took the field through a 4:17 opening mile. Chapa fell back as Salazar and Craig passed three miles in 13:15. "Those times were just off the wall," Craig told the *San Jose Mercury News*. "I was not comfortable with that speed."

Craig and Salazar continued to blaze through the 38-degree chill on darkened streets, swapping the lead several times as they neared a banner of white butcher paper stretched across the finish line. "I thought we had to turn left so I slowed a little for the corner and that's when he got the lead," Salazar said. "Then I saw the paper and sprinted."

Craig, meanwhile, was having trouble with his right contact lens. The lens had dried after being on his eye for 14 hours prior to the 11 p.m. start. "I couldn't really see the finish," he recalled. "I kept looking for a tape or piece of string. The lens started to fall out just as we hit the finish and I threw my hand up to catch it just as I leaned into the paper." The maneuver caused Craig to stumble as he and Salazar broke through the paper together. Both were given a time of 22:13 (4:26.6-per-mile pace), but Salazar was declared the winner. Everyone in the top 10 broke the world record of 23:05. "I was certain 23 minutes would be good enough to win," said mile world record holder John Walker, who finished 10th in 23:04.

With so many under the world record, the course's measurement was immediately questioned, but *Runner's World* claimed it had been measured nine times and certified. As years passed, Craig saw course-measuring standards become more reliable. Even though Craig only won three road races in 1978, *Track & Field News* ranked him the nation's third-best road racer of the year behind Bill Rodgers and Randy Thomas.

Prior to the Mission Bay Marathon in San Diego—which offered neither appearance fees nor prize money—Craig joined the St. Louis Track Club, whose jersey he raced in. On his feet were the shoes of his new sponsor, adidas, which funneled $1,000 a month to him through the club. "That was a way of money laundering to try to keep my Olympic eligibility and I guess you could say maintain my amateur status," he said.

When Craig chose San Diego for his first marathon, he didn't consider the caliber of the field nor the potential for a fast time. "I picked it for the [January 15] date," said Craig, whose confidence was bolstered by the fact he'd logged 15 weeks of solid training. He'd averaged 91 miles per week with a high of 105 and a low of 70. During the 14th week, when Lebanon was socked with two inches of ice, six inches of snow and frequent wind chills below zero, he still managed 95 miles. When he landed in San Diego, he felt he'd stepped onto another planet.

Finding Paradise

Craig awoke at 5:30 a.m. on race day, which featured overcast, 60-degree conditions. Instead of his usual "farm" breakfast, his prerace meal consisted of 10 fructose tablets and three glasses of water. "What I should have had was some pancakes," said Craig, who downed four six-ounce bottles of de-carbonated Coca-Cola during the race. That beverage was in vogue because Frank Shorter drank it during races. Craig bought the bottles from a beauticians' supply house.

Craig started cautiously on the virtually flat course while 31-year-old Ben Wilson charged to the front at a five-minute-per-mile pace. "It was hard to hold back," Craig told the *San Diego Union.* "I knew I couldn't run as fast as I do in the 10,000, and yet my 20-mile runs at home were much harder than the first 20 miles of this race."

Craig spent the early miles in fourth, but was second after 13. He took the lead at 20½ miles and, without hesitation, opened a gap while happily chatting with reporters on the press track. He later told the media, "It was like I was on center stage and I just wanted to say, 'Well, you ain't seen nothin' yet!'"

The race ended at San Diego Stadium, where Craig's sprint finish excited the crowd. He repaid their cheers with an exuberant victory lap. His time of 2 hours, 14 minutes, 40 seconds was the fastest marathon debut in American history, breaking the mark of 2:15:51 set by Randy Thomas in New York in 1977. The world record debut at that time was 2:12:40 by Ian Thompson of Great Britain in 1973.

The next day, Craig's calves were so sore he could barely walk. He attempted to jog, but quit after two miles took 20 minutes. He did find the energy to visit Tijuana, Mexico, where something he ate gave him gastrointestinal distress for three days.

Craig's only indoor track race of 1978 was the Illini Classic two-mile at Champaign on February 23. For the fourth straight year, he finished second, this time to Mark Muggleton, a junior at the University of Arkansas. Muggleton drafted behind Craig until the last lap before breaking Nick Rose's Armory record with an

8:30.80 while Craig clocked 8:34.16. "This race seems to be my Achilles' heel," he told Woods. "Someday, if I win at the Olympics or something, I'm going to say I haven't conquered everything yet. Some day before I retire, I'm going to win this race."

Craig prepared for the March 25 World Cross Country Championships in Limerick, Ireland, by flying to Europe nine days early. After adjusting to jet lag, he won an 8K cross country race in Paris on March 18 in 29:24. That night Craig ate with adidas representative Michel Jazy, a former world record holder in the mile from France. "He introduced me to French champagne," said Craig, who then made his first visit to adidas headquarters in Herzogenaurach, West Germany, where he trained for three days and received massages for a calf injury. Craig's room and board were paid for by adidas, which had its own hotel and accompanying three-star restaurant. Among the celebrities he socialized with there were shot put world record holder Brian Oldfield and tennis star Ilie "Nasty" Năstase. Many Europeans also spoke English so language was rarely a problem for Craig.

Socially, Craig was as comfortable on the world stage as he was at home. "I still feel I can go into a board room with the governor and not feel intimidated and I can go into Joe's tavern in Lebanon and be comfortable there, too," he said. Buoyed by such "people skills," he'd later explore a career in politics.

Craig arrived in Limerick two days ahead of the World Championships to study the course, which soaked up 24 consecutive hours of rain leading up to the gun. He'd describe his start as the worst of his career. Earlier races had tilled the course so when he was cut off after 100 meters, he got "stalled" in heavy mud. He was about 100th after 400 meters, but then weaved through the field of 190 on the 12K course to finish 13th in 38:05, 45 seconds behind repeat champion John Treacy of Ireland. Craig was the top finisher for the eighth-place US team. His lungs hadn't hurt, but his legs had gone dead. It was a frustrating effort he hoped to correct the following year by concentrating more on the start.

Craig remained in Europe another eight days, the highlight of which was the only appearance of his career in Italy's most famous cross country race, the Cinque Mulini (Five Mills) at San Vittore

Olono near Milan. The course wound through roads, fields, ditches, streams, two barns and, of course, five water mills while 30,000 cheered. At the end of the third lap on the more-than-six-mile course, Craig caught the leaders, but wound up third (30:19) behind Belgium's Leon Shots (30:15) and Poland's Bronislaw Malinowski (30:17), who'd placed fifth and second, respectively, in the World Championships the week before.

Boston Recon

After returning home, Craig spent the next three weeks training, but still found time to do promotional work for adidas at the Boston Marathon. "I watched Bill Rodgers break [Toshihiko] Seko on the hills," said Craig, who decided then to run Boston in 1981.

Craig raced five times in April. His second race was the Lions Club five-miler in Highland, Illinois, on April 22 that he won in 23:52. He raced for free as a favor to the co-race director, Dr. Jim Rehberger, whom Craig ranked among his most important benefactors. Dr. Rehberger, Craig's first cousin, provided Craig with chiropractic care and medical advice at no charge. "He was more or less my medical pit crew director," Craig said. "He would see me on a weekly basis and then farm me out to medical specialists as needed."

Craig rationalized that contesting a low-key race such as the one in Highland was actually easier on his body than some of Harry Johnson's workouts had been the year before. Craig later looked back on efforts like that 23:52 as evidence any race, no matter how small, made him too excited to hold back as much as he should have.

Craig wasn't a typical patient for Dr. Rehberger, whose practice consisted mostly of farmers. Craig was different in that he could point out small health problems before they became major. "He could sense that something wasn't right either in how his gait was or how his [foot] plant was or how his posture felt in his lower back and pelvis," Dr. Rehberger said. "That was a big help." In fact, Craig could adjust the position of his pelvis and spine during a race to manage pain. "He was very acutely aware of what his body was feeling like in races as well as in training," said Dr. Rehberger, who considered Craig more like a brother than a cousin. As for not charging Craig, Dr. Rehberger insisted Craig attracted so many new patients, especially runners, he more than covered the cost of his care.

The end of April saw Craig produce the greatest—and perhaps most imprudent—sequence of three races in four days he'd ever attempt. It began on Thursday, April 26, with the only appearance he'd make in the Penn Relays, his first outdoor track race since Brussels eight months earlier. A downpour didn't stop Craig from winning the 10K in 27:59.0, marking the first time an American had broken 28:00 that early in the year.

For his effort, Craig was paid $500. "In terms of America, $500 for a track race was really pretty good at that time," Craig said, "especially when it was cash." He didn't feel guilty about accepting the illegal payment. "I didn't want to declare it because I didn't trust the IRS and I didn't trust the AAU," he said. "When it was that small, I knew I could basically use it to subsidize my training expenses for the next six months. I knew that there were other guys that made probably more money than that in Europe. How they handled it, I did not know, but it did worry me a little bit. Eventually, I wanted to get away from that system and, a year later, I would find a way to do it."

A New King

On Saturday, April 28, Craig was in New York City for the Trevira Twosome 10-miler where he'd face Rodgers, winner of that month's Boston Marathon in an American record of 2:09:27. This was a couples' race in which places were determined by the combined times of a man and woman, but the focus of fans was on the duel between the 23-year-old Craig and 31-year-old Rodgers. "He was king of the roads," Craig said.

Craig and Rodgers reached halfway in 23:13, but it appeared Rodgers was working harder than Craig, who went on to win in 46:32.7, breaking Rodgers' American record of 48:00 set earlier that year. Even though Rodgers had lost to an American on the road for the first time in two years, his 47:36.7 was a career best. Frank Shorter was third (48:34). "All these other guys have been getting publicity, but I've been running well," Craig told *Running Times* magazine. "I came to New York so that the other road runners would know I'm around, too."

Craig's partner, Ellison Goodall, another adidas sponsored runner, won the women's division in an American record 55:37.9 to help clinch the couples' title in a combined time of 1:42:10. Craig had formed his partnership with Goodall at the World Cross Country Championships where she took third in the women's race.

Craig left the postrace party early to fly back to St. Louis for the next day's Famous Barr Gateway Arch Run, a 10K road race put on by the St. Louis Track Club. He attempted to run it like the first 10K of a marathon and that proved good enough to win in 30:28. "I think it shows that my strength and conditioning are there," he told the *St. Louis News-Democrat*. "These last four days have been great for me. But I'm tired, very tired from all the travel and running."

Craig's other comments hinted at his motivation. "I wish I could see that coach's face now," he said referring to Harry Johnson. "I think my results are showing that I knew what I was doing [by leaving Athletics West]. But let the critics decide for themselves."

Chapter 16: American Record

"People identify with you more if you're human, not a machine."

— Craig Virgin

In tiny Lebanon, Craig was a big deal and never bigger than on May 19, 1979, which the town designated as "Craig Virgin Olympic Day." The day doubled as a fundraiser for his Moscow Olympic training expenses. To generate funds, barbecued pork sandwiches were sold on the City Hall parking lot and Craig Virgin Olympic Day T-shirts were on sale at the town newspaper, the *Lebanon Advertiser*. Mayor Bill Best donated one month's salary. Over $5,000 was raised.

Inside the Fairburn Real Estate & Insurance building, a mini-museum of Craig's memorabilia was displayed. The collection included photos and running jerseys along with awards, bowls and glassware won in exotic locales. Outside, the high school band performed.

Amazingly, the day included 16 miles of running and three races for Craig. In a feature story about the day, Dave Dorr of the *St. Louis Post-Dispatch* wrote: "To make the second race, he depended on the CB in his orange, turbo-charged Fiat X1/9 to avoid the smokeys intent on nabbing speeders."

At 5:30 p.m., Craig went to the newly built cinder track at Lebanon High School where the townsfolk watched him run a 4:07.2 exhibition mile, his lifetime best on cinders. Afterward, a proclamation was read dedicating the track in Craig's name. Alas, there was no mention that a sign bearing Craig's name would be erected at the track and it never was.

On the occupation front, Craig had been hired as a marketing associate by St. Louis–based PET Inc., under the Olympic Job Opportunity Program. The program involved 71 companies hiring 94 Olympic hopefuls who'd be allowed time off to train and travel to competitions. Craig's job dealt mostly with the meal replacement drink SEGO, which came in a can. The flavor choices were chocolate, vanilla and strawberry. "When I was there, they just came out with the powder version," Craig said. "You could pack it in with a glass of 2 percent or skim milk." Outside Craig's private office—an 8- by 12-foot space overlooking the Mississippi River and the Gateway Arch—was a plaque that read "C. S. Virgin." His time off work was put to good use on May 26 at Wichita, Kansas, where he beat Herb Lindsay in a stadium record 13:31.7. It was the fastest track 5K Craig would ever run in America.

The center of Craig's social life had become Cindy Wuebbels, who was his brother's grade school music teacher. She and Craig had met at a Lebanon Elementary School open house in the fall of 1978. They frequently went to discos, where Craig felt dancing helped loosen his muscles. The downside of the relationship was that late nights of romance cut into his rest. "I probably did more foolish things in that relationship than any other time in terms of spending money and in terms of staying up late and losing sleep," said Craig, who was "totally smitten" with Cindy. The pretty blonde—a visual amalgam of Steffi Graf and Candice Bergen—had the slim build of a dancer. She jogged, but liked tennis more. She loved music most of all. They had great chemistry, but they'd break up and get back together five times before the friendship finally fizzled in 2004.

On June 2, Craig planned to use a low-key 10K road race in Champaign as a glorified training run. As usual, his competitive instincts refused to be stifled. As he neared the finish inside Memorial Stadium, he spotted a wheelchair competitor who'd had a 9½-minute head start. Craig caught the man to win in 29:14.3. "I killed myself trying to catch that guy," Craig told Woods.

Woods wrote that Craig felt ready to break Steve Prefontaine's American 10K record of 27:43.6 set on April 27, 1974, on a cold, windy night in Eugene. Craig returned to Memorial Stadium later in the day to watch the NCAA track and field championships after which he went for a six-mile run with Oregon's Alberto Salazar and Rudy Chapa. Craig came to view that weekend as the pinnacle of track's popularity in Champaign. Within five years, the track was removed from Memorial Stadium as the sport itself began sliding into out-of-sight, out-of-mind status for the general public.

Streak Ends

Craig's seven-race winning streak came to an end in a 3K at Berkeley, California, on June 9. He stepped into the lead with 800 left, but couldn't hold off eventual winner Sydney Maree of Villanova, who blasted the last lap in 53.7 to set a South African record of 7:43.0. Craig took fourth in a personal record of 7:48.2, which moved him to fifth in US history. "Just by hanging on and fighting with those guys," he said, "my body broke through into another threshold."

On June 17, Craig was on the 10K starting line at the AAU national track and field championships in Walnut, a suburb of Los Angeles and home to the Mt. San Antonio College Relays. Breaking Prefontaine's American record would require a sub-66.4-per-lap pace. Craig didn't expect pacing help from opponents.

The day before his race, a scary thought entered his mind. What if, after eight months of planning, his record attempt failed? The question possessed him to the extent he tried to clear his head with a six-hour walk around Disneyland with Cindy Wuebbels. "That's not the ideal way to prepare for a 10,000, but I had to get my mind off the race," he told John Conrad of the *Eugene Register-Guard*.

Temperatures were in the 60s at race time, but a strong wind on the backstretch made a record seem unlikely. Many in the crowd of 10,627 had left before Craig began his 25-lap journey with a 65.1 circuit. When he passed 800 in 2:09.5, only Paul Geis, in his first year with Athletics West, and Bill Donakowski were near. Both later dropped out along with eight others in the 30-man field. After the sixth lap, Craig was alone. "At that point, my focus shifted to the clock and Prefontaine," he said. "I felt I was racing the shadow of Prefontaine around the track at Mount SAC."

Craig had positioned Mike Durkin and Gary Wieneke outside the fence on the curves at either end of the track to let him know if he was ahead or behind record pace. "I could tell from the announcing that I was under pace for the first eight laps or so and they yelled that I was fast, but I decided just to stay with it and not slow down," Craig told *Track & Field News*. "I felt with the wind I would lose something toward the end and that's exactly what happened."

The pain of Craig's task worsened the final eight laps and he believed the record had slipped away. He reached the bell lap needing a 65 to slip under Prefontaine's 27:43.6. Breaking Frank Shorter's 1975 meet record of 28:02.2 was already a formality. Craig came up with a 61.3 to finish in a 27:39.4, making him No. 12 on the all-time world list.

Craig was voted the outstanding male athlete of the meet and his time would remain the meet record for 25 years until Mebrahtom Keflezighi sped 27:36.49 at the 2004 Olympic Trials. Craig later credited training alone for giving him the mental toughness to chase the record. He estimated a third of his peers also trained alone. The effort earned him the lone US 10K berth for the World Cup II at Montreal on August 24. Fourth-placer Robbie Perkins said, "He really looked at each race tactically with much bigger depth than most of the rest of us. Everybody else would be trying to hang on and see what they had left at the end. Craig was looking to destroy you before it came time to really kick in."

Breaking Opponents

Breaking opponents in a 10K was one thing, but doing so in a 5K was another matter. That much was clear on June 30 in Philadelphia where Craig led until Centrowitz kicked to victory on the final lap in 13:21.0 to become the fourth-fastest American. Craig settled for a personal record of 13:23.6 that made him No. 8 in US history. He was miffed Centrowitz had "leeched off" him the whole race. Worse than losing was the feeling he'd given up the last mile. As was his pattern, he set aside shame and disappointment by focusing on the fact he'd set a PR, which brought enough confidence to think better times were ahead. Another consolation prize was a three-mile postrace cooldown with the sport's 20-year-old glamour girl, Mary Decker.

Even though the nation's road-running boom was in full force, Craig was still surprised his success early in 1979 generated so much media interest. The phones at his parents' home and in his office at PET Inc. rang off the hook with interview requests. Various television outlets sent film crews to Lebanon.

The small newspapers of southwest Illinois even reported on the media hoopla. In the June 28 *Greenville Advocate*, Craig said, "I just didn't dream that it would have that much of an impact in my life." He went on to discuss politics being part of the Olympics. "I just hope politics don't come into athletic competition in these next Games," he said. "No matter how much we hope, it probably will because that's just its form. The whole world is watching and people will take advantage of that."

Craig returned to road racing on the Fourth of July with his first appearance in the Peachtree Road Race at Atlanta, Georgia. While in Europe in 1978, he'd read about the race's massive field. The 10th annual race billed itself as America's largest 10K. A record 20,161 would run in 1979 along with an estimated 3,000 unregistered bandits. Olympian Jeff Galloway, who'd topped a field of 110 to win the first Peachtree in 1970, told the *Atlanta Journal* that Craig had "more potential than anyone since Prefontaine. He has gold medal potential."

For the first 5K, Craig and Roche swapped the lead. When they reached the 130-foot climb of "Coronary Hill," Craig took the lead halfway up and enjoyed a 15-yard cushion at the top. Ahead he could see his girlfriend in the convertible leading the race.

Craig created a 24-second gap by the finish to clock a course record 28:30.5, a 4:35.8-per-mile average. As he leapt through the finish banner, his raised hands both signaled "V" for Virgin Victory. A photo of the moment, with Craig in adidas Marathon 80 racing flats, would appear in full-page magazine advertisements and posters for adidas the next 18 months.

At the start of an hour-long press conference, reporters marveled Craig was able to talk within minutes of finishing. With his arm around Cindy Wuebbels and a beer in his hand, he spoke of the fans' impact. "I just love running and performing in front of the crowd," he told the *Atlanta Journal*. "I guess I'm kind of like an artist or an actor in that respect, but I just like to run in front of the crowd." He'd address the issue again in the August 19 *Chicago Sun-Times*. "A lot of people in running have been colorless and blah," he said. "People identify with you more if you're human, not a machine."

Craig came to view road races as cross country on asphalt. "I could enjoy it," he said. "I could relax. What I learned is I could pace off of the press truck. I would be looking at people's faces and eyes and I would try to listen to what they were saying to each other when I was humming along at the front of the race, pushing the pace. That was a trick that I did to try to deal with the mental pressures and the physical discomfort."

Managing a Career

Craig spent the next two weeks preparing for a seven-race European tour. In the July 17 Bislett Games two-mile at Oslo, Norway, he took third in a personal best of 8:22.0, moving into a tie for sixth on the all-time US list.

A concern for Craig on this tour was making arrangements with meet directors. When he wasn't on the phone trying to confirm race dates, he read John L. Parker's novel *Once a Runner*, which Craig considered the best book about running.

In a July 21 5K at Rieti, Italy, Craig and Henry Rono swapped the lead through opening 1,600s of 4:15.5 and 4:21.5. With three laps to go, Rono bolted and Craig couldn't answer. "I'm disappointed with myself for that," he analyzed after placing second in a personal best of 13:23.3. He spent the next few days at adidas headquarters in West Germany discussing new shoe designs with the research and development staff.

Helping Craig get into European races was Pete Peterson, who was paid by adidas to escort several of its athletes through Europe that summer. He provided coaching as needed. He also dealt with meet directors, arranging travel and athlete compensation. He got Craig $500 to $1,000 for each meet, which was an upgrade from 1978. "First you had to get in. Then they had to agree to pay for your flight and your hotel," said Craig, who found expense negotiations time consuming and energy draining. "Then it was how much more to run.

[Sebastian] Coe and [Steve] Ovett were getting $10,000 or $12,000 to run because they were the world record holders in the mile, 1,500 meters and the 800 meters. So I was still in the upper-middle class in terms of the pay hierarchy, but very happy to still come away with $750 or $1,500 in cash." Craig's reputation for front-running caused some promoters to save the cost of hiring a rabbit because they knew he'd have to set the pace to escape the kickers.

Craig drove with 1972 Olympic gold medalist John Akii-Bua of Uganda four hours to Kauhajoki, Finland, for a meet on July 27. Craig came to appreciate smaller European meets because they put more effort into hospitality. In Kauhajoki, he was provided with the nicest hotel room and meals of the whole trip. Kids at the meet swarmed the athletes, requesting autographs. "Track and field athletes are celebrities over here," Craig wrote.

Craig and his brother, Brent, had their hands full taking care of puppies Pre and Paavo in 1979. The pets were named in honor of running legends Steve Prefontaine and Paavo Nurmi. *(Photo courtesy of Brent Virgin)*

Looking for more speed work, Craig contested the 1,500 and finished second by two-tenths of a second in 3:46.0. In between races, homesickness crept in, but phone calls to Cindy provided relief. "The sad thing for the runners and the bicycle racers in this world is that unless you can take your girlfriend or your family or your wife with you," Craig said, "you basically feel like a soldier going off to war in a distant land."

Craig's tour of duty ended on August 7 in Göteborg, Sweden, where he hoped to crack 13:20 for 5K. A rabbit handled the first three laps, but Craig was in front when he finished the fourth in 4:15.5. With 300 to go, Australian Dave Fitzsimons and Swede Dan Glans passed Craig, who held on for third in a personal best of 13:23.3, which ranked seventh on the all-time US list.

After leaving the idyllic weather of Scandinavia, Craig was greeted with humid, 90-degree conditions for 10 days of training in Lebanon as he prepared for the August 19 Falmouth Road Race. His welcoming committee on the farm included Doberman puppies named Pre and Paavo.

Among Craig's major goals of 1979 was winning Falmouth. *Track & Field News* called the field the strongest gathering of road race talent next to the Boston Marathon. On the eve of the race, a private party for elite runners took place at the Flying Bridge Restaurant. Travel delays caused Craig and Cindy to arrive late. *The Runner* magazine noted they "made a grand entrance, so smooth and handsome that one could see them modeling fall sportswear fashions for magazines." Craig ordered a White Russian and proclaimed, "It makes me think of Moscow."

Falmouth's picturesque course begins in Woods Hole and follows a two-lane road that hugs the coast and winds past the whitewashed Nobska lighthouse and through a forest to Falmouth Heights. A 4:33 opening mile felt slow to Craig. After a 4:37 second mile, the lead pack shrank to five including Craig, who went on to win the 7.1-mile race in 32:19.7, slicing 12 seconds from Rodgers' 1978 course record. The effort drained Craig to the point he forsook his usual leap across the finish. He just wanted to stop. Herb Lindsay was eight seconds behind in second.

Before the awards ceremony, Craig felt chilled and "half sick." With the World Cup only five days away, he decided to shower at the house he was staying at near the starting line. On the way back he got caught in a traffic jam and missed the awards ceremony. "I would think that had to be the only time in Falmouth history that a winner was not present for the awards," Craig said. "I just felt awful. I never missed another awards ceremony." And he never won another Falmouth.

When Craig didn't show at the awards ceremony, Lindsay became its focus. "I didn't have any speech written, but it just flowed out," he said. "I told the story, 'It was a thrill to be running with Craig and Bill. These are people that I've looked up to. It was an opportunity for me to break through.' The crowd gobbled it up. They loved it. It was an appreciative crowd and Craig wasn't there to take the accolades. I took them instead. It was like I stole his thunder." Lindsay saw Falmouth earn him invitations to other major races.

Craig spent the next two days training in Springfield, Vermont, where a friend of Cindy's lived. Craig and Cindy then drove to Montreal for the World Cup II where he'd battle Ethiopian star Miruts Yifter for the second time. Due to the lack of birth records in Africa, Yifter, a lieutenant in the Ethiopian Army, didn't know exactly how old he was, but estimated he was 36 in 1979. *Track & Field News* listed his birth date as June 28, 1947, which made him 33.

Yifter was 5-foot-3¾ and 117 pounds with a hairline that had receded to the point of making him half bald. In his first international meet, the US-Africa dual in 1971, he raced Steve Prefontaine in a 5K, but kicked one lap too soon and stopped. Yifter came back to win the 10K in that same meet. After landing the 10K bronze medal in the 1972 Olympics, Yifter was scheduled to contest the 5K, but when runners left the holding room in the Olympic Stadium, he was in the bathroom. When he came out, he didn't know where to go and missed the race. In 1976, the African boycott kept him out of the Olympics. In the first World Cup at Düsseldorf, West Germany, in 1977, Yifter won the 5K and 10K.

World Cup II events had one entrant from each of eight countries or parts of the world. The eight were the US, Europe, East Germany, the Soviet Union, the Americas, Africa, Oceania and Asia.

The US head coach was Sam Bell and Wieneke was among the assistants. Craig roomed with Henry Marsh to comply with Cindy's strict Catholic moral standards regarding unwed adults sleeping together. She stayed in the room assigned to Craig.

Olive Branch Rebuffed

Marsh relayed a message from Bill Bowerman, who wanted to know what it would take to bring Craig back into the Nike fold. "I listened to my pride instead of my brain back then and I basically told Henry to tell him that it would never happen," said Craig, who later wished he'd asked Bowerman to become his coach then as well as when he left Athletics West in 1978. "I think he would have been an advocate for me in '78 because of the fact he was reaching out to me in '79 through Henry."

The day before his nationally televised Friday race, Craig was interviewed by ABC's Jim Lampley and described how he expected the race to unfold. His insights were later broadcast during the race and proved uncannily prescient. Craig would consider that to be the most watched race he ever contested. On race day, however, his focus was diverted to Cindy, who complained of boredom. When Tom Jordan of *Track & Field News* saw the situation, he invited Cindy to accompany him to a shopping mall. That allowed Craig to rest at the hotel for what he viewed as the race of his life up to that point. "She loved being with a celebrity," Craig said. "She loved getting the VIP treatment. She could appreciate some of what I was doing, but my relationship with her was often a distraction to my demanding training and racing."

After a two-mile warmup and six 100-meter sprints, Craig stretched and went to the check-in room he remembered from the 1976 Olympics. "I feel a lot more experienced, though just three years older," he later wrote. He wasn't nervous because he knew he belonged. Even though the race was at night, the heat was stifling. Calling the race for ABC television were Keith Jackson and Marty Liquori. Liquori noted Craig "has proved over the last three months that he is now a world-class athlete, but he is saddled with the problem that's hit many distance runners before him in that his leg speed is not up to the standards of someone like Yifter, who can run a last lap in a 5,000 or 10,000 meters in 53 seconds. Craig right now is able to do about 58 seconds."

Craig arranged to share the pace with John Treacy to ensure a tempo that would tax Yifter. Treacy would lead the first three laps and Craig the next three and so forth. When Craig pulled wide to let Treacy lead the seventh lap, Treacy couldn't. The pace lagged for 600 meters until Craig pressed on. The race became a duel between him and Yifter the last four miles.

After almost stopping to force Ethiopia's Miruts Yifter to lead the World Cup II 10K at Montreal, Craig was back in front but ultimately finished second to "Yifter the Shifter." *(Photo by Mark Shearman)*

At 6K, Craig accelerated before nearly coming to a stop, forcing Yifter to lead, which he did for 2½ laps. It was the same ploy Craig had used once against Herb Lindsay in college. Liquori told TV viewers, "I've never really seen anybody do that in a meet of this caliber." Yifter proceeded to slow the pace. "He slowed down and called my bluff," said Craig, who took over again at 7K so no one else could rejoin the battle. His surges would briefly drop Yifter, who repeatedly closed the gaps.

Craig cranked the penultimate lap in 65.6. With 300 to go, Yifter dazzled the crowd of 12,567 with a withering sprint to win in 27:53.1. His last lap had required a mere 54.3 seconds compared to Craig's 61.1. Craig didn't think his final lap was so bad, but admitted Yifter "made me look as slow as molasses."

Craig's time of 27:59.6 in second made him the first American to clock three sub-28:00s in the same year. *Track & Field News* would rank him No. 2 in the world behind Yifter in the 10K for 1979. Craig's five career sub-28:00s tied Shorter for the most in US history. Two days after winning the World Cup 10K, Yifter won the 5K in 13:35.9, finishing with a 53.5 last lap.

Craig wasn't disappointed with his World Cup showing. "I feel it was one of my landmark races in my career," he wrote. "I was able to intimidate everyone but Yifter." But the race also showed Craig he'd need a new plan to win in the 1980 Olympics.

Chapter 17: Front Runner Inc.

A World Cross Country title "is worth Olympic gold medal status in my mind, but unfortunately it's not known in America."

— Bill Rodgers

A n increasing number of invitations from road race directors came Craig's way in the fall of 1979. He could ask for and receive several thousand dollars to appear and it didn't matter how well he ran. Accepting the money without jeopardizing his Olympic eligibility became a growing concern.

Craig didn't like that his $12,000, one-year contract with adidas had to be filtered through the St. Louis Track Club. He felt the deal was too restrictive. He saw that Frank Shorter and Bill Rodgers had created running apparel companies. "That's when I came up with the idea of having my own company in sports marketing, promotion, PR and being a consultant so that I could hire out," Craig said.

Craig named the company Front Runner Inc. to reflect his racing style and present a positive image to clients. Race directors would hire Front Runner and Front Runner would assign Craig to do the marketing, consulting, promoting or public relations work. Front Runner would get a check and pay Craig.

Before beginning, Craig sought the approval of AAU president Ollan Cassell, who had the power to revoke Craig's Olympic eligibility. Cassell flew in with a contract to get everything about this revolutionary idea in writing. He'd approved Hilton Hotels paying Shorter in April of 1979, which made Cassell believe Craig's idea could work, too. Under Shorter's deal, Hilton paid the AAU $25,000 and paid Shorter as a consultant for its physical fitness program. "Craig did a different kind of thing," Cassell said. "He wanted to promote events and he wanted to run in them, so that's the reason I came down to his house."

Cassell looked at Craig's educational background as a radio and TV major who took marketing and advertising classes. If there was ever a challenge to Craig's international eligibility, Cassell could defend him by saying "he was qualified" to do promotional events. "That's the reason we approved him to use his name and his athletic ability and everything else in promoting races," Cassell said. "Craig was a pioneer. There is no question about that."

In the March 1980 issue of *Runner's World*, Craig told writer Amby Burfoot, "I think an amateur athlete should be entitled to be an entrepreneur in whatever way he can. If a guy has the determination, the hustle, the gumption, then he's entitled to whatever he can scare up."

As Craig's first adidas contract was about to expire, Spalding approached him about helping to develop a line of running shoes that he'd endorse. Spalding offered a multiyear contract worth $50,000 to $60,000 a year. The four American distributors of adidas told adidas headquarters they wanted Craig to remain as their spokesperson. So Horst Dassler, son of adidas founder Adi Dassler, flew Craig first class to Europe to negotiate a new multiyear contract.

What they came up with was a five-year deal that included a two-year option. Craig would be paid $30,000 to wear adidas shoes and apparel in 1980 and the amount would escalate each year. The penultimate year would pay him $60,000 and the last year $70,000. "As far as I know," Craig said, "at the time that was the longest-term contract anybody had ever signed." He'd later realize long-term contracts had positives and negatives.

Science of Success

When it came to running, Craig planned to spend September recovering. The first week, he wasn't supposed to run at all. The next week called for four miles a day. The third week, he'd run four in the morning and four in the afternoon. The fourth week, he'd cover four in the morning and six in the afternoon. However, he raced five times that month. Many of Craig's "low-key" races became showdowns with top regional runners looking to make a name for themselves.

The science behind Craig's running success had been a mystery until he underwent testing at the physiology lab at the University of Illinois in 1975. Among the things measured was his maximum volume of oxygen consumption (VO^2 Max). His score of 84 was double the average for a man his age. "They were actually scared to publish anything," Gary Wieneke remembered. "They didn't think anybody would believe that somebody could be that good." The head of the lab also told Wieneke that Craig lacked flexibility. Wieneke told the scientist, "Regardless of what your test said, this guy can run."

Craig was tested again at the Cardiac Research and Rehabilitation Lab at Barnes Hospital in St. Louis on September 13, 1979. Among the first tests was a check of his resting pulse rate, which was 41 beats per minute. That was below the average of 45 to 47 for an elite runner. Craig's resting blood pressure was 100 over 67, slightly below the average of 112 over 75 for an elite marathoner. An echocardiogram revealed his heart to be exceptionally large for someone his size. He then did three submaximal runs of three minutes each on a treadmill. The results showed his oxygen consumption was less than other elite runners including Frank Shorter.

The September issue of *Runner's World* included a story written by Craig about the benefits of cross country and how to train for it. "One would think that the so-called 'running boom' in this country would have had a positive spin-off effect on cross-country," Craig wrote. "I personally don't think cross-country has yet felt the impact." Among the points he made: "Cross-country deserves better attention than it receives in the United States. The sport of cross-country has always been regarded as track and field's poor cousin in our country."

The civic leaders of Lebanon didn't want Craig to be poor when it came to Olympic training funds, so they had him organize a four-mile road race in conjunction with the annual Lebanon Fall Festival. Proceeds from the race and festival would go into a savings account to help defray his training expenses. Adidas, which donated shirts and banners, flew in a rep to help organize the race, which drew more than 300 runners. Craig won the October 6 event in 19:07 on a course that became one of his favorite training routes.

Throughout his career, Craig had found most of his fame far from Lebanon, but in early November fame followed him home. Grete Waitz, who held the women's marathon world record, and her husband, Jack, visited the Virgins' farm and stayed overnight at the home of Grandmother Putt. The adidas-sponsored Waitz went for a few training runs with Craig around Lebanon.

In July of 1981, Grete Waitz mailed this photo to Craig's grandmother, Rachel Putt. It showed Grete with Craig after each had won at the World Cross Country Championships in Madrid. *(Photo courtesy of Craig Virgin)*

The focus of Craig's training that fall was the December 2 Fukuoka International Marathon in Japan. The adidas distributor for Japan had asked him to enter. There was also the fact he needed a qualifying time of 2:21:54 or better to enter the US Olympic Trials in case he decided to double in the 10K and marathon instead of the 5K and 10K.

Traveling across 16 time zones to Fukuoka—a city of over a million people in southern Japan—"was a long-ass trip," according to Craig, who arrived the Wednesday prior to the Sunday race. The event was founded in 1947, but didn't become an international race until 1965. In 1979, it also served as Japan's qualifying race for the 1980 Olympics. "They didn't pay us money," Craig recalled, "but they treated us like celebrities."

Visiting entrants were each provided with an interpreter. Craig shared a room in the Nishitetsu Grand Hotel with Canada's Brian Maxwell, who'd later invent the PowerBar. The 112-man field included defending champion Toshihiko Seko of Japan, Bernie Ford of Great Britain, 1976 Olympic champion Waldemar Cierpinski of East Germany and Japanese twins Shigeru So and Takeshi So. Athletics West had four entrants including Tony Sandoval.

The race began with 2½ laps on the track in front of a capacity crowd at Heiwadai Stadium, which also served as the finish. The flat course following the peninsula around Hakata Bay was lined by a half million fans. Craig was in a tightly bunched pack of 30 when he passed 10K in 31:00.

Craig had hoped to race in custom-made adidas Marathon 80 shoes, but they didn't arrive in time. He was concerned his other racing shoes were too wide. "I wanted more support," he said. "So I did an old track trick—I went down a half a size. Instead of 9½, I wore size 9. Well, that works in spikes in a short distance. I didn't realize how much your feet swell in the course of a marathon."

At about 10K, not long before Craig's feet began to suffer, he was tripped from behind and somersaulted to the pavement, leaving behind more skin than he cares to remember. Luckily, he soon regained his spot in the pack. "I'm not sure it wasn't Toshihiko Seko that tripped me," said Craig, who passed halfway with a slight lead in 1:05:13.

Craig hoped his feet could be saved by adjusting his stride and foot plant. Hope turned to hell as blisters began to form. By 25K, he had dropped 10 seconds behind Seko, the So twins, Ford and New Zealand's Kevin Ryan. At 30K, Craig abandoned thoughts of a fast time and focused on getting under the Olympic Trials standard. "It turned out to be the toughest seven miles I have ever run," wrote Craig in a story for the February 1980 issue of *The Runner*.

Craig hung on for 17th in 2:16:59, well under the Olympic Trials qualifying standard of 2:21:54. "I remember my feet were just bloody," said Craig, who asked for his shoes and socks to be cut off. The 23-year-old Seko won in 2:10:35 after outkicking Shigeru So (2:10:37) and Takeshi So (2:10:48). The fourth-place Ford (2:10:51) made it the first marathon with four men under 2:11.

AAU Roadblock

Craig was later shocked to learn Fukuoka's precisely measured course, which rivaled Boston's and New York's in prestige, wasn't sanctioned by the AAU, which didn't accept his qualifying time. "I may have to run another one," Craig told Woods. "Personally, I'm upset about the thing. I don't think I'm being treated fairly in the situation. It's a slap in the face of the Japanese if they [AAU officials] think it's not a creditable course." Craig appealed the ruling and his time was accepted.

As 1979 came to a close, Craig was named the US Distance Runner of the Year by *Runner's World*. He was so filled with confidence he hardly noticed on December 24 that the Soviet Union had invaded Afghanistan. A story by Woods in mid-January of 1980 included Craig's opinions about the possibility the United States might boycott the Moscow Olympics to protest the Soviet invasion. Craig prophetically believed a boycott would hurt the prestige of the Olympics and sow the seeds of a Communist boycott of the 1984 Los Angeles Olympics. He considered the Olympics one of the best ways to strengthen international relations. "For the most part, the athletes will keep on training and racing and the politicians will keep on ranting and raving," he told Woods. "Myself, I don't anticipate a boycott."

Craig returned to Eugene on January 19 for the US Cross Country Trials where the top nine would qualify for the March 9 World Championships in Paris. He stayed out late the night before, renewing friendships from his days at Athletics West and Stretch & Sew. The impact of only five hours of sleep was lessened by the fact the race started in the afternoon. Dan Dillon led the first five miles of the 7½-mile race until Craig took over and created a 150-meter gap to win in 36:43.7. "I knew after one lap [two miles] that it was going to be a super day for me," Craig told the media. "I'd very much like to be the first American to win the international meet."

A week after racing in the 40-degree chill of Eugene, Craig was in the adidas-sponsored Bermuda International 10K Road Race. "To go there for three to five days was a real break weatherwise," said Craig, who fondly remembers filling free time with moped races against fellow runners. During the fifth mile of the actual race, he surged away from Herb Lindsay, Bruce Bickford and Jon Sinclair to win in 29:17. Craig might have run faster except he needed to save something for the following day's half marathon in New Orleans, put on by St. Louis-based Anheuser-Busch, a sponsor Craig wanted to please. "You can get in a compromised situation with sponsors," said Craig, who contested another half marathon in San Blas, Puerto Rico, to please adidas a week after New Orleans.

Craig arrived at the starting line in San Blas wearing an adidas singlet with SEGO written across the chest. Sego was the diet food drink he'd worked for at Pet Inc. It was his first rematch with Miruts Yifter since the World Cup. Heavy rain taught Craig that the hard rubberized compounds of his adidas Marathon 80 shoes didn't grip the pavement properly. Despite slipping every step, he managed to outkick Lasse Viren for third in 1:04:28. Yifter, cheered on by 150,000 spectators, finished 32 seconds ahead.

In February of 1980, Craig revealed Front Runner had signed a one-year deal with the International Management Group (IMG), headed by super-agent Mark McCormack. The deal involved Craig advising IMG about the pros and cons of business opportunities in road racing and track and field. "I wouldn't term this an athlete/agent relationship," Craig told *Track & Field News*. "This is a business arrangement between my company and IMG. They will be assisting my company in finding new opportunities and will offer expertise in doing business in the Big Leagues."

IMG, which signed mile world record holder Sebastian Coe at the same time as Craig, wanted more than a one-year deal, but Craig was hesitant to make a longer commitment. "I said, 'Show me what you can do the first year,' because I was really concerned," he said. "I had plenty of things coming in. I had more than enough on my plate with what was coming in on the phone. There was only one of me and all these opportunities. The situation was that was a tumultuous time in American distance running just when I was hitting my peak."

Bone Chilling

Craig's last tune-up for the World Cross Country Championships was the March 2 Bran Chex 10K Road Race in St. Louis. He beat Don Kardong by 1.9 seconds in 29:37.7, but the five-degree chill—the coldest March 2 in St. Louis in 67 years—may have played a role in Craig straining his left hamstring. He visited his chiropractor cousin later that day for therapy. Within two days, Craig was on his way to West Germany for a three-day stay at adidas headquarters.

Kenny Moore of *Sports Illustrated* would later write of the US cross country team's pre–World Championships bonding and note:

> The only regret was that Craig Virgin, the winner of the U.S. men's trials, was not yet in Paris to enjoy the pre-race idyll. He had recently founded a consulting firm and was in Germany speaking with a shoe manufacturer. An ambitious man, comfortable with the ways of promotion, Virgin is intent on taking full advantage of his success, and thus differs somewhat from the balance of the team, for whom the camaraderie of such a trip and the competition itself are reward enough. While not resented, Virgin's forceful drive gave rise to wishes that he relax a little. Virgin himself admits to feeling "pulled at" by the demands of running and business, but says, "I've been training really hard. Let's let this race decide if I'm holding together."

The IAAF began governing the World Cross Country Championships in 1972 when 15 countries took part. The race was founded in 1903 in England when 41 runners from four countries competed. The "countries" were England, Ireland, Scotland and Wales. The race attracted its first "overseas" squad in 1907 when France entered. Tunisia was the first African entrant in 1958.

Prior to 1980, the best American male results were third-place efforts by both Tracy Smith in 1966 and Bill Rodgers in 1975.

The day before the World Championships in Paris, Craig ran eight miles on the course, studying the final 800-meter straightaway in particular, taking note of landmarks "for gear change No. 1, gear change No. 2 and then, if necessary and possible, a final Hail Mary gear change." A trainer later treated his left hamstring and back, but overall he felt good.

On the bus ride to the starting line, Craig psyched himself up by listening to Linda Ronstadt, Billy Joel and Neil Diamond on the Sony Walkman he'd bought in Japan. The technology was so new, it wasn't meant for export, a fact made clear by the Japanese writing on the case.

The 190 entrants went to the starting line anxious to secure a good position early, which made the ensuing false start of little surprise. Unfortunately, not everyone was ready for the restart when the gun fired again. Most countries went with two men at the front of the starting box, but the ever-democratic Americans wanted as many men in the first and second rows as possible. "I was getting them set up and the starter never said 'ready' and he never said 'set,'" Craig recalled. "He just shot the gun off. My own guys ran me over and nearly took me down."

Someone prevented Craig from doing a face-plant, but by the time he got moving, he was encased in the field. A teammate, Dan Dillon, grabbed the lead as the field began the first of five 2,450-meter laps. England's Nick Rose took over while climbing the backstretch hill on the second lap, quickly creating a 30-meter gap on defending champion John Treacy of Ireland in second.

During the second lap, Craig went from 25th to ninth, but Rose stretched his lead over Leon Schots of Belgium in second. During the third lap, Craig reached the back of the chase pack and his second moment of truth, as detailed in chapter one. He answered that moment of truth and two later ones in the only way that could produce a thrilling come-from-behind victory. Spectators then and viewers of the race video now get caught in a vortex where Craig's imminent defeat turns into assured victory. The process is gradual at first, but suddenly becomes something Hollywood would reject as unbelievable.

Faint Fanfare

American fans, focused as they were on domestic professional sports, paid little attention to Craig's win. The few who heard of his triumph had trouble appreciating its importance. Top US runners, however, knew what Craig had done. "It's worth Olympic gold medal status in my mind," said Bill Rodgers, "but unfortunately it's not known in America."

At the postrace dance, champagne flowed. Moore wrote in *Sports Illustrated* that as Craig surveyed the excitement, he said, "I wonder if the people back home will ever be able to fully appreciate this. Here I've been exposed to 50 million Europeans on TV today, but in my own country I'm sure I'll only draw modest attention."

Moore noted: "To many runners that would be a source of relief, but Virgin seemed concerned." Craig later went out on the town with Fred Lebow, the New York City Marathon race director, who was hoping to host the 1984 World Cross Country Championships. Joining them was Kathrine Switzer, the first "numbered" female finisher of the Boston Marathon in 1967. [Roberta Gibb ran without a number in 1966.] "I didn't get back to the hotel until 3 or 4 o'clock in the morning," said Craig, who caught an early flight to adidas France headquarters in Strasbourg for a press conference. The media wanted to hear Craig's stance on the US threat to boycott the Moscow Olympics.

Every Olympic-year World Cross Country champion prior to 1980 had gone on to win an Olympic medal. "My ambition this year is to go to the Olympics and I'm planning to go with some other athletes to Washington to meet President Carter to persuade him to change his attitude towards the Games," Craig told reporters. "I don't condone what the Soviet Union has done in Afghanistan—make no mistake about that. But the Olympics is still something worthwhile. I appreciate there is good and bad in them, but I think it's important contact between sportsmen and should continue." The can-do attitude that had served Craig so well for so long was about to meet its match.

Back home, the combination of Craig's fame and oratory skills made him a highly sought speaker for club luncheons and school assemblies in the St. Louis metropolitan area. Every time he spoke in early 1980, people asked his views about the possibility of an Olympic boycott. Callers to his 15-minute radio show about running and fitness on KMOX in St. Louis wanted to know the same thing. "I knew the history of prior Olympic boycotts and other types of demonstrations and knew there was nothing that we were proposing to do for Moscow that would make a concrete difference," said Craig, who'd disapproved of Moscow being chosen to host the Games years earlier. "If somebody could have shown me or told me how it was going to make a difference to the people of Afghanistan or to the people in Russia, then I would have gladly considered the sacrifice."

President Jimmy Carter set February 20 as the deadline for Soviet troops to withdraw from Afghanistan or else the US would boycott the Moscow Olympics. The date zoomed past without the slightest compliance by the Soviets.

In an April 21 interview with the *Daily News* of Rolla, Missouri, Craig said, "The only way we can stop Russia from marching over little countries is by military force. Having an Olympic boycott to stop military action is like throwing a glass of water on a burning house."

Among US athletes, support for the boycott was split. Those opposed to it denounced Soviet aggression, but didn't agree a boycott was an effective way to punish the Soviets. "I don't think President Carter understood the full implications, either, or he would have understood it was as much a punishment for America as it was for the Soviet Union," Craig said.

Business as Usual

The Carter administration claimed a boycott would show the Soviets they couldn't commit aggression and expect to do business as usual. The odd thing was most business did continue as usual. There was no interruption in trade between the two countries except for a grain and technology embargo initiated in January of 1980 and discontinued 15 months later by Ronald Reagan. Other sporting events between the countries in boxing and even track and field were held as scheduled. American tourists continued to visit the USSR. In essence, everything except the Olympics went on as usual. The anti-boycott crowd believed that—short of using military action—the USSR couldn't be punished more than when the United Nations condemned its invasion of Afghanistan.

Athletes in favor of the boycott were sure it would make the Soviet people aware of their government's violations of international law. That was a leap of faith considering the Soviet citizenry got its news from state-controlled media. Few Soviet athletes in the 1980 Winter Olympics held in February at Lake Placid, New York, had even heard of the boycott threat. *Track & Field News* came out against the boycott and suggested a better way to protest would be to skip the opening ceremonies. The Athletes Advisory Council to the United States Olympic Committee (USOC) also suggested boycotting the medal ceremonies. Craig liked such ideas and even suggested athletes protest by wearing black armbands.

President Carter claimed the boycott was necessary for national security. The USOC is not legally bound to comply with a president's wishes, but President Carter said he'd take legal actions to prevent the USOC from sending a team to Moscow. He also said participating in the Olympics would have validated Soviet aggression.

USOC delegates met in Colorado Springs, Colorado, on April 12 to consider three options. They could vote to send a team to Moscow, delay the decision until May 24 (the last day for entering the Olympics) or they could agree to the boycott. If there was a boycott, some hoped the International Olympic Committee would change its rules to allow athletes of boycotting nations to compete "unattached" under the Olympic flag.

In a maneuver some viewed as blackmail, the Carter administration threatened to cut a $16 million federal grant to the USOC.
The administration also asked Sears to withhold a $25,000 pledge
to the USOC until it voted to boycott. As noted by Nicholas Evan
Sarantakes in his book *Dropping the Torch*, Sears and 14 other major
corporate donors agreed to withhold a combined $175,000 in pledges.
The White House also vowed to revoke the tax-exempt status of the
USOC. Carter sweetened the deal by offering to cover the deficit
from the Lake Placid Winter Olympics and help fund the 1984 Los
Angeles Summer Olympics. Vice President Walter Mondale told
USOC delegates before they cast their ballots that "history holds its
breath, for what is at stake is no less than the future security of the
civilized world." Delegates voted to boycott, 1,604 to 797.

Speaking Out

Craig was livid, but he'd seen it coming when NBC announced a
week prior to the USOC vote that it wouldn't televise the Olympics.
He'd seen in 1972 and 1976 that the nation fell in love with Olympians
when TV played matchmaker, but now the matchmaker was dead.

Craig was so disgusted with The Athletics Congress (TAC
replaced the AAU as track's national governing body in 1979; TAC
changed its name in 1992 to USA Track and Field) for not standing
up for athletes and negotiating with the White House, he returned
a $200-a-month stipend because he didn't want to feel beholden to
TAC. He also had no interest in going to Europe with a national team
funded by the USOC.

Craig's anger attracted national attention when he said, "US athletes have been sold down the river for a bag of gold. Carter bought
himself a boycott by putting a gun to their [USOC delegates'] heads."
Craig's reaction drew hate mail. One letter read: "If you love the
Russians so much, why don't you go there to live?" Craig bristled at
the suggestion he was unpatriotic for disagreeing with the president.
"Congress disagrees every day with the president, and they're not
considered unpatriotic," he told Tom Jordan of *Track & Field News*.
The ever-optimistic Craig held out hope through May for US participation in the Olympics. By June, his hope was gone.

Craig came to believe his opposition to the boycott was shared by many athletes, who didn't possess his courage to speak out. In the June 6 edition of the *Los Angeles Times*, Craig told writer Mark Heisler, "There weren't enough athletes who had the guts to stand up for what they believed in. A lot of this I blame on the athletes. Many athletes were too wishy-washy. They were too afraid to say what was on their mind. At this point, the ones who didn't, I don't want to hear any bitching [from them] in several weeks, because if they weren't willing to say something at the time it needed to be said, then they deserve to not have an Olympics."

The sad numbers of the matter showed that 466 American athletes and those of 65 other nations boycotted while 5,512 athletes from 81 countries participated. Of the 466 Americans, 219 never made another Olympic team.

Athletes fell into two categories after their Olympic dreams were destroyed. "It drove some on and others just gave up emotionally and mentally," said Craig, who remained emphatically among the driven. He continued to train and race as planned to peak during the Olympics between July 21 and August 1. He knew he'd get another Olympic shot in 1984, but felt sorry for athletes who'd be too old by then. Craig soldiered on, but not without scars. "When they took us out of the Games," he told the *Oregonian*, "they removed the one, sole goal that my life has revolved around for the last three years."

Chapter 18: 1980 Olympic Boycott

*"I came to Paris to beat the American record
and to prove I would have had something to say
in Moscow."*

— Craig Virgin

C raig returned from the World Cross Country Championships knowing he'd scheduled at least three races per month leading up to the June 24 Olympic Trials, which was still the most prestigious track meet in the United States despite the Olympic boycott. The first stop was the March 16 Crescent City Classic 10K Road Race in New Orleans. Race officials put Craig up in a French Quarter hotel where he learned to love raw oysters with cocktail sauce. A little Tabasco made the oysters even spicier. A hot pace in the race's third mile sent Craig to victory in 28:35, 30 seconds ahead of runner-up Bill Rodgers.

On April 27, Craig returned to defend his title in New York City's Trevira Twosome 10-miler, but saw Herb Lindsay top him, 45:59.8 to 46:30.0, as both surpassed Craig's never-ratified American record of 46:32.7 from 1979 and Rodgers' official record of 47:09. "This was the red flag that told me that this was not the same Herb Lindsay from 1978 and 1979," Craig recalled. "It was a huge wake-up call for me because I knew I would see him again at the Olympic Trials."

At the behest of adidas, Craig entered the largest and wildest race of his career to that point, the May 18 Bay to Breakers 7.63-mile road race in San Francisco. Founded in 1912, the race was among America's oldest. It had 200 seeded runners, 24,000 official entrants and a large number of unregistered bandits—some of whom came dressed as gorillas, human centipedes and cops, as well as one woman wearing only a nurse's hat.

Craig wore a yellow-and-black adidas uniform with *Front Runner* across his chest and his name on the back. A story about the race in the August issue of *The Runner* noted Craig's career goals included winning every major road race before he retired. He also said, "I'm here for publicity. Where else can I get this kind of exposure?"

Craig's entry was heralded in the April 27 *San Francisco Examiner* in which writer Glenn Kramon noted Craig's love of fast cars and fast women. "I love sports cars—I've got a turbo-charged Fiat and would like to go to a Porsche soon—and I like driving fast. I have aspirations toward amateur car racing," Craig told Kramon. "I also like going out on dates and having a good time. If there's going to be wine and a fire, I'd rather be doing something other than playing backgammon."

Craig didn't play around on race day, pulling away from the masses early with defending champion Bobby Hodge and Australian John Andrews. Hodge tried to escape on Hayes Street Hill, a half-mile stretch that climbed 150 feet, but Craig countered halfway up and went on to win by 62.9 seconds over Andrews in a course record 35:11.8, a 4:38-per-mile clip.

Speaking to the media afterward while celebrating with a magnum of champagne, Craig said, "Some TV people made it sound like an easy race, but I was hurting the whole way. I never looked back once and just kept driving and driving." In the next day's newspapers, Craig shared front-page headlines with the volcanic eruption of Mount St. Helens.

Requests for Craig to enter events flooded Front Runner Inc., which was first located in a back office of his parents' business building on their farm. He later moved to the second floor of a downtown Lebanon building where rent was under $300 a month. On the other side of a yellow front door emblazoned with the Front Runner logo was a steep staircase leading to a five-room complex. It was managed by Craig's first employee, Anne Meyer, whom he'd plucked from the sports information department at McKendree College.

The walls were covered with a combination of oak paneling and burlap fabric. They were adorned with posters and plaques documenting Craig's career. There were shelves with trophies, and a world map covered with colored pins showing where he'd raced. There was a tiny kitchen and a bathroom with a shower. Plush carpeting was piled high in all the rooms.

Big kickers such as Matt Centrowitz (second from right) were happy to let Craig set the pace as he did in The Athletics Congress National 5K on June 14, 1980, at Walnut, California. Trailing in this photo were Rodolfo Gomez, Steve Plasencia, Wilson Waigwa and John Gregorek. *(Photo by Jeff Johnson)*

Opponents were more than happy to allow Craig to uphold his company's name in the TAC national 5K at Walnut, California, on June 14, which was his second outdoor track race of the year. He hadn't scheduled more because he'd planned to contest the May 24 Olympic Trials marathon, an event the boycott caused him to skip. The pace-setting at Walnut was left to Craig, as usual. With his family watching, he opened gaps in the 28-man field with a 63-second sixth lap. Steve Plasencia, a former University of Minnesota runner who'd faced Craig in college, used a 64.2 to lead the 11th lap. At the bell, Craig was back in front, but too close to Matt Centrowitz, who defended his title in a stadium record 13:33.61 with help from a 56.4 final lap. "Craig was throwing in those fast laps, but I was so far back, I didn't feel it," Centrowitz told the *Eugene Register-Guard*. Plasencia followed Centrowitz past Craig with 200 to go and wound up second in 13:34.83. Craig took third in 13:35.65.

When Craig arrived in Oregon for the Olympic Trials, he could taste the ash from Mount St. Helens and feel it in his eyes. His contract with adidas included performance bonuses such as $5,000 for an Olympic Trials victory. As runners warmed up for the 10,000-meter preliminaries on June 21, they were notified the prelims were canceled due to a lack of entrants. The boycott had caused a number of withdrawals, leaving a field of 20. "I was probably the only one who was disappointed because I was geared towards a hard day," said Craig, who tried in vain to convince meet officials to conduct an exhibition mile.

Craig had yet to reach a fitness peak, but he was getting close. "I was not trying to peak for the Trials," he said. He'd learned in 1976 that one needed to be good enough to make an Olympic team on 85 percent fitness, so a peak could be reached six weeks later at the Olympics. Qualifying for an Olympic team close to 100 percent fitness left one vulnerable to staleness by the time the Olympics arrived. Lindsay decided before the final he wasn't running for second or third. The final would be his Olympics and he would go for the win.

During the Trials, Craig stayed at the luxurious vacation home owned by Herb and Ann Person, the co-owners of Stretch & Sew who'd employed him in 1978. The home was 30 minutes outside of Eugene, but close enough to the McKenzie River that Craig could fall asleep each night to the sound of gurgling water. He believed his top challengers were Alberto Salazar (who'd recently spent time training in Kenya), Paul Geis and Lindsay.

Salazar's fitness had been compromised by a knee injury. "All year I've been thinking about running against Virgin," Salazar told John Conrad of the *Register-Guard*. "I don't think either one of us could pull away from the other. Normally, it would come down to the end and it would take something in the 27:30s to win." Craig wasn't sure he was ready to break 27:40 yet, but he was more interested in setting goals than limits. "I refuse to set limits," he told Leo Davis of the *Oregonian*. "Limits conflict with progress."

Buzz Saw

The Runner magazine publisher George Hirsch, who was scheduled to do television commentary for NBC at the Moscow Olympics, remembered the Trials 10K generated considerable prerace buzz. "Somehow the talk and the buildup was more for that race than any I can remember during those Trials," he said. "What was going to happen when you got the guy who, for all intents and purposes, was unbeatable on the roads at 10K [in Lindsay], running against a 10,000-meter specialist on the track [in Virgin]?"

It rained most of race day, June 24, but stopped before the 10K. The temperature was below 70 degrees, but high humidity made it feel warmer. Even with no Olympic berths at stake, Craig was so nervous he had trouble eating. "For me, at this point, it's for honor and pride," he told Woods. Craig left the cabin without his stadium pass and had to return for it, but arrived at Hayward Field having forgotten his spikes. He warmed up while they were brought to him. In the stands among more than 14,000 spectators, his family and friends from Lebanon had remembered to wear their yellow "Front Runner" hats.

The race opened with Salazar setting a 67-second tempo for three laps. Craig ran the fourth lap in 64.3 to pass the 1,600 mark in front at 4:27.5. "I started at a really brisk clip . . . and then about every 1,200 I would surge," he recalled. "The first surge dropped a few guys. The second surge dropped a few more. The third surge dropped everybody but Lindsay."

Craig reached 5K in 13:43.6 with Lindsay still close enough to clip his heels. Craig then slowed to force Lindsay to lead. *Track & Field News* reported an angry exchange of words ensued before Craig surged to a 10-meter lead. Craig and Lindsay agree the exchange wasn't angry. "He pulled off on the home stretch, pulled off and stopped," Lindsay remembered. "And I stopped with him. He said, 'Come on, Herb. Come, on Herb' and I went back to following him and he promptly threw in another surge. The thing is he could surge away from me and I could catch up, but I couldn't catch up to him fast enough. I would catch up to him, but by the time I caught up with him, he would throw in another surge. He did two miles of that in the middle of the race. I suffered."

Lindsay had just regained contact when Craig's surge for a 4:26.4 fourth 1,600 broke his former Big 10 rival for good. Craig's 62.9 last lap made him the winner in 27:45.61. Meanwhile, the shattered Lindsay faded to ninth in 28:30.2.

Veteran *Track & Field News* correspondent Don Kopriva called it "probably one of the more exciting 10K races I've ever seen." Greg Fredericks, 30, took second in a personal record of 28:03.14 while Salazar gutted out third in 28:10.42. "I just wanted to make the team," Salazar told the *Oregonian*. "I suspected Virgin wanted a fast time and I didn't want to kill myself off chasing him. I think that's what happened to Lindsay."

A rivalry that began in college resumed for Herb Lindsay (left) and Craig in the 1980 US Olympic Trials 10,000-meter run at Eugene, Oregon—with similar results. *(Photo by Jeff Johnson)*

After a victory lap, Craig made a beeline to his family, a cheering section of 16 strong. Photographers formed a semicircle as he embraced his mother, who shed tears of joy. It was the first time Lorna Lee and Vernon had seen their son win a track 10K in person. It was a big deal to Craig that his parents had turned the Trials into a family vacation.

Craig now had six career sub-28:00s, the most in US history at that point. His time, the second-fastest of the year behind Henry Rono's 27:31.8, ranked third in US history behind his own American record of 27:39.4 and the 27:43.6 by Steve Prefontaine in 1974. Frank Shorter's meet record of 27:55.45 from 1976 had fallen and would belong to Craig for the next 24 years.

Even though Craig regretted pulling out of the 1976 Olympic Trials 5K final, he was more than happy to skip the 5K in 1980 because he had the Peachtree Road Race in two weeks. Omni International paid him $5,000 to run Peachtree while race organizers paid for his travel and lodging. His decision didn't sit well with track purists. "Craig Virgin should be in the 5,000 instead of resting up for the Peachtree run," Marty Liquori told Blaine Newnham of the *Eugene Register-Guard*. "To me beating 25,000 joggers is not a great feat. This [Hayward Field] is Carnegie Hall. Road racing is rock and roll; you can make good money at it, but it's still rock and roll."

Craig took the money and ran, which was applauded by Furman Bisher of the *Atlanta Journal*, who wrote that TAC "has just about conceded that runners have to eat, that man cannot travel by foot alone, that he must clothe and care for his body." Craig didn't feel he was in shape to run in the 13:20s in the Trials 5K, but when the top three were Matt Centrowitz (13:30.62), Dick Buerkle (13:31.90) and Bill McChesney (13:34.42), Craig felt he could've qualified. "I could feel my body was going to another level," he said.

Craig's path to becoming the first two-time winner of the Peachtree Road Race, for all practical purposes, became a walk-over when Greg Meyer, Henry Rono and Rod Dixon all withdrew. In a revealing prerace story in the *Atlanta Journal*, Craig noted, "It's easy to be a good winner, but it's hard to be a good loser. I've never claimed to be a good loser, but I try to be a gentleman about it and give credit where credit is due. I never intend to be a good loser because once you become a good loser, it's too easy to lose."

A field of 25,000 awoke on race day to 80-degree heat and 90 percent humidity. Craig coasted with the leaders for three miles before pulling away to win in 28:39.1. The heat sent 30 to the hospital and one runner later died. It was the first of Craig's races to include a fatality.

Next up for Craig were the best six days of racing he'd ever have. He flew to Europe on July 7 hoping to face potential Olympic stars of nonboycotting countries. Unfortunately, he only raced two, Tanzania's Filbert Bayi and Suleiman Nyambui.

Craig's three-race tour opened with a 5K on July 12 in Stuttgart, West Germany. The race featured the withering combination of a fast pace and surges initiated by Craig, who held on for second in 13:19.62, well under his previous personal best of 13:23.3 from 1979. Kenyan Kip Rono won in 13:19.24. "That gave me confidence," Craig said. "My legs felt stronger. My lungs felt more efficient. I felt like somebody had just given me a fifth or sixth gear."

Three days later, Craig was at Bislett Stadium in Oslo, Norway, for another 5K. He loved the venue because the crowd sat close to the six-lane track. Fans would lean over the high wooden wall outside of lane six to pound out a tempo-matching rhythm to propel the runners. Craig put himself in the thick of a fast pack. Even though he only placed fifth, his 13:19.1 was another personal record. His 58.5 last lap gave him the fifth-fastest performance in US history and made him the third-fastest performer behind McChesney (13:18.6) and Liquori (13:15.1). Immediately afterward, Craig felt disappointed, but decades later he felt differently because he never ran faster.

The Protégé

Craig had a special affinity for the affable McChesney and offered to help him any way he could as the 21-year-old broke into the world-class ranks. Craig remembered how Shorter and Liquori had done nothing to help his own climb. "I was mad because no one helped me when I was breaking in a while ago," he told Woods. "We're not going to get better in the world unless we work together. The Africans helped each other. The Americans are so darn selfish."

Craig also complained to Mac McKerral of the *Illinois Alumni News* about the lack of pacing help among Americans. "They are all very selfish, shortsighted and jealous," Craig said. "They aren't concerned with 'can I improve,' but with 'can I win the race?'"

McChesney appreciated Craig talking to meet promoters on his behalf. "He's giving me a lot of information that he had to come by the hard way when he was young," McChesney told a reporter. "I'm going to be in good shape when I get to Europe next summer, and all Craig said was that he wanted to give me some help that older athletes never gave him. He said the only thing he wanted in return was that if I ever met a young kid with a lot of guts, I should take him under my wing the same way."

Craig was in Paris on July 17 for the real reason he came to Europe, an all-out 10,000-meter run to lower his American record of 27:39.4. He ate supper at 5 p.m. and then napped before caffein-ating himself with a large espresso and some chocolate. He started warming up an hour before his race as 10,000 fans jammed into Charlety Stadium. The race began under windless conditions at 10:15 p.m., which wasn't unusually late for a European meet.

McChesney had agreed to help Craig with the 66-second-per-lap pacing. Each was to spend 800 meters out front and then they'd alternate. "I traded laps with him for four miles," McChesney told John Conrad of the *Eugene Register-Guard*. "But then I had to let him go. I just couldn't handle the pace." Craig's recollection is that McChesney lost contact after 3,200 meters.

Although Craig had trained to make surges, he knew the most efficient way to run was with even pacing. His first seven kilome-ters varied only from 2:43.9 to 2:46.5. His eighth kilometer was his slowest at 2:47.2, but the ninth was 2:46.6 and the 10th 2:39.1 to bring him home in an American record of 27:29.16, the No. 2 time in history behind Rono's 27:22.4 world record. Once again Paris had been Craig's "good luck city."

Craig's second 5K of 13:43.0 might have been faster, but France's Philippe Houvion pole vaulted a world record 18 feet, 11¼ inches and danced onto the track to celebrate. He was followed by 30 reporters and photographers. Craig brushed one man and McChesney knocked another down. The mob loitered on the track so long it caused Craig to swerve to lane three on two separate laps. He estimated the detours cost him four seconds, but he still averaged just over 4:24 per mile to best runner-up Fernando Mamede, who clocked a Portuguese record 27:37.9. McChesney took third in 27:58.5, breaking Craig's collegiate record of 27:59.43 set at the 1976 Olympic Trials. Craig recovered so quickly he felt he could've run five seconds faster. "I would feel next year I [should] have a shot at the world record in the 10,000," he'd tell Woods.

Two weeks after Paris, Ethiopia's Miruts Yifter won the Olympic 10K in 27:42.7—more than 12 seconds behind Craig's 27:29.16 in Paris. Little-known Kaarlo Maaninka of Finland took the silver medal (27:44.3) followed by Mohamed Kedir of Ethiopia (27:44.7). "I came to Paris to beat the American record," Craig had told the French media, "and to prove I would have had something to say in Moscow." As in the 10K, all the Olympic 5K medals were won in times slower than Craig's personal best of 13:19.1 with Yifter first (13:21.0), ahead of Nyambui (13:21.6) and Maaninka (13:22.0). Yifter's final laps were 54.9 in the 5K and 54.4 in the 10K.

Speculation

Fans can only speculate what would've happened in the Moscow 10K if there hadn't been a boycott. Craig's former Athletics West teammate George Malley felt Henry Rono and Craig wouldn't have allowed the pace to dawdle. "That race would have been hell," Malley said. "Yifter still may have been able to buck up and get them at the end, but it's really hard to say because, remember, Yifter had been beaten by people before so . . ."

Great Britain's Nick Rose, who placed fifth in his 1980 Olympic 5K semifinal and did not advance, believed the 10K could've been Craig's crowning glory. "I know it's all what-ifs," Rose said, "but he was the fittest he'd ever been." New Zealand's Rod Dixon, the 1972 Olympic 1,500 bronze medalist, said, "I've got a feeling Craig would have beaten [Yifter] or finished a very close second to him."

Former Illinois teammate Mike Durkin, a 1976 and 1980 Olympian in the 1,500, puts Craig among the primary victims of the boycott. "That was his year," said Durkin, who is sure Craig would have medaled. "He had honed himself to a perfect point in terms of sharpening. I really think it would have been a hell of a race to watch him and Yifter." Craig caught hell in the September issue of *Track & Field News*, which published a complaint from reader Steven Fradkin of Portland, Oregon:

Your May issue was enjoyable but why the inter-view with repulsive Craig Virgin? To give print to such an egomaniac is really a shame. Virgin is great by American standards (it's a shame he also has to tell us), but internationally, with no kick whatso-ever, he is no threat at all to a Yifter or a Rono. To keep giving press to repulsive, arrogant athletes like Stones and Virgin seems a disservice to the sport. I never thought that the sport I love so much would turn into a sport with more arrogant, money hungry creeps than baseball.

Three letter writers came to Craig's defense in the November issue of *Track & Field News*. John Behan of Atlanta wrote:

Craig Virgin is the classiest distance runner in the world, whether on the road, in cross country or on the track. He is also the most adept businessman of the running boom, and will be one of the few distance runners who will be well-established long after the boom fades.

Dave Pishnery of Wickliffe, Ohio, noted:

Too bad some readers, like Steven Fradkin, want every international-class athlete to be a model cit-izen and All-American boy. Who says Craig Virgin is arrogant? So what? Somebody loves him. We are all individuals in this sport; that's why we do it. We have the right to say or do or read anything we choose and if people don't like it, they don't have to listen. Ali was cocky, and good. Prefontaine was cocky, and good. The list is endless. By the way, Virgin's 27:29.16 is not sleeping by anyone's standards.

Cleveland's Nathaniel Cross wrote:

> Virgin is not an egomaniac, but instead just tells it like it is. He has the capability to match or over-power anyone's surges. If he is a money hungry freak like many of today's baseball players, then I guess charity workers are thieves!

Decades after the 1980 boycott—when the US had troops in Afghanistan—Craig felt he could've run the Moscow 10K with tactics similar to his Olympic Trials race. He would've gone out hard and thrown a series of surges at Yifter until one of them dropped. Craig guaranteed he wouldn't have sat in the pack as long as Steve Prefontaine had in the 1972 Olympic 5K. "I felt that was a mistake that many people made, for whatever reason," Craig said. "They dumped their usual strategy, the one that brought them to the dance—and ran some other person's race when they got to a big championship meet."

After the Olympics, Garry Hill of *Track & Field News* published his views about which Americans could've medaled. He thought Craig could've won the silver or, just as easily, missed the top three. Hill wrote: "Virgin would have been at home with the Ethiopians' surging tactics, but nobody outkicks Yifter." The world will never know if Craig could've won the 1980 Olympic 10K, but it isn't far-fetched to presume he would've forced Yifter to run faster.

In its December issue, *Track & Field News* published predictions about the inaugural World Track and Field Championships scheduled for Helsinki, Finland, in 1983. The meet was similar to the Olympics except only one sport was contested. Craig and Yifter tied in voting for who'd win the 10K. In its 1980 world rankings, the magazine ranked Yifter first and Craig second. In its American road rankings, the magazine ranked Craig second behind Lindsay.

The day after the Paris 10K, Craig flew home for three weeks of training before he'd make another trip to Europe to take a shot at the American 5K record and the world 10K record. In late July, President Carter invited the US Olympic team to a recognition picnic on the South Lawn of the White House. "It was nice to have my mom and dad and my three siblings along to share that moment with them, although it was a bit frustrating because the Games had started," said Craig, who received official Olympic team clothing from Levi Strauss. "It was bittersweet," he recalled. "We got this beautiful medal, but I'd have given anything to have had the real Olympic medal and not that one."

Most of the 466 athletes came to support each other, not the boycott. Some wore stickers that said, "I'm here to make sure this never happens again." Others refused to shake hands with President Carter or have their photo taken with him. When Craig met the president, instead of scolding him, he shook his hand. "I shook Jimmy Carter's hand out of respect for his position as president of my country," Craig said. "I didn't agree with his decision on the Moscow Olympic boycott or the Russian grain embargo. Years later, I came to respect him more for his true character than for his presidential performance as I saw the many good projects and causes he dedicated his post-presidential time to."

As members of the team-to-nowhere gathered in their hotel, they watched a one-hour Olympic highlight show on TV that included the final two laps of the 10K. Craig loved his sport so he still enjoyed watching with fellow Olympians, but that race would forever be a source of heartbreak.

Chapter 19: World Title No. 2

*"People were gunning for him and that made him a
better athlete and it made us better athletes."*

— Rod Dixon

C raig resumed racing with a 5K in London's Crystal Palace on
August 8. It was meant to be a tune-up for a 5K in Zurich,
Switzerland, five days later, where he hoped to break Marty Liquori's
American record of 13:15.1. "I knew I had four seconds to go, which
I thought was well within my reach," Craig said. "They were going
to have rabbits [at Zurich] because there were two other guys who
wanted to go at about that pace."

Somewhere in the second mile, Craig was following Ireland's
John Treacy when the spike plates of their identical adidas shoes
momentarily locked together. Craig almost fell as he sprained his
right ankle. It hurt to put weight on it, but he managed to limp through
two laps before getting back to a 64-second pace. He worked his way
as high as eighth before fading to 11th in 13:53.7. Treacy went on to
win in 13:27.9, edging out Olympic 800 gold medalist Steve Ovett
(13:27.9) and third-placer Bill McChesney (13:30.8).

Craig's ankle swelled to the size of a grapefruit, prompting him
to skip Zurich and return home. "That was a really weird ending to
the best summer I had in Europe," said Craig, who continued to train
on the bad ankle, which in the domino-effect world of injuries meant
he soon had a sore knee above it.

The competitive calendar Craig chose for the rest of 1980 was
dominated by 11 road races—four against elite foes—and his diary
makes frequent mention of pain above his left knee. He opened his

self-proclaimed recovery month of September with a 10K in steamy Baton Rouge, Louisiana, where Rod Dixon finished 63 seconds ahead of Craig's 29:48 in second. "I heard he was running this race so I kind of came in at the last minute to try and knock him off his perch," Dixon recalled. "People were gunning for him and that made him a better athlete and it made us better athletes."

As Craig searched to remedy his knee problem, he learned his left leg was 2 percent weaker than his right, so he purchased a $2,000 quadriceps exercise machine called a Cybex Orthotron. It remained part of his workout routine for the next four years. "I would use it as part of my weight training to strengthen both the quadriceps and the hamstring," he said. "I believe the whole theory behind the Cybex equipment was isokinetic; the more I pushed against it, the more it resisted back, and there were adjustable settings." During this time, Craig did most of his thrice-weekly weight training at health clubs near Lebanon.

Craig also began to wear one-pound weighted exercise gloves during his morning runs. "My kick was getting stronger and stronger, and my arm drive was getting stronger and stronger," he recalled. "I got to the point where I think the gloves did me a world of good."

Craig watched in frustration on October 26 as Alberto Salazar ran 2:09:41 to win the New York City Marathon, an event Craig was forced to skip because of the damage done by the Zurich ankle sprain. Salazar's time would remain an American debut marathon record until Ryan Hall ran 2:08:24 in 2007.

Craig's rivalry with Nick Rose resumed in a 10K road race at Bowling Green, Kentucky, on November 15. Craig served as race consultant and even provided 1,500 race T-shirts. The second employee hired by Front Runner, special events coordinator T. L. Simmons, drove the T-shirts to Kentucky in Craig's Lincoln Continental Town Car. The tank-sized vehicle, with vanity plates that read "USA 10K," was so full of T-shirts, there was hardly room for Simmons.

A crowded lead pack shrank from nine men to two when Craig and Rose pulled away after two miles. Near the third-mile marker, a course marshal dropped her hat and stepped on the course to retrieve it. Craig collided with her, losing several seconds in the process. "That sort of thing is just part of road racing," he told the media. "It really didn't throw me off that much." By the fourth mile, Rose had a 40-second lead before coasting to victory, 28:15.8 to 28:27.1. It was Craig's second-fastest "road 10K" of his career.

Craig was pleased with his time, but didn't realize until years later that running sub-28:30 10Ks in November wasn't sustainable over a career. "Where my strategy backfired was that on some of these races that brought me in, they started going faster and faster," he said. "It's one thing to run in the 29:00s. It's another thing to run in the low to mid-28:00s year round."

Office Politics

The third person hired by Front Runner was Bonnie Robinson, who'd previously worked as a secretary at McKendree. She replaced Anne Meyer, who wanted a job in marketing. Craig needed an administrative assistant and the detail-oriented Robinson fit the bill. The fit was less than good between Robinson and Simmons, however, as they sometimes clashed when Craig left town. "There was a bit of a jealousy thing going on there and a bit of a power struggle," Craig said. "My mom had to intervene several times when I was traveling."

Office politics, like most travails, didn't bring Craig down for long. The *Clayton* (Missouri) *Times* published a four-page story about him in which his optimism and confidence shine through. Among the revelations was his dream of becoming the first athlete to design leisurewear. "I like nice clothes," he told writer Donna Venturini. "I don't like to wear a sweat suit all the time. I'd like to design some sportswear that will retain its value."

As for Craig's confidence, he noted, "I believe in myself. I believe in taking chances. I want to do unordinary, untypical things." Venturini also observed: "Talking to Virgin, you forget that he's a young man but three years out of college. He's a smoothie, he's glib; he talks like an old man, never at a loss for an answer because he's heard the same questions a hundred times before. He comes off as just a wee bit rehearsed."

The time limits of an interview are too short to fully capture anyone's essence. Craig's former college teammate, Dave Walters, said in 2009, "I think Craig has been misunderstood for quite a while."

While some saw Craig as self-centered, Walters saw him as extremely focused. "He was very selfless," Walters said. "I think a lot of people didn't see that side of him because he was so driven, and driven people can be kind of one-sided at times. I think complicated people are also in a sense driven. I think they are misunderstood by a lot of people." Walters viewed Craig as caring and loving. "I think there are people that don't see that side of him," Walters said. "They see him as so focused on this or that they don't understand what Craig is all about."

Another one of Craig's friends, George Hirsch—the former publisher of *The Runner* and *Runner's World* magazines—said, "Craig was brash. He was confident. Certainly some would have probably said arrogant. I don't think that hurt his performance. It probably helped it. I don't think he was intimidated by anyone."

In the November/December issue of *Running* magazine, a five-page story about Craig by Paul Perry revisited themes common to features about Craig such as his love of cars, his reliance on radar detectors to avoid speeding tickets and his whirlwind schedule of business and training. Front Runner's Simmons, a former *Metro-East Journal* photographer, told Perry, "Craig is as direct as a rifle shot. Most people set themselves off like shotguns. They aren't sure about what they want to do. He is specific. He looks to the future. This is a company we are trying to make stand after Craig Virgin can't run anymore. This place isn't just a post office box. This is a future." Simmons also noted Craig "never thinks of the negative, only the positive. His good attitude plus his determination and focus set him above the rest."

Training Formula

Craig didn't rest in December, averaging 102 miles per week. His two-a-day workouts began with a 6:30 a.m. run of four to six miles. His second session was at 4 p.m. Each week included two interval workouts. Monday or Tuesday featured 12 reps on a quarter-mile hill near his Lebanon home. He'd run up the hill from the west or the east, depending on which direction the wind provided a boost. The hill was so steep that a time of 70 seconds was equal to 60 on flat terrain. On Thursdays or

Fridays, Craig might do 12 quarters on a track, starting at 66 seconds and ending at 57. He often mixed in 880- and 220-yard reps. Another favorite workout was a 10-mile run featuring six miles of fartlek in the middle. He'd sprint to a landmark like a telephone pole and then slow until he almost recovered before sprinting again.

Craig did 95 percent of his training alone, but sometimes Kansas State half-miler Lennie Harrison from Kirkwood, Missouri, tagged along. There were seven other occasional training partners, who might pace Craig halfway through his 400s or 800s. Running alone wasn't all that different for Craig than his days with Athletics West when he led workouts.

As Craig bid adieu to 1980, he learned he was among 10 finalists for the Sullivan Award honoring the nation's top amateur athlete, but "amateur" didn't remotely describe him. His business was supporting his running, and his running was supporting his business. Supporting both was the belief he was "ready to race top notch again." The Sullivan Award went to speed skater Eric Heiden.

Craig was approached early in 1981 by the St. Louis–based Ralston Purina Company, which wanted to put on a nationwide series involving running, bicycling and walking to promote its Bran Chex cereal in conjunction with local YMCAs. Front Runner would be paid to organize the races and Craig would be paid to run in them. The first event would be a 10K road race in Clearwater, Florida, on January 18. "It was a good deal for us financially," said Craig, who envisioned filling the winter months "working" and training in Florida and Arizona.

What Craig quickly discovered was how much work it took to coordinate a road race and prepare to run in it, even with help from Front Runner employees. Among Front Runner's tasks was subcontracting course measurement, timing and finish-line management to local running clubs. Front Runner also provided documentation: entry-form templates that YMCAs would copy, distribute and process, and typed job descriptions for YMCA race volunteers.

On the day before the Clearwater race, Craig's "duties" included a short run before breakfast, a TV interview before lunch, a speech during lunch, two more interviews after lunch, an interview/run after that and a track workout at Clearwater High School, followed by weightlifting at the YMCA and a whirlpool before supper.

In a race-day article about Craig, the *Clearwater Sun* played up the fact he was unknown to the public compared to athletes of his rank in baseball, football and golf. Writer Craig Stanke noted: "If Dave Winfield were a runner, Craig Virgin would lap him, several times. If Virgin were European, he would be a hero. Around here, Winfield's wallet is the idol—Virgin's exploits are loose change, clinking around in the bottom of the sporting pocket." The story also noted Craig was hurting his road-race ranking by also contesting cross country and track.

Racing was the easy part of Craig's trip to Clearwater, where he used what he calls steady state or threshold training pace to win by over 2½ minutes in 29:31.6. "Steady state" running was done at an even pace well below the speed that would create oxygen debt. He tried to subvert a headwind the final three miles by signaling to the pace car driver to break the wind for him, but the driver thought Craig wanted him to keep his distance.

Postrace Popsicles

A cold snap the previous night had sent temperatures crashing to 28 degrees, freezing the orange juice and milk meant for 457 participants after the race. At the awards ceremony, Craig joked over the public address system that straws could be stuck into the frozen juice to make Popsicles. The frozen milk, however, meant people had to eat their Bran Chex dry. Despite such initial setbacks, Craig remained involved in the Bran Chex series for the next two years.

Craig ran four races in January of 1981. When he looked back on his loaded postcollegiate schedule, the over-racing he did in high school and college didn't seem so bad. "It's hard to tell people 'no,'" he said. "I would say I really don't want to go run for less than $5,000. I thought that would deter them and they kept coming up with it."

Craig kept going in February with three races, beginning with his final appearance in the Millrose Games at New York City. A loaded field dragged him to an indoor 5K personal best of 13:38.3, but he only finished seventh behind the world record 13:20.4 by Suleiman Nyambui of Tanzania and the American record 13:22.6 by Alberto Salazar.

Two weeks after Millrose, Craig escaped brutal weather in Illinois to attend a running symposium put on by 1978 Boston Marathon champion Gayle Barron at Kiawah Island, South Carolina. He won a 10-mile road race there in 47:33.6, but the best thing about the trip was the chiropractic treatment he received. "I felt so much better in the race from whatever technique this guy used on my hips, low back and joints," Craig remembered. "I felt balanced and I felt more efficient."

Craig was still feeling the benefits of the treatment when he returned to the Illini Indoor Classic at Champaign six days later for a two-mile against Clemson's Hans Koeleman, who'd become a two-time Dutch Olympian. Craig was highly motivated after placing second in this meet in 1975 (to Nick Rose), 1976 (Rose), 1978 (Niall O'Shaughnessy) and 1979 (Mark Muggleton). In all those races, Craig had led most of the way before getting outkicked. With energy suddenly flowing again through his lower back and legs, he won in a meet record and indoor personal best of 8:30.0. He'd asked for and received pacing help from Koeleman. "He's responsible for the time as much as I am," Craig told old friend David Woods. "There aren't that many Americans who would have done that."

Craig had long felt the governing bodies of his sport did little to help athletes. That feeling doubled in February of 1981. He'd contacted the chairman of the US Long Distance Running Committee, Bob Campbell, the previous fall asking about the date for the 1981 US Cross Country Trials. Campbell inadvertently told Craig an incorrect date. By the time Campbell told Craig the correct date was March 7 in Louisville, Kentucky, Craig had already committed to a March 7 road race in Dallas.

The fact that the reigning world champion was even being asked to qualify was the subject of an Associated Press story by Bert Rosenthal, who asked Campbell why Craig couldn't receive an automatic berth as world champions from other countries did. The US team rulebook didn't address the issue. "If he didn't have to run, there would be an awful stink from all the other runners in the country," Campbell said. Craig reluctantly withdrew from the Dallas race, which had been using his name in its advertising.

Rose's Backyard

The US Cross Country Trials were organized by Louisville's Victory Athletic Club, whose members included Nick Rose. Even though it was a US qualifying race for the upcoming World Championships in Madrid, Rose was allowed to run so he could impress selectors of the British World Championships squad. He was selected, but flu kept him from racing in Madrid.

The soggy turf at E. P. Sawyer State Park seemed to bog down Craig, who was only 30th at 2K, but churned his way through the field to reach Rose's side in the race's second half. Over the final 4K of the 12K race, the pair repeatedly traded the lead until Craig pried open a tiny gap the final 100 yards. Much of that gap disappeared when Craig stepped in a hole four steps from the finish. Somehow he maintained his momentum to edge Rose, 36:09.8 to 36:10.0. "Man, it was great," Craig told the *Louisville Courier-Journal*, referring to the final 4K. "He'd have the lead, then I'd take it. It was beautiful."

It was also what Craig had expected. "We run so close together every time we race, this didn't surprise me at all," he said. "But the ending definitely surprised me. To go so hard for 7½ miles and to end like that. Amazing." Rose rued his impetuous early pace. "His split times were really close, consistent, whereas I went out really quick and lagged in the other splits," Rose told the media. "That's the sign of a super runner. And Craig's the best there is."

In the March 13 edition of the *St. Louis Post-Dispatch*, Craig discussed his plan to contest the April 20 Boston Marathon. To be considered one of the best all-around runners, he felt he needed a "very good" marathon result. He predicted it would take sub-2:10 to win, but he believed that was within reach. "My speed level is up real well, and strength has always been my forte and I'm able to run at a consistent pace for long periods of time," he told the newspaper. "That course, under the right conditions, can be lightning fast. I think that the US and even the world record could be broken someday at Boston."

Thirty years later, Craig's prediction came true when Kenyan Geoffrey Mutai ran a world best 2:03:02 at Boston while Ryan Hall ran an American best 2:04:58 with help from an 18-mph tailwind. Neither mark was ratified because the course drops too far in elevation.

Craig's trip to the World Championships included his customary detour to adidas headquarters in Herzogenaurach where he talked business in between massages and sauna visits. He flew to Madrid to inspect the course, which was again at a horse-racing track. While on the course, he spoke with Miruts Yifter, whose Ethiopian team along with Kenya was entered for the first time as a record 39 countries took part.

The 12K La Zarzuela course had two sets of 27-inch-high log obstacles, one on the backstretch and one on the homestretch. A four-month drought in Madrid ended with eight hours of rain the day before the race. With no toilets near the starting line, Craig added to the soggy conditions by emptying his bladder behind a racehorse starting gate. He thought he was being discreet, but two months later a British magazine published a photo of his nature break. "The English publish a lot of things that the Americans wouldn't publish," he laughed.

The 236-man race opened on a gradual downhill with Rod Dixon and Fernando Mamede pushing the pace, but Craig was near the front when the leaders passed 2K in 5:32. "All I did was float in that top 10 for the next four or five miles," he recalled. "Nobody could make a move that I couldn't see and that I didn't cover."

In the fifth kilometer, seven of the eight Ethiopians gathered on the outside of the 18-man lead pack. Craig felt the Ethiopians' tactics were meant to intimidate. "I refused to be intimidated," he told the media. "The Ethiopians are no supermen. But they could give athletes in America and probably those in Europe a lesson in teamwork and their readiness to work for each other." Yifter, for one, didn't look intimidating when he tripped and fell midway before quickly rejoining his teammates.

Are We There Yet?

What happened next ranks among the bigger gaffes in the history of international athletics. The Ethiopians upped their pace on the fourth of five laps. Craig thought it was a surge and went with them, but he'd planned to go at that point anyway. "The thing was, the surge never let up," said Craig, who lost contact 600 meters from the end of lap four. "They surged over the whole penultimate lap and finally, when we were coming into the homestretch, they not only maintained the surge, but they picked it up a gear. I basically conceded defeat to them and said, 'You've got bigger balls than I do.'"

Craig wears a mask of pain after correctly counting the laps in the 1981 World Cross Country Championships at Madrid. Later, he'd see the victory as one of his greatest achievements. (*Photo by Mark Shearman*)

As the Ethiopians approached the end of the fourth lap, they swerved to the right and sprinted. Despite prerace instructions and lap counters, they thought they were nearing the finish when in fact they had another 2,500-meter lap to go. As officials blocked off the finishing chute, Yifter came to a stop, wearing a bewildered expression at the realization he had another lap to go. Mohamed Kedir and Dereje Nedi were the first to notice the mistake as Craig surged into the fifth lap followed by Australia's Rob de Castella. "My instincts told me I had to go and I had to go right then," Craig said. "I ran right through the middle of them and took advantage of their confusion and their discouragement."

Through 2016, no American male had climbed atop the awards podium at the World Cross Country Championships since Craig in 1981. Joining him on the podium that year were third-placer Fernando Mamede of Portugal (left) and runner-up Mohamed Kedir of Ethiopia (right). *(Photo by Mark Shearman)*

About 400 meters into the fifth lap, Craig heard the footsteps of Kedir, who'd led the field at 5K (14:30) and 10K (29:29). "He had given a lot of effort to catch back up to me," Craig recalled. "I just kept the pressure on." Kedir led with a kilometer to go and remained in front until the final 200 meters when Craig launched what he regarded as the best kick of his career. His sprint broke the finish line in 35:05, two seconds clear of Kedir, whose team defeated the USA for first, 81–114, with Kenya third at 220. Yifter managed 15th in 35:42.

Ethiopia's coach was livid, claiming organizers had misled him about the number of laps. "When the Ethiopians began sprinting so early, I knew they had made a mistake and I started laughing," Craig told the Associated Press. "But they have no excuses because there were signs all along the course marking the distance in kilometers. They can read like I can." Ethiopian protests were hurt by the fact two previous races, one for women and one for junior men, had both included a bell to announce the last lap.

Making the victory extra sweet for Craig was the fact his sister, Vicki, was among the 10,000 spectators. She was a University of Illinois student spending the spring semester studying in Bath, England. She and three friends had traveled to Madrid via ferry and train, arriving the day before the race. "That is a very special memory that I have personally as a sister to a brother," Vicki said. "I remember how wonderful it was to get to the hotel and, of course, Craig took us out to dinner."

A cheerleader in high school and college, Vicki made posters supporting Craig and carried them into the stands where her friends jumped and screamed for him during the race. "It was a very, very exciting race," Vicki recalled. "When we met up with him afterwards, he was elated." Vicki joined Craig and his teammates for a celebratory dinner at a tiny restaurant where the owner, swept up in the excitement, treated the group to champagne and fresh strawberries topped with whipped cream. "For me, being 20 years old, it was also kind of my initiation into being old enough to be more than just a kid sister," Vicki said. "I remember him really treating me like an adult."

As decades passed, the memory of Madrid continued to glow for brother and sister. "That's kind of a special something that Craig and I shared that he will often remind me of or just say, 'You were in Madrid with me,'" Vicki said. The self-coached man, who trained alone, had reached the top again, far from home. But this time his joy could be shared with someone he loved. What could be better? For a truly optimistic person, the answer was worth pursuing.

Chapter 20: 1981 Boston Marathon

"I'm not coming to Boston to go for second."

— Craig Virgin

There was time to bask in the glow of a second World Championship, but Craig didn't take it. Instead he went to New Orleans to try to defend his Crescent City Classic 10K title, but lost to Kenyan Mike Musyoki, 27:55 to 28:06. "That race was a shocker," Craig recalled. "I should have been able to go with him and didn't."

At the urging of adidas, Craig entered the Boston Marathon, even though his contract didn't include performance bonuses for anything other than Olympic Trials victories and Olympic medals. He hadn't done traditional marathon training. All he'd done was add an 18-mile run every 10 days to his usual 10K training. He'd found a cinder-and-dirt path on an abandoned railroad line between Edwardsville and Granite City on which he'd do nine miles out and nine back. "I found out that was a great way to do an 18-mile run and not have it beat up my legs so much," he said. "One time I would do it medium pace and the next time I would do it hard."

To prepare for Boston's hills, Craig trained on a monster called Lindeman Hill in Kirkwood, Missouri, 10 days before the race. Three days later, he ran 18 miles faster than he ever had, averaging 5:16 a mile.

Craig arrived in Boston the Saturday before the Monday race. He drove over part of the course and ran the last four miles. He'd planned to bike the course, but that didn't happen. Later, he wished he'd inspected the course more. He spent part of Easter Sunday doing publicity work in the adidas booth. Unlike most of his carbohydrate-loading competitors, Craig's last supper before the race featured prime rib.

Upon reaching the starting line with 6,844 others representing 50 states and 32 countries, Craig stood side by side with Japan's Toshihiko Seko, the prerace favorite among Boston newspapers. Seko, who owned a 10K best of 27:43.4, was the only entrant who could match Craig's speed. A three-time Fukuoka Marathon winner, Seko held track world records for 25K and 30K. "He has the ability to follow in a high-pressure race and then take over the race at the right time and execute his game plan," Craig told the *North Andover Eagle-Tribune*.

Overcast, 50-degree weather and a breeze blowing toward Boston lifted spirits skyward where 14 TV helicopters looked down, vulturelike, ready to cast judgment about who was weak and who was strong. Craig remembered how shocked he was by the course's narrow streets compared with other major road races.

Goofing Around

Adidas' wish for Craig to put its logo at the front of the race was sabotaged when Gary Fanelli, dressed in a Blues Brothers costume with a picture of Disney's Goofy on his behind, bolted from the starting line, taking the press truck away from the contenders. Fanelli would later claim his 4:29 opening mile was meant to set up a world-record pace for others.

Craig coasted effortlessly through the opening downhill miles, never far from the contenders. The 85th Boston Marathon still clung to its amateur traditions in 1981, which meant few portable toilets at the start and water located at too-few spots that had nothing to do with runners' needs. Plus, time splits were announced at obscure, but traditional, points.

Craig wore a short plastic straw on a chain around his neck so he could sip liquids he got at aid stations or from spectators. He wore the straw as a favor to inventor Phil Benson, who hoped his product would catch on with runners. By sipping through a straw, runners could avoid stomach distress caused by swallowed air, according to Benson. "I wore that for a few races, but the trouble was it kept bouncing around," Craig said. "It wouldn't tuck down inside my shirt."

Runners depended on spectators for drinks in between the "official" water stops. "Grabbing a cup, you never knew if it was going to be water, Gatorade or a vodka tonic," Craig recalled. "Running at Boston was the closest thing to one giant tailgate party because that's what it was."

The 1981 Boston Marathon was a two-man battle the final six miles, but Japan's Toshihiko Seko (right) pulled away to win in a course record 2:09:26, which was a minute ahead of Craig. *(Photo by Leo Kulinski Jr.)*

The miles between 10 and 18 reminded Craig of the movie *The Magnificent Seven*, in which desperadoes kill off the main characters one by one, only this time it was the pace that killed. Between 17 and 20 miles, Greg Meyer led Craig and Seko. After that it became a two-man race in which Craig tried to copy Bill Rodgers' 1979 strategy by surging a minute before the summit of Heartbreak Hill near Hammond Street, but Seko, wearing a placid expression, wouldn't break. Now within 40 seconds of record pace, Craig had a three-step lead when he reached 21.5 miles. At 21.6 miles, it was clear the heat of battle hadn't altered Craig's friendly nature as he shared a drink with Seko. A correspondent for the *Chicago Sun-Times* wrote that Craig tried to unnerve Seko with small talk about the US-Japan auto war:

"Hey," said Virgin, "do you know who Lee Iacocca is?"

"No," Seko replied dispassionately.

"Well," said Virgin, "I just want you to know I've got the United Auto Workers on my side."

As the duo charged on, the deafening crowd drew closer because there were no restraining barriers. "I started to get claustrophobic," remembered Craig, whose shoulders bumped several spectators. As a live TV audience in Japan watched Seko, Craig's family in Lebanon kept tabs on the race via telephone reports from friends in Boston.

The 24-year-old Seko was aware of Craig's track credentials and knew he couldn't leave the outcome to a final sprint. On a stretch nicknamed the Haunted Mile because of the adjacent Evergreen Cemetery, Seko's coach, Kiyoshi Nakamura, signaled for his pupil to surge. Seko accelerated past Bill Rodgers' running store and built a 25-yard gap in the space of 400 yards.

"I went to hit the throttle and it wasn't there, but I didn't panic," said Craig, who tried to recover. "For a mile, that worked. With two to go, I hit the wall. I went from 4:50-something pace to running 5:30s. I felt like I was running in molasses." Craig's form changed from floating to plodding and his feet slapped the pavement. His fatigue was such he had to walk the 90-degree turns in the final blocks. "It was almost surreal," he lamented. "I couldn't run and turn at the same time."

Seko ran the 23rd mile in 4:32. His 150-yard lead in the 24th mile gave him time to acknowledge Japanese flags in the crowd. He reached the finish in 2:09:26, one second under Rodgers' course record and a minute ahead of Craig in second. Seko had produced the fifth-best time in history and the best ever in the Western Hemisphere. "I just ran in rhythm," he told *Track & Field News*. "I didn't occupy myself with my adversaries because at Boston it's impossible to know where one is. No indications of the kilometers are given."

Only five Americans had ever run faster than Craig, who clocked 2:10:26. By the end of 2016, he'd fallen to 25th among US marathoners all-time. "Everything was going well until 23 miles, then the bottom fell out," he told *Track & Field News*. "Damn! That last mile was long." His time would've won 81 of the 84 previous Boston Marathons with the exceptions being Rodgers' wins in 1975, 1978 and 1979. The 33-year-old Rodgers, slowed at 17 miles by a side ache, rallied to take third in 2:10:34. Craig's disappointment was eased by the fact he beat Rodgers. "For me to beat him on Boston's course was a feather in my cap," Craig said.

A finish-line photo of Craig shows a tortured man. It wasn't a moment he wanted to treasure, but the photo later adorned the National Distance Running Hall of Fame plaque he received in 2001. Feeling nauseous after the race, Craig went to the medical tent. "I was probably in the medical tent a good 20 to 30 minutes until they got me up on my feet and I was able to leave," recalled Craig, who was later troubled to see blood in his urine. He told *Track & Field News*, "My kidneys and the rest of my body can't take too many marathons. One or two a year is all I want to run."

Craig hated to miss the postrace press conference where Seko told the media through an interpreter, "I ran my own race, set my own pace. I've been training for the hills, and they didn't bother me today. I just didn't want to have a fight at the end." Then Seko turned to Rodgers and said, "I'm sorry I broke your record."

Craig felt better during the awards ceremony at Hynes Auditorium. While most runners were still in warm-ups, he wore a three-piece suit. Given a chance to address the crowd, it was obvious he knew his audience, which roared in approval when he said, "You can expect a lot of great races from Rodgers in the future."

The media caught up with Craig over the next six months. *The Runner* magazine put Craig on the cover of both its June and July issues in 1981. "I got more attention in this country for second at Boston than I got for my first and second World Championships in cross country," said Craig, who made a national TV appearance with Boston women's champion Alison Roe of New Zealand on ABC's *Good Morning America* the day after Boston.

Other than a trophy, Craig received no compensation for his Boston efforts. The organizing Boston Athletic Association was five years away from offering prize money. "They should at least reimburse the top 10 finishers for their expense money," Craig told the *Patriot Ledger*. "I'm very professional about my training. Why shouldn't I be compensated for it? The Metropolitan Opera doesn't make its singers perform for free."

Road Shock

Craig could hardly walk the day after Boston. His only exercise was two miles of jogging and fast walking. "The downhills on Boston will kill," he said. "That's what makes Boston one of the top two or three worst races to recover from, because the downhills are at the end. If you've lost total control of your legs, you tend to pound them more." Two days later, after a media interview in St. Louis, leg pain forced Craig to descend a staircase backward. He described three miles of running that day as a crawl. He wondered how long it would take to return to normal. The question needed an answer because he'd committed to run the Trevira Twosome 10-Miler in New York City just six days after Boston. His legs were still sensitive to road shock when he jogged 1:00:40 at Trevira, where Nick Rose won in 46:08.

Craig's friend Brion Boeshans, an occasional training partner beginning in 1979, came to believe Boston took more out of Craig than anyone realized. "There was something about that race and he was never, ever the same after that," Boeshans said. "He did not know 'slow down.' He did not know 'quit.' He just went so far with his body that it tore him up, I think. He just never had that extra 'thing' anymore. It just pulled it out of him. He's a friend, but I think Boston hurt him."

Rod Dixon agreed Boston's jarring topography and the hot pace changed Craig. "I still think to this day it might have done a little bit of damage to him," Dixon said. "He never seemed to be right after that." Alberto Salazar, in his 2012 book *14 Minutes* with John Brant, wrote: "Once you run a marathon you can't return to the track with the same consistent short-distance speed that you exhibited before running 26.2."

Craig hoped his Boston performance would earn respect from the East Coast distance-running establishment. He undoubtedly earned some respect, but he didn't win over everyone judging by a scathing account in the 1994 book *Boston Marathon* by Tom Derderian, who was a runner, coach and journalist. In the 1970s and 80s, Derderian worked for adidas' rival, Nike, a fact worth remembering.

Virgin grew up in the midwest farming community of Lebanon, Illinois. Runners, writers, and fans described him as the most professional and media-conscious of all the top runners. But as he grew famous he did not grow worldly; he assumed instead the costume and manners of what he thought constituted a successful athlete and businessman. But he misinterpreted those mores and became a caricature of a politician. To postrace gatherings he wore a cream-colored three-piece suit, his hair coiffed into a bouffant. He worked the crowd of runners and friends who dressed in casual clothes, blue jeans, or running clothes. He overcompensated for his typical long-distance runner's introversion with an extreme and awkward extroversion. In his attempts to overcome shyness, Virgin treated fellow competitors like fans, friends like political contributors. He shook too many hands and smiled too much as he gazed over the head of the person before him to find another, apparently more important, hand to shake. His oppressive friendliness did not gain him many friends. Virgin incorporated himself into a business that he called Front Runner, which sold its only product, himself. He raced in a yellow adidas singlet, perhaps to help his fans locate him in lead packs and to celebrate himself after the fashion of the Tour de France, where the previous winner traditionally wore a yellow jersey. He represented adidas running shoes. Despite his distasteful self-promotion, Virgin trained with a maddeningly fastidious, aggressive, intelligent plan. Craig Virgin sprang as much from the values of the American midwest—God-fearing, hardworking, and honest in the face of adversity—as Seko rose from the disciplines of the samurai.

Critic's Corner

Derderian's analysis hurt Craig. As a public figure, he accepted that people would make assumptions about him even if they didn't know him. One way to avoid criticism is to do and say nothing, which is the antithesis of Craig's philosophy of life. He suspected East Coast writers were reluctant to applaud those besting their hero, Bill Rodgers, just as West Coast writers failed to celebrate those surpassing Steve Prefontaine.

Derderian's biggest issue with Craig seems to be the sin of self-promotion. Derderian makes Front Runner sound tacky instead of an innovative way for an athlete to survive in that quasi-amateur era of running. "I had a good thing set up," Craig said. "I couldn't understand why the rest of the guys weren't doing it."

Craig returned to his winning ways on May 17 in the 70th Bay to Breakers at San Francisco, where he broke his year-old 7.63-mile course record by four seconds with a time of 35:07.8 despite a headwind. With 27,000 official entrants and an estimated 13,000 unofficial ones, it was the largest road race in American history.

The *San Francisco Examiner* noted Craig had drawn criticism for focusing on a mass-participation race. "This is the biggest road race in the country and the only time I could run in San Francisco this year," Craig said in his defense. "Being the defending champion, I wanted the challenge of winning again. And I want to be the top-rated road racer in the US. I plan to use Peachtree, Falmouth and the Bay to Breakers as my credentials for that title."

As Craig prepared for a seven-race track season, his diary entries included suspicions he might be overtraining and complaints of training lost to business obligations. "This is not the way to train for a world record," he wrote two days before flying to London. Awaiting him to contest a 3K at the Crystal Palace on June 3 was Olympic 800 gold medalist Steve Ovett. Craig had hoped to ease into his track season, but that was impossible in a race involving Ovett and Nick

Rose. Craig boldly told London's *Daily Mirror*, "I can beat Steve. I don't go into any race looking for second place."

The big kickers left the pace-setting to Craig for six of the race's seven and a half laps. He reached 1,600 meters in 4:17, but when it came time to kick, five men steamed past, leaving Craig sixth in 7:56.90, well off his career best of 7:48.2 from 1979. Ovett won in 7:54.11 while Rose took fourth in 7:55.17.

Ring Bearer

Craig was discouraged by his London result, but grew optimistic heading into a 5K on June 7 at Gateshead, England. On the way to Gateshead, however, his luggage was broken into at Heathrow Airport. Among the jewelry lost were his 1976 and 1980 Olympic rings, which he routinely traveled with. "I wasn't that big on jewelry, but I would wear them on occasion as accessories," he said. "I was probably stupid to be carrying them all at one time."

Craig theorized thieves targeted the bag because it had a first-class tag. A boarding agent in Chicago had recognized him and upgraded him from coach to first class. "Now I wish I had flown coach and still had my rings," he said. His race fortunes were no better as he finished eighth in a tactical 13:32.60, more than 11 seconds behind winner Barry Smith of Great Britain. Craig needed to find out why he felt dead and couldn't get loose.

Craig knew the answer wasn't in Florence, Italy, where he'd planned to race on June 10, so he flew home for chiropractic relief. "I've definitely got something wrong," he wrote. "It's starting to affect me psychologically, also." Craig's airport woes in England continued as a pickpocket relieved him of $200.

Craig's confidence was restored by a June 13 workout in which he ran a 4:08 mile, a 1:58.3 half mile and a 57.3 quarter. A workout four days later included an encouraging 4:03.7 1,600. He felt the hot weather helped him reach his optimal weight, a "lean and mean" 140 pounds heading into the TAC national meet at Sacramento on June 20.

Craig, who last raced at Hughes Stadium in 1972, could've entered the 10K, but he knew the weather would prohibit a good result. "There was no sense in throwing away a 10,000 in bad weather," he said. So on a 101-degree day, he entered the 19-man 5K along with two-time defending champion Matt Centrowitz. On the penultimate homestretch, Centrowitz bolted from fourth to first. His 56.2 last lap gave him the victory in 13:28.86 while Craig took second in 13:31.64.

The meet doubled as a selection event for the US team that would face the USSR in a dual at Leningrad (now St. Petersburg) in July. The fact the meet still existed while Soviet troops remained in Afghanistan made the Olympic boycott of 1980 seem even more of a waste to Craig and others. Alberto Salazar, who won the TAC 10K, told *Track & Field News*, "I think it stinks that we're going to Leningrad. Nothing has changed in Afghanistan, but all of a sudden they [the governing bodies] want to pretend nothing happened, that there was no Olympic boycott. It's been less than a year since the boycott, and now it is supposed to be business as usual. I have mixed feelings about the boycott itself, but I sure don't think it is right that the athletes were the only ones to make a sacrifice, and now we're supposed to forget it ever happened." Many US stars including Salazar, Centrowitz and Craig declined to run in Leningrad where the US men still won, 118–105.

Craig got home from Sacramento at 2 a.m. on June 21 and awoke at 6:30 a.m. for a local five-mile road race, which he ran in approximately 26:00. Later that day he flew to Paris, but the airline left his luggage stateside. With no running gear, he was finally forced to rest.

On June 24, Craig returned to the Sport 2000 International Meeting for a 5K at Charlety Stadium in Paris where he'd set the American 10K record the year before. He expected to run sub-13:30 against a field that included new European 10K record holder Fernando Mamede of Portugal and old rival Suleiman Nyambui of Tanzania.

After 1,600s of 4:17 and 4:22, Craig made a bid for the front with a kilometer to go, but "chickened out and waited for the kick," as he later wrote. With a final 400 of only 59 seconds, Craig had to settle for fourth in 13:24.83 as Nyambui won in 13:21.10. Craig chalked the loss up to a lack of confidence and aggressiveness.

Two days later, Craig returned to the Bislett Games in Oslo, Norway, for a 5K in which he wanted to make a stronger commitment.

He opened with 1,600s of 4:18 and 4:20, but when McChesney and Julian Goater of Great Britain surged on lap seven, he couldn't respond. Craig blamed his third-place finish in 13:25.73 on having "no guts." An injured Miruts Yifter took 12th in 13:47.07.

Cascade Change

Two days after the Bislett Games, road running in America changed forever and not in a good way for Craig. The Cascade Run Off 15K in Portland, Oregon, became the first in a new series of six US road races to offer prize money. The series was governed by the newly formed Association of Road Racing Athletes (ARRA), whose president was 1976 Olympian Don Kardong. "Open racing will add excitement," said Kardong at a prerace press conference.

The race, sponsored by Nike, offered $50,000 in prize money, but a runner had to declare beforehand if he or she would compete for money. Craig was all for runners making money, but this series outlawed appearance money so everyone was paid based on their performance. "Most athletes weren't earning it (appearance money), but I was," said Craig, who'd made as much as $5,000 a race regardless of where he finished. He felt the prerace promotional work he did at races deserved compensation. "I had every right to be paid," he maintained. "I had a name and credentials and I was earning my money as a public relations spokesperson, but they were about eliminating all appearance money and making everything straight prize money."

Craig's former Big 10 rivals Greg Meyer and Herb Lindsay finished first and second in the Cascade Run Off, earning $10,000 and $6,000, respectively. Women's champion Anne Audain of New Zealand also won $10,000. Fourth-placer Bill Rodgers, who admitted earning $250,000 annually from running-related activities, had announced beforehand he wasn't running for prize money because he didn't want to risk losing his "amateur" standing and thus his Olympic eligibility. "I can make more under the table," he told *Track & Field News*.

The Athletics Congress (TAC), the national governing body for track and field, threatened to declare all 6,000 participants to be professionals including those earning, but not accepting, prize money. Most top runners just wanted to receive their money above the table instead of under it. "It was basically like coming to unity, almost like a union of athletes to say, 'We're not going to accept this shamateurism anymore,'" Lindsay said.

Craig viewed ARRA's agenda as too radical. "In my short experience, TAC and [director] Ollan Cassell could be negotiated with," Craig said. "I found I was having more success working with TAC." Craig didn't participate in any of ARRA's pro races in 1981 and later sensed resentment from some runners for not using his clout on behalf of their "prize money" cause. The unintended consequence of prize money was that it lured more foreigners to American roads, making it more difficult for American runners to make a living.

TAC ordered 13 of the Cascade Run Off participants to appear at a hearing in Chicago on August 22 to answer charges they had accepted prize money. The "Cascade 13" included Meyer, Lindsay, Rodgers, John Glidewell, Benji Durden, Mike Layman, Ric Rojas, Charley Vigil, Pete Pfitzinger, Ed Mendoza, Patti Catalano, Cindy Dalrymple and Jan Oehm.

The case against them was complicated by the fact they had done different things with their prize money. Meyer had donated his check to his running club. Lindsay had not deposited his check, but placed it in the office of his attorney. Most had cashed their checks.

Lindsay was the only one to appear at the Chicago hearing. He and Rodgers retained their "amateur" standing while Meyer, Catalano, Rojas, Durden, Dalrymple, Mendoza, Glidewell and Pfitzinger were ruled ineligible. Confusing everything was the "contamination rule" in which runners risked being banned for competing against ineligible runners. "There was turmoil for a while, but it all settled out," Lindsay recalled. "Everybody was exonerated and no problems came from it."

Trust Funds

ARRA's pressure to professionalize running led to the creation of TAC-administered trust funds into which athletes hoping to maintain their Olympic eligibility had to deposit prize money and make withdrawals to cover their training expenses. Being forced to funnel earnings through a TAC trust fund was something Craig resented as much as the loss of appearance fees.

In Ollan Cassell's book *Inside the Five Ring Circus*, he wrote: "Craig Virgin defied the road racing community by not supporting their divisive policy of challenging the national governing body and not competing in the Cascade Run Off. Like Shorter, he believed he could do more for

After winning the 1981 Peachtree Road Race in Atlanta, Craig's career began a decade-long slide to retirement. *(Associated Press photo)*

the athletes by working with the national governing body than against them." Cassell also noted Craig's athletic credentials "made him one of the most popular road racers in the world."

With the benefit of hindsight, Craig wished he'd had the political savvy to work with fellow appearance-fee heavyweights Shorter and Rodgers to negotiate a better solution with ARRA and TAC officials. "When I look back on it now, I was politically ignorant," Craig admitted. "It's one of those things—woulda, coulda, shoulda. That's how it was."

Hindsight would also lead Craig to believe his career peaked at his next race, the Peachtree Road Race in Atlanta. Many good results still lay ahead, but none would outshine those that came before that Fourth of July tipping point.

A field of more than 25,000 was greeted by a rare 69-degree morning with 87 percent humidity. As TBS broadcast the 10K live nationally for the first time, viewers didn't have to wait for excitement as several athletes in the front row fell at the start, including Mary Decker. Craig planned to push the tempo, but didn't need to as the leaders passed the first mile in 4:20. Ric Rojas and Adrian Leek, who'd later break the British 15K record, tacked on a 4:22 second mile and soon had a 50-meter lead.

Craig reeled in Leek at 4½ miles and ran scared as he entered the last mile with Rod Dixon, a 3:51-miler, only 12 meters behind. That mile in Piedmont Park included a series of curves through a tunnel of fans pressing against restraining ropes on both sides of the street. While out of Dixon's view on each curve, Craig surged for three seconds. Before Dixon realized what was happening, Craig had a 30-meter lead with only 400 to go. With his whole family looking on, Craig sprinted to a third consecutive Peachtree title in 28:03.4 with Dixon second in 28:11. Craig had shattered his 1979 course record of 28:30.5 and his own (point-to-point) American record of 28:06 set at the 1981 Crescent City Classic. Despite the hilly course, 14 finishers broke 29:00 and 46 broke 30:00, prompting *Track & Field News* to call it "one of the highest quality events ever." Craig ranked his effort equal to a sub-27:40 on the track.

While Craig's running had been a success at Peachtree, his financial arrangements could have been better. In 1980, when he'd received a $5,000 appearance fee, he noticed the race had T-shirts for entrants, but no official commemorative T-shirts that people could buy at the race expo or order through the mail. So in 1981, he asked to be the commemorative T-shirt supplier. Peachtree officials agreed as long as he ran for free. Craig accepted, but failed to take into account the Bible Belt customers he was aiming for when he created a T-shirt that read: *I CHASED THE VIRGIN AT PEACHTREE.*

The wording on a commemorative T-shirt Craig sold in 1981 was too racy for some. *(Photo courtesy of Craig Virgin)*

The idea for the wording came from a newspaper headline from 1979 that read: "30,000 Chase Virgin Down Peachtree." The headline had been provocative enough to get mentioned in *Playboy* magazine and by Johnny Carson on the *Tonight Show*. Craig sold less than

$1,600 worth of the T-shirts. With no appearance money and no prize money, Craig avoided losing his shirt by earning several thousand dollars for wearing a Coca-Cola hat to the awards ceremony.

In a postrace TBS Sports highlight show, Craig was asked about the Cascade Run Off and road racing's first steps toward professionalism. "We're right in a transition stage between a completely amateur hypocritical system (and) some sort of a system like tennis where professionals and amateurs compete side by side," he said. "I don't think I'm any less of an athlete than, say, the tennis, basketball, football (and) baseball stars. I'd like to be compensated. I attack my sport as professionally as I can in my attitude."

As Craig cautiously awaited change, he took stock. He'd just finished his 16th race in 120 days (more than 108 miles of racing) in an American record over a premier foe in Dixon. Craig's strength was back. He could be competitive in anything from a cross country race against Yifter to a marathon against Seko to a 3K against Ovett. Craig had become the ultimate "Renaissance Runner." Unfortunately, there was no one to tell him the title came with a price.

Chapter 21: Tough Times

*"Plenty of people are willing to help you when
you're on top."*

— *Craig Virgin*

C raig had gone to the well at Peachtree. The next day he went
to Europe, track's most lucrative stronghold, for the fifth time
in 1981. He arrived in Milan, Italy, for a July 8 5K feeling lethargic.
His glands were swollen, but he warmed up hoping to take advantage of the paid pacesetter, Irishman Ray Flynn, who was asked to
run 63-second laps through 3K. Within three laps, Craig began to
struggle as his back and neck became strangely fatigued.

Craig faded to seventh in 14:06.69, more than 39 seconds behind
winner Alberto Cova of Italy. Craig soon had a raging fever brought
on by a virus. In the middle of the night, a doctor gave him a shot to
ease nausea. Craig had planned an assault on the 10K world record
in Oslo, Norway, on July 11, but canceled and made the 17-hour trip
home feeling miserable.

Ten days of lackluster training and some antibiotics later, Craig
still felt sluggish when he won a hilly 5.5-mile road race in Kirkwood,
Missouri, in 27:25. He was sick to his stomach afterward, but later
tacked on an eight-mile training run to give him 92 for the week. "I
started doing some more intensive mileage with an eye toward the
New York City Marathon," he said. "Adidas was subtle about it, but I
knew they wanted me to run New York. I knew with ABC televising
it that it would be a wise move."

Craig ended his track season on July 27 with a 5K in the National
Sports Festival at Syracuse, New York, in a field that included Alberto

Salazar and Matt Centrowitz. The temperature was good, the wind bad and the track soft as Salazar set the pace. With three laps to go, Craig used a 64.2-second circuit to take the lead. He held on for a meet record 13:35.4 with Salazar second (13:38.2) and Centrowitz fourth (13:49.9). "I covered every single move he made and basically put him away in the last lap," Craig said of Salazar. "I was worried because I knew that Alberto was coming along in late 1980 and 1981. I knew that Alberto was going to be a great one."

By kicking with nearly three laps to go, Craig felt he'd won fair and square. "I've had guys sit on me all the way," he told famed *Boston Globe* writer Joe Concannon. "That's a chicken way to run. If he had anything left, I wanted him to have a shot at me." It was the last one-two finish between the two that Craig won.

Craig ended 1981 with 10 road races, the most competitive being the Maggie Valley Moonlight five-miler in Waynesville, North Carolina, on August 1 and Falmouth on August 16. With 1,700 entrants, Maggie Valley was run at night on an out-and-back course that began with two miles slightly downhill. Dixon won in 22:43 followed by Perkins in 22:53, while Lindsay edged Craig for third, 22:59.3 to 22:59.5. All four finished under Lindsay's 1980 course record of 23:11. "I've been running against Craig Virgin for 15 years," Perkins told the *Asheville Citizen-Times*. "And this is the first time I've ever beaten him."

At midnight during the postrace party, a cake arrived to help Craig celebrate his 26th birthday. He'd tell a reporter, "If I die tomorrow, I'll have experienced as much in 26 years as some people do in a lifetime. I wouldn't feel cheated at all."

Craig had been among the best in the world in his age group for most of a dozen years. Jack Shepard of *Track & Field News* is of the opinion that—with few exceptions—a track athlete only has seven years at the top. "If you want to be an age-group star, then you may no longer be a star by the time you finish high school," he said. "If you are a high school star, you may only be great through college. Or if you developed into an NCAA champion late in your college career, we may see you on the world scene for a few years past college." Craig was five years past his expiration date and the clock was ticking.

A heavy race schedule had Craig on ice after the 1981 Pepsi National 10K Championships road race in Purchase, New York. *(Photo by Leo Kulinski Jr.)*

As he trained for Falmouth, Craig battled fatigue daily. On race day, he had a bad start made worse by misleading splits. A 4:23 sixth mile sent Salazar on to a winning 31:56 (a 4:30-per-mile average), well under Craig's 1979 course record of 32:19.7. Craig ran 32:50 in fifth to finish behind Dixon (32:16), Mike McLeod (32:33) and Kirk Pfeffer (32:43). Despite beating Lindsay in sixth (33:00) and Perkins in eighth (33:04), Craig called the outing "depressing." In his heart, he felt he should've forced himself to maintain contact. His diary notes: "All I did was fool myself."

An October visit to the St. Louis Sports Medicine Clinic revealed Craig's left leg to be 55 percent weaker than normal. It was decided he should take anti-inflammatory medicine to go along with physical therapy that included ultrasound, electric muscle stimulation and alternating applications of heat and cold.

Craig made it to the New York City Marathon on October 25, but only as a commentator on the lead vehicle for ABC television. When it came to addressing a national audience, Craig was a natural. His eloquence combined with his ability to think on his feet made him fearless. He told viewers that Alberto Salazar was lowering Derek Clayton's 12-year-old world record of 2:08:34 to 2:08:13. It was a display of strength that impressed Craig, but not to the point he didn't feel he could match it.

Three years later, the course was measured again and found to be 148 meters short. Statisticians rated Salazar's effort as being worth only 2:08:41 for a full marathon, but they couldn't take away the three years of positive publicity he garnered in the meantime.

American Tourist

Craig cautiously returned to two-a-day workouts the day after New York. A week later, he won a pain-free 10K in 30:03 during his first visit to Dallas. "I like to go places in the country that I haven't been that much," he told *The Dallas Morning News*. "That's really one of my major considerations when I choose a race to run in."

Craig hadn't faced elite competition since Falmouth when he arrived in Rock Island, Illinois, for the November 28 Scrub Shirt Classic 8-miler to face Tony Sandoval, the 1980 US Olympic Trials marathon champion. Evidence of Craig's sporadic training showed up in his inability to stay on his toes as usual. His calves grew sore the final three miles as he finished second to Sandoval in 38:38.

Over the next six months, Craig only raced nine times, the least of any such span in his career. Five of those races were part of the Bran Chex/YMCA series, which paid him $7,000 a race plus a little extra for his staff to organize things. He could usually run easy, as slow as 33:32, and still win. "I probably was reliable to a fault in that year or so to Ralston Purina and Anheuser-Busch," Craig said. "I was loyal to my sponsors and to my clients almost to the point where it jeopardized my future. A year or two later, when I wasn't the fastest kid on the block, they didn't give a damn [about me] anymore. I learned the hard way over the next four to six years that that loyalty that I had always tried very hard to give to races and to sponsors was probably misplaced. In a lot of cases it was not a two-way street."

Craig could see his days of winning winter road races at training pace were near an end. "We started to have an influx of foreign athletes beginning in 1981 that really started to pick up steam in 1982," he said. The foreign stars could peak for three or four races and be replaced by others throughout the year.

The winter of 1981–82 also saw ibuprofen become a daily part of Craig's training as a way to manage knee pain. He'd later blame overuse of the drug for further damaging his kidneys. Another problem was training in sub-zero weather and trying to race at 70 degrees or warmer. "The weather difference between Lebanon and what I had to compete in, it really threw my body for a loop," he admitted. The weather was so bad on one business trip to Chicago, Craig ran more than 10 miles indoors at the prestigious East Bank Club.

The potential for bad weather was the main reason Craig, while at the TAC Convention, voted against Pocatello, Idaho, hosting the February 15 US Cross Country Trials. Pocatello was picked anyway and race day arrived with the course a mix of mud, snow and standing water. Some water-filled potholes were glazed with ice. Every step held the potential for injury. "This was a survival thing, not a race," Craig told *Track & Field News*.

While wearing a longsleeved shirt and gloves, Craig ran cautiously, but stayed with leaders Alberto Salazar and Dan Dillon until they broke away with 3,600 meters left on the 11K layout situated at more than 4,200 feet above sea level. Salazar went on to win in 36:52.4 followed by Dillon (37:03.1) and Craig (37:23.4). "Alberto was on a roll. I was sputtering," remembered Craig, who had secured his spot on the nine-man US team headed for the March 20 World Cross Country Championships in Rome. He had every intention of battling for a third consecutive world title.

Deserving Better

The poor organization of the Pocatello race made Craig resolve to put in a bid to host the event himself one day. "It was put together in an organizationally weak and frustrating way compared to other professional events that I attended," he said. "It was run like a high school triangular." He had no doubt he could find a better locale in February for a race he deemed so important. "The guys were giving up income to go there," he noted. "We athletes deserved better."

Craig's final race before Rome was a Bran Chex/YMCA 10K in New Orleans on March 6. Three days earlier, he developed a fever and lung congestion. During a March 5 press conference to promote the race, he collapsed in a restaurant bathroom and had to be helped to his hotel. He was still sick on race day when he staggered over the course to win in 33:32. "I should not have run that race," he admitted. "I shouldn't have even been at the press conference. It was set up and I was a good soldier."

After the race, Craig went to a hospital emergency room complaining of stomach pain. He spent the night in the hospital, but flew home the next day. By March 9, he questioned whether he could make the trip to Rome. He was ready to notify US team officials to replace him with an alternate. Feeling marginally better five days later, he decided to go. "I really loved that cross country team," he said. "That was the thing I looked forward to all winter long—the Trials and the World Championships and having that team together for a week. In retrospect, I was too sick and shouldn't have gone."

Craig's journey to the World Championships included his customary prerace visit to adidas headquarters where he awoke on March 17 with a fever and back pain. He could tell he had a urinary tract infection or something worse so he visited a urologist the next day. By day's end, he could hardly walk as his temperature soared to 106 degrees, where it would remain for three days. He was so ill, the trip from his bed to the bathroom felt like a marathon.

The day before he hoped to win his third consecutive world title, Craig was examined by Dr. Thomas Wessinghage, who was a world-class miler sponsored by adidas. He took one look at Craig, who now had swollen lips and a swollen tongue, and sent him to the hospital via ambulance to see a specialist. Tests showed his right kidney was swollen and a massive infection raged in his urinary tract. A tube was inserted through his back to drain the kidney. On the first day of his six-day hospital stay in Erlangen, West Germany, Craig blacked out after three hours of torturous medical tests involving an oversized catheter. "The pain kept coming in waves at me," he recalled.

On March 24, doctors determined the right kidney "was worth saving." If it had less than 20 percent function, they wanted to remove it, but they found it was operating at over 50 percent. The next day, Craig was taken to a plane in a wheelchair and flew home.

With a nephrostomy tube still exiting his back, Craig checked into Barnes Hospital in St. Louis on March 28 for three days of tests, which included a renal scan and a Whitaker pressure test to determine if the tube could be safely removed. The tube came out March 31 and doctors allowed Craig, though not yet released from their care, to jog in nearby Forest Park. He couldn't go faster than a shuffle as his tight legs were sensitive to road shock. Nevertheless, he jogged and walked a total of six miles with friends, who, for once, didn't struggle to keep up.

Doctors believed the kidney became infected because of two blockages in Craig's ureter. Dr. Robert Royce told the media Craig's left kidney was functioning at 55 percent of capacity while the right was at 45 percent so surgery was unnecessary.

What Doesn't Kill You...

Months later, Craig was philosophical about his ill-fated trip to Rome. Adversity, after all, isn't necessarily a bad thing. "Maybe it's good," he told Julie Ward of the *St. Louis Globe-Democrat*. "Well, not good . . . but it hardens you, number one. It tests your commitment, let's put it that way. It tests your resolve because a lot of people can deal with success, but success has its own problems. I've seen some people who couldn't handle success, but also if you've been successful to have to handle being subpar or not being the best is very difficult. It makes you a little humble. It makes you appreciate when things are going good and what it means to be successful."

Craig also offered Ward his take on what it meant to be a champion, noting, "For all these guys who do have flashes of success, one of the things that separates those short-term champions versus the guys who are long-term champions is the ability to come back from adversity because there is nobody that stays at the top really long that hasn't known illness, injuries or setbacks."

Craig's final Bran Chex/YMCA race came May 1 in Cleveland after Bran Chex decided not to renew its two-year contract with Front Runner. Besides the financial loss, Craig also lost the race to Ted Rupe, who'd run against Craig in college. Craig managed a 4:40 first mile, but couldn't maintain that tempo. Rupe went on to win, 29:33.1 to 29:51.8. "I'm facing my biggest challenge as far as running goes in coming back from this infection," Craig told the *Cleveland Pr*ess.

After Cleveland, Craig didn't race for more than a month. He stayed busy fulfilling a contract with General Electric to promote its portable videotape system at road races on the national circuit. The program involved videotaping runners from three angles while they ran on a treadmill. As the videotape was played back, the runners' form would be critiqued by Craig or another expect. "That was in the early days of VHS," Craig said. "This was a portable deck you could put on a strap over your shoulder and shoot just like professional TV people did."

Craig promoted the system at Bay to Breakers with a public relations account executive who later sent him a thank-you note that read:

> It always makes my job easy and fun to work with a professional and articulate spokesperson. Your ability to relate to the media on a personal level made for effective interviews, and the enthusiasm you generated for General Electric products resulted in impressive client plugs. In addition to the media tour success, we at Burson-Marsteller appreciated your willingness to work

at Saturday's demonstration—above and beyond the call of duty—coaching runners. Ultimately, your participation in this program translated to a happy client!

The struggles Craig had been going through made him sympathetic to the athletes who were injured during the years he was on top. "I found I was indeed human and vulnerable, and it hurts physically and from the mental point of view when you can't stay with those guys," he relayed to Woods, who wrote of Craig's indestructible optimism. "If I can work myself out of this hole," Craig told Woods, "I can work myself out of anything. A lot of guys are surprised that I'm racing already. But I can't stay away from it this long."

Final USA Title

Four months of frustration ended for Craig in The Athletics Congress National Championships 10K at Knoxville, Tennessee, on June 25 with what would be the final national track victory of his career. The 35-man race was his first track 10K since he'd set the American record in Paris in 1980.

Craig's preparations had gone well thanks to new training partners Steve Baker and Jeff Roth. Baker, who was getting into the college coaching field, was a British citizen spending the summer in St. Louis. Craig told Baker of his problems changing gears during sprint finishes. Baker agreed to design workouts Craig would run with Roth two or three times a week. "Steve was the one who taught me that when you really want to do true speed work that you need to give yourself more rest," Craig said. "I was treating my speed work like 'strength' speed instead of 'speed' speed. He taught me some things about working on changing gears—some techniques and some drills. We talked about form."

The opening 8K in Knoxville featured 10 different leaders including Craig, who reached midway in 14:20.4 while spending more time than usual tucked in the pack. "Thankfully, nobody really forced the pace," recalled Craig. He momentarily lost contact with the leaders, who were more worried about playing tactical games than getting rid of him. "With a mile to go, they slowed down up front and I was able to make contact with the back of the lead pack," he said. "That was their fatal mistake."

After officials reluctantly allowed him to enter The Athletics Congress National 10K at Knoxville, Tennessee, on June 25, 1982, Craig proved he belonged by winning in 28:33.02 ahead of UCLA's Steve Ortiz. It was Craig's last national title. *(Photo by Jeff Johnson)*

At 9K, the lead pack dissolved to include only Craig, Steve Ortiz, Mark Curp, Robbie Perkins and Bob Hodge. UCLA's Ortiz had been the top American earlier that month while placing sixth in the NCAA 10K. Ortiz surged to a five-meter lead with 500 to go with only Craig and Perkins giving chase. Each had his accelerator floored the final 250. "I felt something inside me that I hadn't felt in a long time," Craig recalled. "With three or four laps to go, it was like my memory kicked in, my tradition kicked in and my past achievements kicked in."

Craig overtook Ortiz 80 meters from the finish and held on to win by .56 in 28:33.02. Craig told Bert Nelson of *Track & Field News* that with eight laps remaining, "I almost gave up and walked off the track. That's how much I was hurting."

That race also left Craig hurting from the way he'd been treated by meet officials, who weren't going to let him enter because he had no qualifying time from 1981. "I had to jump through all kinds of hoops to ask them for special permission and dispensation to get into that 10,000 despite everything I had done," said the American record holder and two-time world champion.

Craig's request was sent to a committee that included Tennessee coach Stan Huntsman, the meet director. "He didn't think I should be allowed to run in it," remembered Craig. "I had to conduct a PR campaign and call all kinds of people to put some weight on my appeal. Finally at the 11th hour, they relented and let me get in the field."

Craig was especially miffed that he'd been supporting the national meet with his attendance since 1975 when other stars had skipped it to focus on lucrative European meets. "I just felt disrespected and I was ticked off," he said. "I got along with Stan before and after that, but for some reason I don't know why he took that position that he did. It was wonderful revenge to take that victory lap."

Chapter 22: One Marathon Too Far

"Everybody's got problems, but you've got to hang in there and tough it out. Pretty soon the sun starts shining again."

— Craig Virgin

The day after Craig's victory in Knoxville, his American 10K track record of 27:29.16 fell to Alberto Salazar, who ran 27:25.61 in Oslo, Norway. Nevertheless, Craig's spirits were lifting as he headed to Atlanta in an attempt to win a fourth consecutive Peachtree Road Race. He repeatedly told the media he could win even though his fitness level was only at 85 percent. "But if I lose," he told the *Atlanta Constitution*, "they will know that I'm there."

Craig had been to Atlanta in June of 1982 to film several 90-second television commercials promoting the Peachtree broadcast by TBS. The promos included running tips and doubled as adidas advertisements. During a June 7 Eastern Airlines flight to Atlanta, the pilot recognized Craig's name on the passenger manifest and asked a flight attendant to have Craig autograph a running magazine. "This flight attendant was real cute and looked like a facsimile of Cheryl Tiegs with the haircut, the eyes and the cheekbones," remembered Craig of his introduction to Sandy Pitts. "She came back later to follow up and visit with me. She was going to be doing Peachtree for the first time. She was a snow skier and she also did barrel racing in small rodeos."

Sandy would tell the *Atlanta Journal-Constitution* that prior to that day she "had no earthly idea who Craig Virgin was." As Craig left the plane, he mustered the courage to ask her out for dinner or coffee or something. "We were going up the concourse and she finally, reluctantly, agreed," he recalled.

What Sandy agreed to was drive Craig to his rental car and then meet him for beer and oysters the next night. The fact that she lived in Marietta, Georgia, a nine-hour drive from Lebanon, did not deter Craig. Later that week, he asked her out again. When she hung up the phone, she asked her roommate, "Why did I tell him I'd go out with him?" They had dinner and she took him to the airport.

When he returned for Peachtree, Craig met two-time Olympian Dick Buerkle and his wife, Jean. "A beer and three kamikazes later, she [Sandy] shows up. That's when I fell in love," Craig told the *Atlanta Journal-Constitution*. "We ended up starting a pattern where we'd see each other every couple of weeks. Either I would fly down there or she would fly up to St. Louis or we'd meet on the road at a race." Nine months later, they married.

Craig may have been distracted when he arrived at the Peachtree starting line without his race number. After being issued another, he labored through the opening mile in 4:30, a harbinger of the sixth-place finish to come. His time of 28:47.9 was nearly 32 seconds behind winner Jon Sinclair. "I stayed in the back of the leaders' pack, going as fast as I could pedal, and it just wasn't fast enough," Craig told the media. Still, he remained optimistic.

Craig's enthusiasm about his comeback boiled over in July when he committed to be the spokesperson and celebrity entrant for the September 26 Chicago Marathon, which fell in the middle of his never-observed "rest" phase. He'd later confess, "I just didn't see the error of my ways."

At the end of July, Joe Concannon of the *Boston Globe* wrote a story to promote Craig's return to the August 15 Falmouth Road Race. The piece brought up Craig's impatience about rehabbing while Salazar set the American 10K record. "It's been frustrating," Craig said. "You can't leave the dance floor for too many dances otherwise someone steals your girl."

As Craig turned 27, he made sure he was part of the action in August, racing five times beginning with the Maggie Valley Moonlight five-miler in North Carolina. He and Sandy made the winding, 2½-hour drive from Atlanta in her new navy-blue Chevy Camaro Z28 with T-tops. "She and

I really had a good time driving up there through the mountains of north Georgia and North Carolina," recalled Craig, who arrived at a starting line that included Rod Dixon, Mike Musyoki, Rob de Castella, Robbie Perkins and Herb Lindsay. Giving them extra incentive was a $1,000 bonus if they broke Salazar's 1981 world record of 22:04.

The downhill opening two miles on the out-and-back tour of US Route 19 were scorched in 4:09 and 4:21. Over the flat third mile, which Craig covered in 4:39, he moved into the top three behind Musyoki and de Castella. After covering the uphill fourth mile in 4:49, Craig was the first to surge, opening a 10-meter lead. In the final 100 meters, Musyoki rallied to within four-tenths of a second but got no closer as Craig won in 22:46.9. "If I can outkick Michael Musyoki, I've come a long way back," Craig told *Southern Runner*. Musyoki admitted to the *Asheville Citizen-Times*, "I had to spend everything to stay with him."

Planet Salazar

A week later, Craig returned to the 7.1-mile battle of Falmouth where future Olympic marathoner Keith Brantly brashly cruised the first mile in 4:23. The lead group of Mark Curp, Dixon, Musyoki, Salazar and Craig passed two miles in 9:02 and three miles in 13:36. At 5K, Salazar took off and was never caught. Craig wound up second in 32:12.3 while Salazar's 31:53.3 was 2.3 seconds under his 1981 course record. "Alberto was like me in 1980, he was on another planet," Craig said. In the race's 10-year history, only Salazar had times faster than Craig's 32:12.3, which topped his winning 1979 mark of 32:19.7. "Things were going well for me," Craig said. "I was falling in love with a sweet girl from Georgia who looked like a smaller version of Cheryl Tiegs. I was also coming back in my running."

Craig then left for a three-race, seven-day European tour. The first stop was Berlin on August 20 where he took third in a 3K in 7:56.10. Ahead of him were Bill McChesney (7:45.55) and Henry Rono (7:47.23). Craig contested another 3K two days later at Cologne and was slightly faster at 7:55.96, but only seventh.

Craig ended the trip with a 10K in Brussels, Belgium, where his 28:07.88 left him second to McChesney's 27:50.82. It was Craig's best time since he'd set the American record. He'd end 1982 with the sixth-fastest time in the United States and the 28th best in the world. But after Brussels, he never stepped on another European track. "I had to run under 13:30 [for 5K] or I'd just be embarrassing myself," he said. "I never got that fast again so I didn't go back."

The trip overseas helped Craig sort his feelings for Sandy. He took it as a sign when he phoned her for $100 worth of talking. "I thought, I'm not very loose with money, and I just spent $100 on a phone call to a girl. This must be something," he told the *Atlanta Journal-Constitution*.

Craig finished his final 18-miler a week before the Chicago Marathon feeling strong after averaging 5:00 a mile. "I don't have as much of a base as I had in the past, and I'm trying to work out some minor aches and pains," he told the *Associated Press*. Soon after that last long run, Craig began to experience the symptoms of a kidney infection. He should've gone on antibiotics immediately, but didn't because they made him lethargic. Instead of antibiotics, he drank cranberry juice, but that didn't work. As he performed his promotional duties leading up to the race, he had recurring low fevers along with an aching lower back.

Contenders with Craig for the $12,000 first prize included Greg Meyer, Joe Nzau of Kenya and John Halberstadt of South Africa. A field of 6,049 assembled under cloudy, 55-degree conditions for the 9:30 a.m. start. "I knew two miles into the race that I was having a terrible day," Craig lamented. "I had a urological infection and it just was getting worse. The one thing you don't want to do with a urological infection is get dehydrated, because it just aggravates it." With 24 miles to go, he began to doubt he could be competitive, but hoped for a second wind.

Three sub-4:50 miles leading up to the six-mile mark gave Nzau and Garry Bjorklund a gap on a pack that included Meyer and Craig. "We were all keying off Virgin and that made us go too slow," Meyer would tell Phil Hersh of the *Chicago Sun-Times*. Bjorklund faded as Nzau reached seven miles on 2:07:18 pace.

Obligated to Endure

At eight miles, Craig knew his only goal was to finish. At 16, the nine-man chase pack, which still included Craig, disintegrated. "They expected me to make a move and I felt awful," he said. "Suddenly the whole front of the pack blew up and I fell back." He'd tell Hersh, "They scattered across the road like birds." In the final half mile, Nzau folded and Meyer posted a 2:10:59 to 2:11:10 victory. It was a personal best for the 27-year-old Meyer, who'd sliced three minutes off the course record.

After fighting the urge to quit the final 10 miles, Craig's torture ended in 2:17:29. He finished in what he called "a mild state of shock." There was blood in his urine after the race, which he blamed on irritation caused by a stone in his right kidney. His 16th-place finish missed a slice of the prize money by one spot, but he'd received $15,000 for running in and promoting the race. "It was just a horrible, horrible experience," he remembered.

Loyalty stopped Craig from dropping out—loyalty to Chicago-based race sponsor Beatrice Foods, loyalty to his college teammates who came to watch, even loyalty to the schoolchildren he'd talked to while promoting the race. He'd been told as early as 1981 that he had a kidney stone. "I would have bouts where the stone would get in the wrong place and cause an irritation and cause an infection," he said. "It just was haunting me." Eleven months later, after more infections, the stone was surgically removed.

Craig's ailments dating back to mid-1981 were detailed in a story he wrote for the November 1982 issue of *The Runner*. The piece has the tone of a confessional as he recounts the poor decisions that followed each setback. It's also a warning to those dreaming of living the glamorous life of an elite runner.

Craig noted: "Life in the upper echelon of the running movement is not always the rose garden that some people imagine it to be." He also wrote: "If you like job security, don't plan on being a world-class distance runner." He admitted to overtraining and ignoring feedback from his body. He was especially critical of his attempt to mount a six-week crash program to prepare for the 1981 New York City Marathon. "Good things always take a long time to develop," he wrote. "Don't gamble if you don't have to."

The plot of Craig's personal life thickened late in 1982 when he and Sandy became engaged. "When I met Sandy, I met somebody who matched up with a lot of the things that I was looking for," he said. "That was one positive thing that happened in a year of ups and downs." Befitting their on-the-go lifestyles, Craig's marriage proposal took place in an Eastern Airlines employee parking lot prior to them catching separate flights.

The couple picked March 12, 1983, for their wedding, a bold choice a week before the World Championships and just two after the US Cross Country Trials. "I was pretty ambitious," conceded Craig, whose other big goal for 1983 was the inaugural World Track and Field Championships scheduled for Helsinki, Finland, in August. In the December 1982 issue of *Track & Field News*, a panel of forecasters picked nine potential 10K medalists including Craig.

Firing a Friend

In late 1982, the contentious relationship between Front Runner employees Bonnie Robinson and T. L. Simmons came to a head. Craig knew one of them had to go. "I decided I needed Bonnie's administrative services more than I needed T. L. to work on the races," Craig said. "I paid him through the end of '82, so that gave him like six weeks to get another job. That was the first employee I ever had to terminate. That was tough, because we were good friends."

Much less difficult was agreeing to conduct running clinics on Oahu prior to the Honolulu Marathon on December 12. It was Craig's first trip to Hawaii. A story in the *Honolulu Star-Bulletin* referred to him as "Captain America" and "Mr. Personality." Craig told writer Jack Wyatt, "Beginning marathoners need all the encouragement that they can get." Wyatt noted: "Island women, in particular, are awed by Virgin's presence."

Craig's focus heading into 1983 was the US Cross Country Trials, an event so shabbily organized in previous years that he asked The Athletics Congress to allow him to host it. It would be February 20 on the campus of Southern Illinois University—Edwardsville. He sold more than $10,000 worth of sponsorships, which was bigger than anything Front Runner had yet conducted. He put more than $15,000 of his own money into the event in the form of cash or his six employees' time. TAC contributed nothing.

Craig ran the 1983 US Cross Country Trials in more ways than one. *(Photo by Randy Sharer)*

Craig designed the 12K course and instructed the university's grounds crew on how to maintain it. He also organized more than 200 volunteers to work the race and hired Boston-based commentator Toni Reavis, a St. Louis native, to handle the finish-line announcing. The St. Louis Track Club staffed the finish line. SIUE students were hired to videotape the race.

At the Collinsville hotel where most runners stayed, Craig organized a Sunday morning religious service (coordinated by his mother) so runners wouldn't have to leave the hotel. The Rev. Jeff Wells, a race entrant, gave the sermon. Shuttle buses ferried runners from the hotel to the course. "I incorporated everything into that race that I thought people would ever want or need," said Craig, who did all the above while also training. "How he was able to put this whole thing together and still train for the race itself is beyond me," Reavis told the *Belleville News-Democrat*.

On top of everything, Craig also tried to recruit the nation's best runners to participate in the US Cross Country Trials, a practice he began in 1979 and continued throughout his career. Hindering his sales pitch was the fact runners had to pay their own way to a race that offered no prize money. "We were not always getting our best guys out for the team," said Craig, who felt his recruiting paid off between 1980 and 1986, a stretch in which the United States finished second, second, sixth, second, second, third and third in the World Championships.

From what Craig could see, runners who made the US team began to feel it boosted their careers. A group of frequent qualifiers including Pat Porter, Dan Dillon, Ed Eyestone, Guy Arbogast, Bill Donakowski, Jeff Drenth and Mark Stickley developed an esprit de corps that attracted new teammates.

Ten days before the US Cross Country Trials, the weather in Edwardsville was rainy. Five days of good weather, however, dried the course, making it firm and fast despite its many turns and short hills. Craig had designed the course to be fan friendly by looping it repeatedly through a central viewing area. The meet also had a junior race and a race for the public.

The weather was almost too good on race day as temperatures climbed to 73 degrees. Craig's strategy was to remain in contention for three miles and then push. "I am going for the win," he told Julie Ward of the *St. Louis Globe-Democrat*. "I always do. I really am hoping I can pull a big upset in front of my home fans." In prerace newspaper articles, Salazar, suffering from a cold, downplayed his role as favorite. "This is not the biggest race," he said. "A month from now is when we want to run our best races. To qualify is the No. 1 goal. Winning is No. 2."

Fan Fair

On race day, an estimated 5,000 spectators dotted the sun-splashed course. "Seeing all those people turn out for me brought tears to my eyes as I crossed the finish," Craig would tell the *Edwardsville Intelligencer*. After Lebanon coach Hank Feldt fired the starter's pistol, Salazar dropped deep into the field of 70 before slowly advancing. By two miles, the field had strung out behind the front pack of Salazar, Craig, Porter and Donakowski.

Salazar's plan at two miles was to see who wanted to stick with the leaders. Craig did, but his body protested. "I was tired after the first lap and I thought to myself, 'Whoa, if I'm this tired and there's still 5½ miles to go, I'd better conserve myself a little bit,'" he told the *Post-Dispatch*.

Just before five miles, the race became a two-man battle between Salazar and Craig. With two miles remaining, Salazar opened a five-yard lead without trying. He took that as a signal to push. It wasn't long before his advantage was 75 yards and Craig was hoping for a second wind. "I thought I could roll up on him a little bit," Craig told the media. "I wanted at least to get close and then try to get strong again on the last lap."

After he tried and failed to slice the deficit, Craig focused on finishing, which he did in 36:51, 17 seconds behind Salazar. Rounding out the US team for the March 20 World Championships were Porter (37:09), Donakowski (37:20), Mark Anderson (37:39), Doug Brown (37:39), Ed Eyestone (37:45), Thom Hunt (37:45) and John Idstrom (37:52). Missing the final berth by four seconds was Rev. Wells.

Craig had been soundly beaten unless you consider what came next. "During the awards ceremony, almost every one of the guys who accepted the award . . . said how amazed they were that we had pulled this off and how they had never experienced a Trials like this," Craig remembered. Even Doug Brown, who'd slammed Craig for leaving Athletics West in 1978, was kind in his remarks. Only a victory could've made Craig feel better. "It's one of my prouder accomplishments to this day because it's never been duplicated," he said.

Salazar and Craig had a lopsided rematch on March 6 in the nationally televised Continental Homes 10K at Phoenix. Salazar lowered his American record to 28:01 while Craig, feeling ill, finished 17th in 29:13 as an estimated crowd of 10,000 looked on.

The leaders in the 1983 US Cross Country Trials at Edwardsville, Illinois, became legends. Craig (1) and Pat Porter (22) were the last challengers to let eventual winner Alberto Salazar (2) break away. *(Photo by Randy Sharer)*

"For a while, I didn't think I would be able to finish the race," Craig told the *Belleville News-Democrat*.

The event wasn't a total loss, though, as Craig arranged to promote Panasonic. The deal would earn him $5,000 and three audio systems for his cars if the Panasonic insignia he wore was visible on television for at least 20 seconds. He taped a Panasonic logo on his race number and wore a Panasonic sign on his back. He also wore a Panasonic cap while warming up, cooling down and during postrace interviews with CBS, ESPN and a Phoenix TV station. The CBS production staff, which had worked with Craig elsewhere, gave him some good-natured teasing about the hat that had suddenly appeared during his interview.

Craig and Sandy's March 12 wedding took place in a chapel at Callaway Gardens resort in Pine Mountain, Georgia. Craig considered the locale a beautiful place to run. The only attendees were a few Atlanta-area friends and the immediate families of Craig and Sandy, who wanted a small wedding. Two years older than Craig, Sandy would change her last name to Pitts-Virgin.

The newlyweds, who'd signed a prenuptial agreement, wouldn't have a dinner alone together for another month because they were soon on their way to the World Championships in Gateshead by way of adidas headquarters in West Germany. "They gave us the VIP, celebrity wedding, honeymoon treatment there," recalled Craig, who received similar hospitality in Gateshead where the US team stayed in a castle. "They gave us the honeymoon suite. We're talking about a four-poster bed with the tapestries and the window treatment. The rest of the team really gave Sandy and me a warm welcome."

Craig hoped to return the favor by being a steadying influence on the squad. He tried to build team morale and help his teammates realize how good they were. Salazar, for one, needed no pep talk judging by the importance he placed on the race. "You have all the best runners from the mile up," he told the *Post-Dispatch*. "It's the only world championship where all the best runners are running one common distance."

That distance on March 20 was 12K on the muddy turf of Riverside Park behind Gateshead International Stadium. The lingering effects of a sinus infection and months of erratic training had robbed Craig of fitness and confidence. Despite that, his goal was a top-three finish, but as the race unfolded in chilly conditions, he never cracked the top 30. He wound up 42nd in 38:06, six seconds faster than he'd run on a scouting expedition four months earlier. He was the team's fifth man while the fourth-place Salazar (36:53) led the US to second. Ethiopia was first and Kenya third.

Craig left the World Championships with his worst result in five appearances, but another World Championships beckoned— the first ever in track and field was slated for August in Helsinki. Beyond that—12 months beyond—Craig could hear the call of the 1984 Los Angeles Olympics.

Chapter 23: Life on the Run

*"I respect a champion who can taste the sweet and
the sour and still be able to come back."*

— Craig Virgin

After returning from their Gateshead honeymoon, Craig and Sandy lived a commuter marriage. He rented a home in Lebanon near McKendree University and she owned a house built by her father in Marietta. They'd stay one place or the other for two weekends a month and be together on the road the other weekends. It was an unconventional lifestyle for an unconventional couple. "It was exciting, but it presented challenges and complications," said Craig, who felt tied to his Lebanon-based business and its employees.

Sandy received an Eastern Airlines employee discount that allowed her and Craig to fly for $15 one way if a seat was available. When flights were full, they got bumped to later flights. Maintaining two homes, two lawns and two refrigerators of fresh food grew to be a hassle. Plus, there was one more thing. "She did not like my hometown as much as I liked Atlanta," said Craig, who hoped Sandy would enjoy nearby St. Louis. Complicating matters were Sandy's concerns about getting bumped from return flights and missing work assignments in Atlanta.

As he waited for his flights or hers, Craig often ran in or around airports. Travelers staring at him speeding through concourses may have thought he was late for his flight. While Marietta provided better weather for winter training than Lebanon, it was very hilly and had far worse traffic. "I took my life into my own hands," remembered Craig of his 6:30 a.m. workouts on narrow roads with minimal shoulders and no sidewalks. "My biggest problem with Atlanta was always vehicular traffic." Another drawback was the absence of his cousin-led medical team.

Craig had never taken former Brigham Young University miler Paul Cummings seriously as a distance runner until the May 8 Rock N Run 10K in Los Angeles. On a course around the UCLA campus that Craig later suspected was short, Cummings won in 28:08, six seconds ahead of Craig in fourth. A 3:56 miler, Cummings was near the end of a six-week training phase in which he was averaging 130 miles a week in preparation for a June marathon.

While in Los Angeles, Craig scouted for housing he and his family could use if he qualified for the 1984 Olympics. The Rock N Run was sponsored by Kangaroos shoes, a St. Louis–based company which had asked Craig to enter. Several celebrities were on hand including rock star Mick Fleetwood of Fleetwood Mac. Kangaroos shoes were known for their key pouch. "For rock-and-roll people," Craig laughed, "it was used to put their marijuana and other drugs into."

Boxed In

In mid-May, Craig made his third and final appearance in San Francisco's Bay to Breakers. The prerace promotions featured Craig and Rod Dixon wearing boxing gloves for *San Francisco Examiner* photographer Katy Raddatz. Her photo includes a scale, as if the two were weighing in for a fight. Such hype fit Craig's philosophy that the public needed rivalries to draw its interest.

In a feisty prerace interview, Dixon told the *Examiner*, "I don't care if Craig is training to jump over the moon, Rod Dixon is going to be in 100 percent shape at Bay to Breakers and he's going to beat the record. Rod Dixon is coming to win, and if Craig Virgin is in the race, the victory will be so much the better."

In a spunky retort, Craig noted, "I'm an individualist, and I always react aggressively when people say, 'You can't run this fast. You can't come back this fast.' I don't like limits. It's like waving a red flag in front of a bull." The proverbial checkered flag went to Dixon, who did break his 1982 course record of 35:07.6, clocking 35:01.3 on a route that was 75 yards shorter than in 1982 to make it exactly 12K. Craig captured third in 35:15.0.

Craig returned to Indianapolis on June 18 hoping to defend his TAC National 10K title. Standing in his way was Salazar, whose dominance was beginning to wane. The meet was doubly important because it was the qualifier for the inaugural World Track and Field Championships in Helsinki in August. To advance, Craig needed a top-three finish and a time under the qualifying standard of 28:03.0. If he made the top three, but didn't run under 28:03.0, he had until July 28 to get a qualifying time.

The race began after sunset on a hot day that saw the humidity spike late in the afternoon. Of the 36 who started, only 27 would finish even though the early pace was slow. Craig and Salazar found themselves at the front of an eight-man lead pack after a 2:54 opening kilometer.

As runners entered the homestretch approaching 4,500 meters, a downpour on the backstretch forced fans to sprint for cover. "The people on the homestretch were laughing at the people on the far side," recalled Craig, who remembered the torrent was notable for the giant size of its chilling raindrops. "I had never experienced anything like that where a sheet of rain just crept a foot at a time across the infield and then finally ended up on the home stand." As runners made knee-high splashes, officials darted between them to squeegee pools out of lane one.

With five laps left, only Mark Nenow, who'd become the US 10K record holder in 1986, remained with Salazar and Craig. "With 600 to go, I was trying to figure out how to play this because I just couldn't seem to drop anybody," Craig said. "I was more scared of the kick of Nenow than I was from Salazar based on the fact I had beaten Salazar just two years earlier in that [Syracuse] 5,000 meters. I knew he wasn't in the same shape he had been in earlier."

Rigor Mortis

Craig chose to kick with 400 left, a move he'd later wish he'd postponed another 200. The trio became a duo on the final curve when Nenow faded as Craig built a slight lead over Salazar. At that point Craig could sense he was tying up. "It was like, 'Oh my God, this is not the right time for this,'" said Craig, whose body locked up the entire final 75 meters. "I desperately tried to get my angle of attack corrected because I was starting to [lean] back too far."

Salazar sprinted past to win in 28:11.64. He later joked to reporters, "It's the first time I've outkicked someone in seven years. It will probably be another seven years before I outkick someone again." Craig ran 28:13.06, which *Track & Field News* suggested would've been under the Helsinki qualifying standard of 28:03.0 in good weather. Salazar and the third-place Nenow (28:14.37) had earlier met the qualifying standard, but Craig would need to find another 10K in which to chase the standard.

Before he could attend to that, Craig wanted to run in his pseudo-hometown of Atlanta in the Peachtree Road Race even though organizers refused to pay him. Being told no didn't affect Craig as it did others. He'd noticed Peachtree, which was offering $25,000 in prize money, didn't have an official lead vehicle. He told race officials he'd run for free if they allowed Audi to supply the lead car. "Audi was excited about that," said Craig, who received a promotional fee from the automaker.

What Craig didn't get was another strong showing to continue his momentum from Indianapolis. Barely a half mile into the 10K, he felt limp and unable to get up on his toes. The result was a sixth-place finish in 29:08, 46 seconds behind winner Mike Musyoki. Craig's misfortunes multiplied when he helped Audi employees take down their booth. As he tilted a handcart piled with heavy boxes, the load shifted and the handcart rolled over his right foot, damaging ligaments in his ankle.

Craig hoped for a miracle as he flew to an All-Comers meet in Eugene on July 22 to try for a Helsinki 10K qualifying time. He'd planned to run in Eugene the previous week, but was forced to withdraw because of his injury. That race he missed saw former University of Oregon standout Jim Hill win in 27:59.5 with Salazar second in 28:06.1. Other elites who would've made that a perfect pace-sharing race for Craig were Rudy Chapa and Matt Centrowitz.

That left no one in Eugene to help Craig set a 28:03 pace except Bill McChesney, who had a qualifying time from the summer of 1982 and would get to run in Helsinki only if Craig didn't. Craig asked McChesney to run, but understood when he declined. Nevertheless, Craig was miffed no other elites were available. "If you are not an Oregon graduate, Athletics West member or sponsored by Nike, it puts you at a disadvantage in getting someone to run with you around here," he told the *Register-Guard*.

With a crowd of about 150 watching him outclass a field of no-names, Craig reached 5K 10 seconds behind his goal pace of 13:55. He could see his quest was futile and stopped. There'd be no World Championships for him. "It was obvious the foot was only getting worse," he told the *Register-Guard*. "I didn't want to risk a super serious injury that would keep me out for more than just a few weeks."

Rolling Stone

By the time the World Championships were underway, Craig was in St. Louis' Barnes Hospital on August 10 getting his kidney stone removed. He viewed the operation as a must if he hoped to qualify for the 1984 Olympics. The nephrostomy procedure involved inserting a tube through his back into the kidney and leaving it there for several days. The half-inch stone was removed through the tube without the need to cut through muscle. As he healed, Craig watched the World Championships on TV feeling excluded. "When there was a meet that big," he said, "I should be involved in it." The 10K was won in 28:01.04 by Italy's Alberto Cova.

A story in the September 1983 issue of *Indiana Runner* magazine rehashed Craig's rocky year. When asked why he tried at all considering everything he'd been through, he noted his success of 1980 and 1981. "Once you've tasted it, you don't want to be a has-been," he said. "There are a lot of champions that have had adversity. I think the real, true champions are the ones that have had the adversity and have been able to come back from that to return to their form." Now 28, Craig considered himself too young to retire. "In America I'm a grizzled old veteran, but in the rest of the countries, I'm still a rookie," he told the magazine.

As 1983 came to a close, the weather in Lebanon turned horrific with temperatures often below zero and wind chills at face-freezing levels. For the first time, Craig suffered frostbite. He interrupted some workouts to push stranded motorists out of ditches. At other times the conditions were so bad, he had to skip workouts entirely. His optimism took a beating as he tried to pound out 100-mile weeks. Things were better when Sandy was available to time his splits. After a 15-mile run on New Year's Day of 1984, however, he wrote: "Battled a great deal of emotional anxiety (i.e.) 'what am I out here doing this for?'"

The answer in the January 7 Red Lobster 15K Classic at Longwood, Florida, was "winning" in 44:28, a 4:46-per-mile pace. "It wasn't quite as fast as I expected," Craig told the *Orlando Sentinel*. "I guess I'd forgotten just how long a race 9.3 miles is. I was a little rusty when it came to concentration for a race that long. Still, I'm very happy with the progress."

What Craig really needed was a potion to alleviate the tendonitis of the vastus medialis muscle above his left kneecap, which had become a daily complaint in his diary. He bought a portable electro-galvanic stimulation unit so he could treat his knee. He'd attach pads to his leg and the unit would alternately force the muscles to contract and release.

A deep field awaited Craig in Paradise Valley, Arizona, in the January 29 Runner's Den/KOY 10K Classic. There were 25 entrants with PRs under 29:00. Craig expected to break 29:00, but questioned whether he could run sub-28:20 to win. He wound up third in 28:33.5. Seventh-placer Tom Ansberry, a 20-year-old University of Arizona runner, told the *Arizona Republic*, "I was kind of scared being in the lead pack. It kind of puts you in awe running next to these guys like Virgin."

Craig's aura of excellence faded in the February 4 Orange Bowl 10K in Miami. He went in hoping for a time in the low 28:20s. He told the *Miami Herald* in a prerace interview, "I feel like a test-car driver who has just rolled a new chassis out of the body shop. It's just great to be healthy."

The 4 p.m. race was held in humid, 80-degree conditions. Craig stayed with the leaders until the third mile when he lost contact on his way to a 12th-place finish in 29:29. He was baffled about why he felt weak so early in the race. He found out four days later when a measles-like virus gave him a rash, which required Prednisone, a corticosteroid. He'd later have to declare to US Cross Country Trials officials he'd taken the drug so they wouldn't suspend him for using a performance enhancer.

Funk Master

The misery of Miami left Craig in a funk for two days. On the third day, funk changed to determination as he prepared for the February 19 US Cross Country Trials in New Jersey, where he rated Pat Porter and Alberto Salazar as the favorites. The 12K course at the Meadowlands Racetrack had many turns, two hay bale hurdles and a plywood hill covered in carpeting. A light rain added mud to the mix. Although Craig struggled to find the proper stride and foot plant, he managed third in 35:18. Porter, who won in 34:47, told reporters his 4:18 opening mile felt like a 4:30. "I think to win the World meet someone is going to have to go out and run the kind of race Pat Porter ran today," Craig told *Track & Field News*.

Craig told the *New York Times*, "I felt a lot better physically over the final three miles, but Pat was too far ahead to even hope to overtake." In a column for the *Atlanta Journal-Constitution*, Dick Buerkle wrote that Craig wanted to regain his panic. "I used to panic if I wasn't in the lead," he told Buerkle.

The March 1984 issue of *Track & Field News* previewed the 5K and 10K for the US Olympic Trials. The magazine's five-man panel ranked Craig first in the 10K ahead of Jim Hill and Porter. The panel picked Craig eighth in the 5K, where the top three spots went to Doug Padilla, Jim Spivey and Matt Centrowitz. The magazine's assessment of Craig was: "Competitively smart. Lacks great speed, but varies pace to lessen that disadvantage." Craig told the magazine, "I plan to run the Trials the same way I'll run in the Games, and that's the same way I did in the '80 Trials—where Herb Lindsay and I fartleked through a 13:43 5K. That kind of race takes the sting out of the kickers."

In that same issue, Craig addressed the question of why slow kickers run in slow packs at major meets with no hope of winning when they should be forcing the pace to tire fast kickers. "There's a certain element of courage and sheer guts when you're out there," he said. "You can't just press a button and do it. There's an essence of gambling to leading. You can't have negative thoughts. You've gotta be confident."

NBC sportscaster Ahmad Rashad and his crew visited Craig in Lebanon on March 15 to film a piece that profiled Craig and Pat Porter and aired during the World Championships broadcast. The video shows Craig jogging through downtown Lebanon while talking about the importance of his hometown roots. He calls the challenges of Midwest weather an advantage instead of a handicap.

When asked about his health problems, Craig's hopeful response was: "One of the hardest things for any runner who has been at the top has to battle, and this applies to any athlete, is to all of a sudden . . . after you struggle so hard to get to the top of the pecking order, the top of the hill, the top of the ladder, to have to come back and start all over one or two years later when other guys have taken your place and you are starting at the bottom of the heap and you have to scratch and crawl your way back up. It's taken me two years and I'm getting close and I know if I do the right things then maybe I can make the Olympic team and maybe can return to my former goals."

Seeking a Miracle

Craig arrived in East Rutherford, New Jersey, for the World Championships—held in the Western Hemisphere for the first time—with no clue about his fitness and no question he lacked momentum. All he had was a nothing-to-lose attitude. He confided in his diary: "A top-10 finish would be a miracle." As a crowd of 17,418 watched, Craig hustled to an early spot in the top 20 of the 7.3-mile race, but struggled to move up. He faded to 22nd, but surged on the final lap to finish 17th in 34:07, one place and one second behind Ethiopia's Mohamed Kedir. Portugal's 37-year-old Carlos Lopes won in 33:25.

Craig had topped his Trials' time by 71 seconds and beaten notables such as Rob de Castella (21st, 34:08) and Portugal's Fernando Mamede (23rd, 34:09). In his postrace critique, Craig noted: "It was good (but not great) considering all the health problems I've had over the past month. Finished in good company." He was the No. 3 man for the United States, which placed second behind four-time defending champion Ethiopia. No US team would place that high again until the 2013 squad took second to Ethiopia.

During three years of abysmal health since winning his second World Championships, Craig had fallen to 17th, a spot for which he had little respect. But a case can be made that 17th under his circumstances was more impressive than his victories. He was getting insufficient power from his left leg because of knee pain. His immune system was compromised as viral infections inter-rupted his training. He'd been over-racing since 1969. Why could only 16 of the world's best beat him? Could it be some 1980–81 magic remained along with enough mental toughness to make up the difference?

Chapter 24: 1984 Olympic Games

*"I may write about the pressures of being an
Olympic wife. It would be a best seller."*

— Sandy Pitts-Virgin

With his cross country season complete, Craig returned to
the sizzling road race circuit for the April 1 Crescent City
Classic 10K in New Orleans. He placed a disappointing 10th in 28:38
after Mark Nenow blew things open on his way to an American
record 27:22.

As Craig often did, he mailed the race director thanking him for
being invited. Such letters included Craig's analysis of his own performance and suggestions for how the race could be improved. After
Crescent City, he also wrote: "It will be interesting to see whether the
athletes running so fast this past month can still be as competitive in
June or August."

Three days after Crescent City, Craig was hospitalized with a
103-degree fever and a white blood cell count over 16,000. A normal
white blood cell count would be between 4,500 and 11,000. A test
for mononucleosis came back positive and he was started on intravenous antibiotics. His left ear was surgically punctured to relieve fluid
pressure. Another test showed a loss of hearing and some inner ear
nerve damage. On Craig's growing list of travails, these blended into
the background of his emotions as if camouflaged. After two days
in the hospital, he resumed running with an easy four-miler. He was
accompanied by his dog, Brownie, who didn't mention there were
only 71 days until the Olympic Trials.

Craig visited Dr. David Martin's Georgia State Laboratory for Elite Athlete Performance on April 18, but could only produce a VO^2 max of 84.8, well off the 88.8 he'd posted the previous October. Such tests were so exhausting Craig could only psych himself up for them by trying to exceed his previous time on the treadmill. He'd hoped to last 17:00, but only made it to 15:59. He did raise his pulse to 198, but it was clear his aerobic threshold was falling.

As Craig (1) prepared for the 1984 US Olympic Trials, he enjoyed socializing with recreational runners in road races such as the May 24 Olympic Federal five-miler in Bloomington, Illinois. (*Photo by* The Pantagraph)

Craig made a breakthrough on May 10 during a workout in Champaign under Gary Wieneke's supervision. It featured a six-lap drill that opened with an 800 in 2:10 and was followed by four laps of alternating 200s of 29 and 37 seconds to mimic the surging tactics he planned for the Olympic Trials. The training to surge continued with four laps that began with a 2:10 800 ahead of alternating 200s in 30 and 35. Next came six laps beginning with a 2:19 800 followed by two laps of 200s in 30 and 35 before finishing with a 2:14 800. "I always got excited going back to Champaign," Craig remembered. "It just felt good to go back there, plus I enjoyed performing in the workouts for Coach."

Two days later, Craig's legs were still stiff from that workout when he won a five-mile road race in Bloomington, Illinois, in 23:24 as he averaged under 4:41 per mile. "I'm starting to feel the rhythm where I don't think about my running," he told the *Champaign News-Gazette*. "A distance runner will float at race speed when he's in that kind of rhythm. I think I may be able to look back on that weekend and say that was the turning point."

May of 1984 found the Soviet Union still occupying Afghanistan. On May 8, the Soviets announced they'd boycott the Los Angeles Olympics because of security concerns and what they saw as anti-Soviet sentiments in the United States. Seventeen other countries, mostly Eastern Bloc allies of the USSR, also did not compete. *Track & Field News* estimated the boycott would keep 50 percent of the potential track medalists away. By comparison, the magazine noted the 1980 boycott kept an estimated 20 percent of the medalists away.

This latest boycott hit Craig as hard as the first. "You don't settle differences between countries—whether they're military or political— with athletics," he said. "Four years after our boycott, what has changed? Nothing. It was a useless sacrifice. The sacrifice was to the Olympics and the athletes. It wasn't Russia that sacrificed." Craig's solution was to create a permanent site for the Olympics with Switzerland being his top choice.

Hoping for a 13:30 5K, Craig entered the New England Track Championships on May 31 in Boston. It would be his last race before the June 16 10K preliminaries at the Olympic Trials. He'd arranged to alternate 800-meter shifts in the lead with Bruce Bickford, who hosted Craig at his Boston home. Craig wanted to run 65-second laps, but in rainy, 49-degree conditions he could only will himself to do 66s on his first shift. He got slower from there, finishing second in an abysmal— for him—14:02 behind Bickford's 13:37.

Craig's diary report was extra brutal as he noted: "This was one of my most embarrassing moments in my career!" Dissection of the painful truth continued the next day when he wrote: "Last night's nightmare race is still vivid. It is frustrating and depressing. I recovered too fast afterwards. Have I forgotten how to race and hurt?" He just wanted one more positive race before the Trials. "That was a huge deal for me, ending on a bad note like that," he said. "My confidence was shot."

With Sandy along for support, Craig arrived in Los Angeles on June 14 with his left knee hurting and his mind spinning. He planned to contest the 10K and 5K, which meant he'd run five races in 10 days over 87½ laps for a total of 35,000 meters, just 4½ miles short of a marathon. There'd be a prelim and a final in the 10K along with a first round, a semifinal and a final in the 5K. Fifty laps into his chore, Craig told a noontime press conference after the 10K final, "I don't know many sportswriters who can walk 50 laps."

Taco Sauce

Sportswriter Charles Pierce wrote that Craig "always was the taco sauce in the mellow wheat germ of distance running." On the eve of the 10K prelims, Craig received a free massage from old friend Ilpo Nikkila of Finland, who'd known Craig since his Athletics West days in 1978. Nikkila was flown in for various meets by Salazar for several years. It seemed to Craig that Nikkila could wave his hands across a muscle and feel where heat caused by inflammation was coming from. "It was almost spooky," Craig said.

Craig drew the first of three 10K heats. He saw eight good names in his 15-man heat. He told a reporter beforehand, "The ideal race strategy is 'start fast, surge up the middle and run like hell at the end,' but I can't get into a situation where I have to sprint at the end." He took the lead with a 65.8-second 16th lap and then backed off a lot to win in 28:19.59. It was the fastest 10K prelim in Olympic Trials history and will remain so since 10K prelims were discontinued after 1996.

Craig's heat had the most qualifiers with eight while the second and third heats only advanced five each. Following him were Paul Cummings (28:19.63), Mark Nenow (28:19.66), Bruce Bickford (28:19.68), Charlie Bivier (28:32.46), Steve Ortiz (28:34.69) and Mike Buhmann (28:43.94). The second heat was won by Ed Eyestone (28:34.37) and the third by Pat Porter (28:29.34). Other big names advancing were Herb Lindsay (28:34.38), Garry Bjorklund (28:34.50) and Tony Sandoval (28:40.52).

Craig could've run faster, but he eased up the final eight laps, ending with a leisurely 71.2 final circuit. He passed 5K in 13:59.3, which made his 14:02 in Boston even harder to fathom. "When I made my move, I made it," he told David Woods. "I wanted to be a .44 Magnum instead of a pop gun."

With two laps to go in the 1984 US Olympic Trials 10K, Craig was in position to react to the moves of Paul Cummings (278), Garry Bjorklund (336) and Pat Porter (573). *(Photo by Jeff Johnson)*

Craig was happy to advance, but concerned about the depth of talent he'd face three days later in the final. The next day he was treated by Nikkila and received chiropractic adjustments from internationally known Dr. LeRoy Perry. On the eve of the final, Craig wrote: "Am finally getting excited and feeling some positive vibrations. I guess the performer in me is coming out."

Craig warmed up for the 7:45 p.m. final on the Los Angeles Memorial Coliseum's top level so he could watch other events. His race opened at a moderate 28:37 pace the first seven laps. Nenow changed that with laps of 64.3, 65.2 and 66.5 that forced Craig to run his third 1,600 in 4:25.8. His first two 1,600s took 4:35.0 and 4:31.8. "I remember how I suffered from that, but I had no choice," he said. "The whole pack went." After reaching 5K in 14:06.1, the pace slowed as Nenow was supplanted at the front by Porter before Bickford took over for three laps. The group of four ran so tightly, Craig would finish with seven bleeding spike wounds on his right shin. He was bumped off the track twice.

Between 6K and 7.5K, the injury-plagued Nenow dropped back. Craig was in a six-man pack led by Mark Curp that passed 8K in 22:33.5. As Cordner Nelson of *Track & Field News* described it, "30-year-old Paul Cummings ran a little wide as if itching to launch his drive. Also eager to race was Craig Virgin, who had seemed washed-up from injuries and kidney trouble." Also in the mix was old rival Bjorklund, a 1976 Olympian. Bickford was shed with three laps remaining. Bjorklund fronted a five-man band with 600 to go and shared the lead at the bell with Cummings while Curp fought to hang on.

The bell seemed to ignite Cummings, who unveiled his miler's speed. Craig pulled the trigger on his kick and kept Cummings within 10 meters until midway through the last turn. At that point Cummings finished off a 55.9 last lap to win in 27:59.08. Meanwhile, Craig, running scared, notched a 59.6 good for second in 28:02.27.

Craig hadn't led a single step because each time he considered leading, someone else went to the front. That left him with enough power for a 13:55.7 final 5K, a 4:20.4 last 1,600 and a 2:05.0 final 800. "I just kept pumping that (last) straightway," he told Dave Dorr of the *St. Louis Post-Dispatch*. "It seemed so damn long. I was scared as hell."

Bjorklund, who'd failed to make the Olympic marathon team in May, was passed on the backstretch by Porter, who took third, 28:03.86 to 28:05.83. "I really didn't think Craig was going to be there," Bjorklund told Woods. Craig couldn't blame anyone for thinking that. "I had absolutely no momentum going into that race," he said. Among those who'd been whipping Craig the previous six months, Curp took fifth (28:06.80), Bickford sixth (28:18.86), Perkins ninth (28:38.64), Nenow 11th (28:53.78) and Eyestone 12th (28:55.78). Other notables were Lindsay in 14th (29:03.72) and Sandoval in 15th (29:06.45).

"Second place wasn't the biggest battle," Craig told Dorr. "Getting here, getting well and my mental state were my biggest battles.

Cummings had explosive speed. I stayed out of trouble, but my legs felt heavy [in the homestretch]." After the race, Craig was uncharacteristically stoic as he compared his achievement to those from the 1976 and 1980 Trials. "The last three years have been the hardest of my career," he said. "So these Trials were the most satisfying. I owe a lot to eight different sports medicine people."

Craig's 28:02.27 would rank 27th in the world for 1984. It was his fastest time since 1980 and it made him the first American to qualify for three Olympic teams in the 10K. In 2016, Galen Rupp became the only other American-born runner to make three Olympic 10K teams.

Pizza Party

Craig had to get drug-tested the same night he qualified, select an Olympic uniform and fill out forms. By the time he got done, it was after midnight. Friends greeted him at his hotel with champagne and pizza. "Of course when you make an Olympic team, you're kind of giddy," Craig said. "I could feel no pain by that point in time and life was good."

Craig owed a lot to his wife. "She never knew me when I was successful," he told the *Los Angeles Times*. "She met me during the slump period. Now I hope she'll see me during some good periods." The Trials had brought them together for 12 straight days, a record for their marriage.

Craig had bought himself six weeks to prepare for the Olympics. "I can't do anything but get faster," he told Woods after qualifying. It was a good thing Craig didn't need to extend himself in the first round of the 5K two days later, because he'd paid a physical price in the 10K. He chose to enter the 5K because he needed the speed work and he wanted to qualify in another event in case he got sick at the Olympics like he did in 1976. The top six in each of three heats advanced along with the next six fastest. Craig clocked 13:50.62 to finish third in the second heat.

The next day, the top five in each of two semifinals advanced along with the next two fastest. Craig qualified sixth in the first semi in 13:40.30, which would've won the second semi. He'd never run that fast again. The semifinal winners were Don Clary (13:35.22) and Steve Plasencia (13:42.35). Joining Clary and Craig among those doubling back from the 10K were Bickford and Steve Ortiz.

After a day off, Craig knew by the second lap of the final he'd gone stale. "It was just too many races too close together," he admitted after placing eighth in 13:41.63. He was still in contention until the leaders ran the last three laps under 3:00. Doug Padilla won in 13:26.24 ahead of Steve Lacy (13:27.72) and Clary (13:28.6). The dreaded first non-qualifier was Bickford (13:33.78). Craig was sad to see the Trials end, but he'd gotten what he came for, an Olympic berth. "When I got to that stage," he recalled, "a switch would click and I would turn into something."

In a July 24 *Atlanta Journal-Constitution* story, Sandy told writer Jack Wilkinson she went crazy after Craig qualified. "I didn't know what I was gonna do, or was supposed to do, if he didn't make the team. If he didn't, it was probably gonna be the toughest thing I was ever up against. But when he did, I just cried from my toes. It hurt. It was like somebody had finally let some of the tension out. I went to call Craig's folks right away, and after I told them, they asked, 'Who was first? Who was third?' I didn't even know." Sandy went on to tell Wilkinson, "I may write about the pressures of being an Olympic wife. It would be a best seller."

Inner Depression

Sandy hadn't known Craig at his peak, but thought that might have benefitted their relationship. "I don't like cocky people," she told Wilkinson. "But now that I know him, he's not like that. Craig just has confidence." The confidence, however, had been interrupted by moody stretches where Craig was in a funk. "It's been an inner depression," Sandy told the biggest newspaper in Georgia. "Maybe Craig and I only know about it. People don't realize the ups and downs we've been through the last two years. He's got a lot of pride, but it's been hard for him to hold his head up sometimes."

Craig's pride drew little benefit from lackluster results in the Peachtree 10K (4th, 29:02) and the Prefontaine Classic 5K (7th, 13:54.5) before spending the last two weeks of July at an Olympic training camp in Santa Barbara, California. He'd run on the beach or on dirt roads near President Ronald Reagan's ranch.

Craig hadn't forgotten the cramped living conditions in the Olympic Village at Montreal. He hoped to avoid that by renting an apartment—sight unseen—in Los Angeles near USC. Another reason to rent was the fact Sandy wasn't permitted in the Olympic Village for security reasons. The apartment, however, was in a rough neighborhood, had no air conditioning and was so shabby, Sandy cried when she saw it and Craig "had to fight depression." They stayed at the Santa Monica home of a family acquaintance instead.

The opening ceremonies, which had taken too long for Craig's taste in Montreal, were even more drawn out in Los Angeles, which also had more layers of security. Athletes were held in an arena next to the Coliseum for four hours before they were allowed to march in. Craig was struck again by the joyous atmosphere of the opening ceremonies. "Everybody was in such a good mood," he remembered. "Nobody had had their hopes and dreams dashed and it was just a very positive time. It really makes you believe in the power of the Olympics."

The opening ceremonies made Craig proud to be American, but they also left him drained physically and emotionally. By the time his 29th birthday arrived, so had his parents for a party in Santa Monica. His Olympic preliminary was the next day. He marked the occasion in his diary with: "I finally get the chance that was denied me in 1980. I wish I was in the same shape."

Craig thought the best he could hope for in the Olympics was a top-10 finish. He'd allowed himself three days of tapered training instead of his usual two. There were three heats with the top five in each advancing to the final along with the next three fastest. All three of the time qualifiers including Pat Porter (28:19.94) would come from the third heat.

Craig was in the first heat. As he jogged onto the track in front of the biggest crowd of his career at 90,000 strong, he thought, "I guess it was all worth it . . . all the pain, all the strain, all the sacrifice, all the training and all the things that I gave up. It was an overwhelming feeling, like 'I can't believe I'm here and in this race.'"

Craig ran in the top five the first four miles, which saw the pace gradually slow. His opening 1,600 splits were 4:33.6, 4:33.9, 4:38.2 and 4:40.1. As he covered the 18th lap in 64 seconds to take the lead at 7K, the Coliseum roared its approval. He didn't recover well from that surge, though, as his lower back and hips began to tighten. "The surge was supposed to shake up my opponents, and instead I was sucking air," he recalled.

Running in the first of three 10K preliminary heats in the 1984 Los Angeles Olympics, Craig finished ninth in 28:37.58 and failed to advance. His heat was won by Portugal's Fernando Mamede (second from left). *(Photo by Mark Shearman)*

When Craig wanted to surge again with four laps left, his back began to spasm. "I was starting to feel like the tin man that got left out in the rain," he said. "The last three laps on that track were three of the longest I've ever run and three of the saddest." He wanted to quit, but couldn't with his parents and wife in the stands.

Craig slogged onward to finish ninth in 28:37.58. The fifth and final qualifying spot in his heat went to England's Mike McLeod in 28:24.92. The slowest time qualifier for the 18-man final scheduled three days hence ran 28:20.26. Of the 41 finishers in the three heats, 20 were faster than Craig, who felt like crying.

The 10K final was a reunion of stars Craig had beaten or lost to the previous four years. Italy's Alberto Cova won in 27:47.54 after clocking 13:27.0 for the final 5K. Finland's Martti Vainio took second in 27:51.10, but was disqualified a few days later when he tested positive for the steroid metenolone.

Admittedly naïve about the prevalence of performance-enhancing drugs in distance running, Craig said, "I lost my innocence that day." McLeod (28:06.22) replaced Vainio as the silver medalist while Kenya's Mike Musyoki secured the bronze (28:06.46). Other prominent finishers were Ireland's John Treacy in ninth (28:28.68), Nick Rose in 12th (28:31.73) and Porter in 15th (28:34.59).

Craig awoke the next morning depressed. Sandy and his parents gave him space because he was inconsolable. He couldn't understand why his back had tightened so badly. "I felt like I was running in quicksand," said Craig, whose funk lifted 24 hours later. He spent the last week of the Olympics trading uniforms with athletes from other countries.

As the closing ceremonies neared, Craig and Sandy decided to watch them on TV in Santa Monica before leaving on a six o'clock flight the next morning. "I regret I didn't stay in the Olympic Village overnight at least one night and I regret I didn't participate in the closing ceremonies," he said decades later.

Craig's final races of 1984 convinced him his left knee needed surgery for his career to continue. He consulted with Atlanta orthopedic surgeon Dr. Rick Hammesfahr to schedule arthroscopic surgery for October. MRI tests showed signs of long-term inflammation on Craig's left quadriceps tendon while his left knee showed irritation on the undersurface of the kneecap.

Craig thought his knee surgery would go as smoothly as it had for Joan Benoit, who won the 1984 Olympic Trials marathon 17 days after surgery. His surgery, however, was more than arthroscopic as the surgeon made a two-inch incision on the left side of the kneecap and slit the retinacular tissue. This allowed the kneecap to move to the right, where it was more in the center of his knee. This procedure, known as retinacular release, is performed less often nowadays. "It caused the whole recovery to last a lot longer than what I was anticipating based on testimony that I had heard from other athletes," said Craig, who did find one positive from the surgery. He could now sit pain-free in an airplane with his knee bent. Before, he always had to have an aisle seat so he could straighten the knee.

Plate Full of Change

In December of 1984, Craig closed the Front Runner office in Lebanon and moved it to Marietta, where he planned to reside full time. He had to hire an administrative assistant to replace Bonnie Robinson, who didn't want to move to Georgia. Sandy sold her Cobb County home so she and Craig could lease a Marietta condominium. "There were a lot of decisions on my plate that fall coming out of the disappointment of Los Angeles," recalled Craig, whose five-year shoe contract had reached the point where adidas could drop him or pick up an option for two more years that would bump his annual salary to $70,000.

Craig had been paid $50,000 in each of the previous two years. The trigger date came and went and Craig didn't hear from adidas. "I said, 'Well, I guess I'm in adidas for the next two years and they are going to be paying me $70,000 a year,'" said Craig, who knew he wasn't worth the new salary, but also knew he'd been a bargain earlier when he was paid $30,000 a year.

Despite everything he'd been through in 1984, he didn't consider retirement. The possibility of qualifying for the 1988 Olympics at age 32 was worth chasing. He was encouraged by the fact Olympic marathon champion Carlos Lopes was already 37 and 10K world record holder Fernando Mamede was 33.

Craig had qualified for the Olympics on basically one good leg after three years of start-and-stop training. His health-wrecking kidney stone was already gone. Surgery would make his knee as good as new. He'd rejoin the best in the world and share the jet-setting lifestyle of a star with his very own Cheryl Tiegs. It was a script for happiness no optimist could resist.

Chapter 25: Starting Over . . . Again

"Mingling with people pumps me up for the race."

— Craig Virgin

After four months without a race since knee surgery, Craig began a 24-race campaign in 1985 in the January 12 Red Lobster 15K Road Race in Orlando, Florida. Despite feeling rusty, he took fifth in 46:04, which was 95 seconds behind winner John Tuttle.

Craig's January to-do list included moving Front Runner Inc. into an office on Marietta, Square in the center of Marietta where his first executive secretary was Lin Murakami, a former Nike employee. On February 16, he got moving in the US Cross Country Trials to earn a record eighth consecutive berth in the World Championships, which would be held in Lisbon, Portugal, on March 24. He'd run the final two miles on guts because there was little fitness to draw on. He sliced through 30-mph winds on the hilly 12K course at Waco, Texas, in 37:03 to finish fifth.

Craig thought residing with Sandy full time would be a winning idea, especially since they were talking about starting a family. But within two months he saw their relationship turn rocky. He didn't realize how challenging it would be to give up his support systems in Lebanon. The move left him discombobulated for several months, a fact he didn't think Sandy realized.

Craig was at his best when the personal, business and athletic aspects of his life ran smoothly, but now all three were in flux. Prior to living together, their marriage had enjoyed the excitement of perpetual dating. "When I look back on that period, we both

made mistakes," he said. "I can honestly say I did not do enough
to reinforce her about where she was in the priority of things. From
a relationship standpoint, you need to still make dates even when
you are married."

**Ever optimistic, Craig held out hope throughout the 1980s that he could
return to his 1980 form.** *(Photo by T. L. Simmons)*

Craig's marriage to distance running continued on its relentless path with a 19th-place effort in the World Cross Country Championships. He was cut off on the initial sprint and passed 1K trailing more than 200 men, but rallied to clock 34:12 on the 12.19K course. "I did feel very strong during the middle of the race, probably the best I have felt in three years," he later wrote to a race director. As the fourth American, Craig helped his team place third behind Ethiopia and Kenya.

Craig felt there was something about his biomechanics that helped him run faster than most over rough terrain. "I love [cross country] so much I can be in half-ass shape and then go out and still be able to beat most people," he said. "I think that growing up on the farm and running and walking in the pasture, which was always rugged footing, made me stronger."

Head-on photos of Craig running show his leading thigh directly in front of his trailing thigh, creating the illusion he only has one leg. Such a rotation by his hips to allow one thigh in front of the other may have given him a few extra inches per stride, but those inches came at a cost. "There might have been something about that that gave me a disadvantage in terms of serious injury that eventually would terminate my career," he said.

Craig's career was marked by loyalty to particular races. That loyalty paid off in terms of familiarity with local media. The *Times-Picayune*, for one, referred to him as "Mr. Crescent City" prior to his fifth appearance in the March 31 New Orleans race, where he managed eighth in 29:02 while Lopes won in 28:17.

Lopes, who announced he'd retire after 1985, inspired Craig, who told *Track & Field News*, "He was a top world-class runner in the mid '70s, had a series of injuries and missed a few seasons. His story provides hope that you can come back and continue to achieve, even past 30. People tend to think of him as a marathoner because of the Olympic win. But look, the guy has just come off winning the World Cross Country title, too. Right now, he's the best in the world, period."

Super Sub

Craig finished an encouraging second in the April 27 Trevira Twosome 10-miler in New York City, clocking 47:33 to earn $4,000. He was 15 seconds behind defending champion Dave Murphy of England. When Eamonn Coghlan injured his ankle the day before the race, Craig replaced him as the partner of Grete Waitz. She set a women's course record of 53:19, giving them a winning combined time of 1:40:52. Waitz told the media, "I was looking forward to having Eamonn as a partner, but I did get an excellent substitute."

During his March trip to Lisbon, Craig had landed a business opportunity when former 10K world record holder Dave Bedford of Great Britain asked him to run in the IAC City Centre Series in England. Besides being paid to run, Craig was paid to bring other top Americans. British officials, whose stars had been competing in the United States for years, hoped the series would reverse the flow of road race talent between their country and America.

The series was made up of three 10Ks in 28 days. The entrants included Portugal's Fernando Mamede, the track 10K world record holder, and Welshman Steve Jones, the marathon world record holder. Americans Paul Cummings and John Tuttle, whose appearances Craig finagled, would also appear. *Athlete's World* called the assembled talent "probably the highest quality fields ever seen on the roads of the United Kingdom."

In the series opener at Glasgow, Scotland, on May 5, Craig took eighth in 28:24. Eight days later in Cardiff, Wales, he ran 10th in 27:59 on a course he suspected was short. Winner Eamonn Martin was credited with a UK record 27:42. With his left knee feeling better, Craig returned to Marietta prior to the series finale on June 2 in London. A virus and 102-degree fever sidelined him on May 15, but he returned to training on the morning of May 17. During a fartlek workout, he sped around a corner and stumbled over construction debris on a sidewalk, spraining his left ankle, scraping his knee and bruising two ribs. The ordeal cost him six days of training and forced him to withdraw from the May 27 Bolder Boulder 10K. Instantly, months of recovery by his left knee were erased by having a weak left ankle.

In the May issue of *Track & Field News*, Craig was quoted as saying, "I have two holes in my knee where scar tissue was taken off the top of the quadriceps tendon. It has taken me longer to come back from the surgery than it did from all the kidney problems I had a few years ago." He also made the May issue of *Runner's World*, which had an article about the top 20 moneymakers in the sport for 1984. Carl Lewis topped the list at $700,000 while Craig was at the bottom with $110,000. Craig hadn't reported his income to the magazine, but he actually made $120,000, roughly a third of which came from road racing.

Craig made it to the IAC City Centre Series finale in London, where he ran 10K in 28:51 for 10th. He summed up the series to *Athlete's World* by saying, "It's a whole different scene here to back home. We are used to tactical races but your top 10 or 12 guys are very gritty runners and they don't take any prisoners."

Craig needed more than grit to overcome the power loss and imbalance caused by his ailing left knee. That was clear in his second and final track race of 1985, the TAC/Mobil National Championships in Indianapolis on June 15, where he placed ninth in the 10K in 28:49.91, a time that would rank 25th among Americans for the year. He told *Track & Field News*, "The artist in me still wants to run fast on the track again."

As he turned 30, Craig produced his best effort of 1985, a fifth-place finish in the August 24 Maggie Valley Moonlight Race. Over the final two uphill miles, he moved into fifth and hung on to clock 23:03.3. In a letter to the race director, Craig noted: "This summer has been especially frustrating for me. I had such a bad experience in my previous four races that it was a real pleasure to feel strong and pick off runners coming back up the hill."

Pit Crew of One

Sandy picked Thanksgiving in Atlanta to contest her first marathon. Craig played the role of pit crew boss as she clocked 3:44:40. He supplied his 32-year-old wife with water bottles and even ran alternate miles with her at an 8:00 mile pace through 19 miles. He also ran the final four miles as she shattered her goal of four hours. "It was worth all the training," she told Dick Buerkle of *Runner's World*. "I couldn't have done it without Craig's help." Craig was impressed by her effort in humid, 70-degree heat, noting, "She's worth 3:20 on a good day."

Craig's next race on November 30 offered the worst footing of his career as rain turned the TAC national cross country meet course in Raleigh, North Carolina, into soup. The quagmire, combined with his ailing left knee and a tender right hamstring, relegated him to 14th in 31:44.5 for 10K. He'd overcome a poor start to crack the top 10 midway, but faded from there. Pat Porter won his fourth straight title in 30:33.1 to earn an automatic berth in the World Championships scheduled for Neuchatel, Switzerland, in March of 1986.

The first of Craig's 15 races in 1986 was the Charlotte Observer 10K in North Carolina, where he ran 28:56 to finish one second behind winner Jim Cooper, a Charlotte resident. Craig's last-ditch sprint was in vain, but earned him $1,000. He told the *Charlotte Observer*, "The last three weeks have not been good for me. I tried one brief surge . . . and didn't get anything at all. I said, 'So much for that.'"

A week later, Craig returned to the Red Lobster 15K in Orlando, which offered a $25,000 bonus for anyone breaking a world record. Twelve men covered the wind-aided first mile in 4:48. Craig led the next four miles, but a 15-mph breeze put the 1983 world record of 42:27 by Mike Musyoki out of reach. "Once I got out in front, there was no room to go back," Craig told the *Orlando Sentinel*. "I should have pleaded age. I looked over my shoulder, and I saw a close-knit pack of world-class runners, and I knew I had to run hard to win."

At the six-mile mark, Mexican Olympian Mauricio Gonzalez stopped to cough up a mosquito. Between six and seven miles Craig answered a surge by Mark Stickley and took the lead for good with a mile to go, winning in a course record 44:05. Runner-up John Tuttle, the defending champion, was seven seconds back. Craig felt "tired, but ecstatic" about his first major road race victory since Maggie Valley in 1982. It was his last triumph against an elite field.

The good times kept rolling on January 23, 1986, when Craig reported to Tempe, Arizona, for a *Runner's World* photo shoot in the desert with Lisa Martin, who'd later win the 1988 Olympic Marathon silver medal. He wore adidas gear and a smile that hid his chronic pain. Lisa wore a skintight one-piece Nike uniform made of Lycra that was cut high enough at the hips to send the April issue flying off store shelves.

Limited Shelf Life

During a four-race February, Craig lined up for the US Cross Country Trials in Waco, Texas, eager to qualify for his ninth World Championships team. In a *Waco Tribune-Herald* preview he said, "One thing I'm seeing . . . is that most runners usually only have about two to three years at the top. Something breaks after that. You look at Alberto Salazar, Bill Rodgers, Frank Shorter—they all lasted about two or three years at the top. But then nobody ever said being a semi or pro athlete was easy."

The race was held on the Cottonwood Creek Golf Course, where the solid footing seemed less of a problem for Craig's knee than mud would've been. During the opening two miles, he showed little pop, but he looked stronger the final three miles, leading the chase pack behind Pat Porter and Bruce Bickford. Craig elected to coast the final half mile to avoid unnecessary strain, which caused him to drop from third to fifth, but he qualified with room to spare. His time of 35:32.81 was 26 seconds behind the winning Porter. "I just knew how to pace myself over 12 kilometers," Craig explained. "I could take a limited amount of gas and make it go a long way."

Craig went farther than he should've in the six weeks leading up to the World Championships, contesting a half marathon, two 5Ks and a 15K. "Considering my knee wasn't 100 percent, I probably overdid it even though some of those were 5Ks," said Craig, who remembered being scared awake by a 3 a.m. dream the night before his "road" personal record of 14:05 in a 5K at Rockledge, Florida. In the dream, he was back in baseball, a sport he hadn't played since grade school. "It scared me because it was almost like somebody was trying to tell me my running career was over," he said. "It had come full circle and it was almost like a bad omen."

Craig's eighth-place finish at the March 8 Jacksonville River Run 15K was only made memorable by a particularly bad incident and resulting argument with Sandy. "We hit a low point in our marriage on that weekend that we never ever totally recovered from," Craig said.

As Craig tried to regain his form, he missed retired comrades. He told the *Harrier*, "I look around now at a lot of these meets and I no longer see my friends. I see new faces, but I can't let that intimidate me. I'm stubborn. A survivor. And I guess I'm proud that I have persevered over all these years. You don't see too many exceptional high school runners who have had continued success. I can say I have." Pat Porter said in the same article, "I really respect Craig. He's there year in and year out. Just when people say he's out, he comes back and proves them wrong."

As Craig trained for the March 23 World Championships in Switzerland, he took heavy doses of ibuprofen to cope with left knee pain. It hurt more to land on his left leg than push off it. "I was taking three Advil three or four times a day," said Craig, who never went a day without it. "That was the only thing helping me keep that edge off that knee."

A downpour the night before the World Championships left the 12K course soggy and extra difficult for the weak kneed. Voted captain by his teammates, Craig fought his way into the top 50 early, but abruptly ran out of energy. He struggled to his worst finish yet, 81st in the field of 337 in 37:26.4. Kenyan winner John Ngugi finished 1:53.5 ahead. "That was the first World Championships where I just didn't feel competitive at all and I didn't feel like the same runner that I had been in the past," recalled Craig, the No. 6 scorer for the United States, which placed third behind Kenya and Ethiopia. He later wrote to US coach Joe Vigil: "I'm not sure what hurt more during the race, my body or my pride."

Rotten Attitude

Craig's running continued to deteriorate the following week as both hamstrings became knotted and his left knee screamed as never before. In his diary under a section titled "mental attitude," he wrote:

"Rotten, ready to retire!" After a discouraging 14th-place finish in 29:11 at the April 5 Crescent City Classic, he might've retired if he'd known things were about to get worse.

Craig had been experiencing trouble with his contact lenses the previous month. As he was doing promotional work for adidas at the April 21 Boston Marathon, he passed his left hand in front of his left eye with the right eye closed and noticed the hand disappeared prematurely. Five days later he underwent surgery in St. Louis where a procedure known as scleral buckle was used to repair a detached left retina. To this day, a thin silicone band encircles the sclera of his eye.

Doctors couldn't determine why the retina detached since Craig hadn't sustained a blow to the head. He later told Loren Tate, "There's no guarantee that the procedure will work, and it could be three to six months before we can determine how much sight has been lost. Right now there's no white in my left eye. The swelling has gone down but it looks like chopped liver. You'd think I stepped in front of a line drive."

Craig's career was at a standstill. Doctors forbade him from lifting anything. He couldn't bend from the waist or do anything that would send blood rushing to his head. He couldn't fly. Above all, he couldn't risk jarring the retina. May and June of his season were gone and the late summer hung by a thread. Given the circumstances, it took an ultimate optimist to tell Tate: "I know I've had a lot of things go wrong, but I'm a fast healer."

Chapter 26: Wounded Warrior

"There is a front side and a back side to every career. In most cases, there is no storybook ending."

— Craig Virgin

Two weeks after eye surgery, Craig was cleared to ride an exercise bicycle and lift. He returned to running on May 21 and was up to eight miles a day by June 10. Ready or not, he resumed racing on July 4 at Peachtree. The race program included a story about Peachtree's history, noting that Craig had become more identified with the event than anyone else. It also noted: "His vibrant, confident personality was a perfect expression of the spirit of the race."

The wounded hero story angle was a hit with newspapers promoting Peachtree in 1986. Craig told the *Marietta Daily Journal*, "When the gun goes off and I won't be able to sprint out with the leaders, that's when it's going to hurt. I'll be running for fun and it's going to hurt." His lack of fitness was accurately reflected in an 87th-place finish in 31:29.

Craig made sure he didn't run for free by landing two nightclubs as sponsors, Sneakers in Marietta and Elan in Atlanta. *Marietta Daily Journal* writer Andy Friedlander astutely noticed that Craig "doesn't demand to be left alone. For it is here, in a crowd, not out there alone on the track or the road, that Craig Virgin is truly in his element."

Among Craig's dreams for 1986 was to organize 20 of America's top sub-marathon road races into a circuit for 1987. He believed the races' futures could be enhanced along with runners' incomes if a circuit was available to provide stronger marketing and promotion. He wrote to Don Kardong, "I believe strongly that the events need to be promoted and sold as a package. There would be efficiencies in such a setup that could benefit everyone."

In July of 1986, Craig contracted with Red Lobster to organize a five-race series he'd also run in. The overall and masters male and female winners from four races would receive an all-expenses-paid trip to the finale, which would be the Red Lobster 10K Classic in Orlando, Florida, on February 21, 1987. The finale would offer a $50,000 purse. Craig knew major races couldn't be created as quickly as Red Lobster needed, so he suggested Red Lobster become the title sponsor for races that already existed. "I would negotiate the terms with an existing race, identify the objectives that Red Lobster could ask for and get, and then I would go in five days before and make sure they got what they asked for," Craig said. "I would be a media spokesperson. I would oversee the race that morning and then run in the race." Besides Orlando, other races were set for Cincinnati, Chicago, Dallas and Washington, DC. The series only lasted one year, though, because Red Lobster withdrew its support.

Craig's three remaining races in 1986 included his final appearance in the August 23 Maggie Valley Moonlight Run where he finished 22nd in 24:27 for five miles, a whopping 2:06 behind the winning Musyoki. In the Alumni All-Comers cross country meet in Champaign on September 6, he placed fourth in 14:51 for 5K, tying his worst finish in that event.

Five months, three doctors and thousands of dollars in medical bills later, Craig still wasn't healthy. An MRI of his lumbar area showed a slight bulge in a disc, but it was ruled out as the cause of his discomfort. One doctor blamed Craig's problems on tight muscles and recommended a program of stretching, swimming and physical therapy. Another doctor recommended orthotics.

In a letter to Larry Ellis, the 1984 US Olympic track coach, Craig noted: "My hamstrings were so bad in the fall that I had difficulty not only in running but even when I would walk or sit for periods of time."

As 1986 came to a close, Craig and Sandy purchased a 1½-story country French-style home in Cobb County. They remodeled the upper story into a fitness center, giant closet and deluxe "man cave." With his two-year adidas contract extension now expired, Craig resumed "gentle comeback training" on January 1 of 1987 with help from drug and exercise therapy.

Mementos from his past brought a smile to Craig's face in 1994. *(Photo courtesy of Craig Virgin)*

Craig resumed racing on January 31 in Miami's Orange Bowl 10K where he clocked 30:26.88 to finish seventh among Americans, but only 22nd overall. Winner Mauricio Gonzalez was more than 87 seconds ahead. Most of Craig's training had been in a pool while wearing a snorkel, mask, webbed gloves and old racing flats. "I was searching for answers," he said.

Leg pain put to rest Craig's hope to run in the US Cross Country Trials in February. It was the first time he'd missed the race since 1979. On April 4, he didn't skip another old favorite, the Crescent City Classic, but perhaps he should have as his weekly training of "50 to 60" miles could only get him 25th in 29:21. Sandy also ran, clocking a respectable 40:23.

Craig set April as the start of a 15-month drive to peak for the 1988 Olympic Trials. His goal was to become the 12th American to qualify for four Olympic Games. Only one other runner had qualified four times, George Young, who competed in the steeple-chase, marathon and 5K. In an April letter to a road race director, Craig was at his optimistic best when he wrote: "After a year off from the national circuit I am finally ready to jump back into the thick of things again come May. My short term goal this summer is the National Track Championships at the end of June. I hope to qualify for the 10,000 meter event there and if I can place in the top three I will qualify to represent the U.S. at the Pan Am Games in August and the IAAF World Championships in September."

Craig began a four-race track season on May 9, 1987, at Atlanta's Griffin Invitational where he finished second to Herman Beltrand of Venezuela, clocking 14:08.89 in a 5K while feeling "very rusty." Two weeks later, Craig contested his first track 10K since June of 1985, winning at the hot and humid Gatorade Classic in Knoxville, Tennessee, in 29:29.05. That was well off his goal of 28:50, the time he needed to qualify for the National Championships.

Craig's appeal to enter the June 25 National Championships at San Jose, California, without a 10K qualifying time was accepted. He finished 12th in 29:03.4, 28.3 seconds behind winner Gerard Donakowski.

For his twice-weekly summer speed training, Craig used Georgia Tech's track, which was the easiest on his legs of any artificial surface in Atlanta. To gain entrance, he'd squeeze through a gap in the fence caused by construction near the tennis courts. It was another sign the glamorous world of the world class wasn't all it was cracked up to be.

Craig made the last of his three appearances in the US Olympic Festival on July 26 in Durham, North Carolina. Originally called the National Sports Festival, it served as the nation's largest amateur multisport event in non-Olympic years between 1978 and 1995. Craig ran fourth in the 5K in 13:57.32, more than nine seconds behind winner Keith Brantly. It was the last time Craig would break 14:00. "It was very depressing," he recalled. "I used to run faster than that coming through en route to the 10K."

By August, Craig had had enough and elected to undergo arthroscopic knee surgery to remove scar tissue that had developed after his previous surgery. His only outward scars this time were four dots evenly spaced around his left kneecap. "I told Dr. [Rick] Hammesfahr, 'If I'm going to make a fourth Olympic team, we've got to try to make this knee stronger,'" Craig said. "He went in and this time he did not do as much as he did in late '84."

Undiminished Ambition

Craig rested for a week before gingerly beginning again at two miles a day. By early September, he was up to 25 miles a week in addition to swimming and biking. On September 12, he finished third in the Alumni All-Comers meet at Champaign, running 15:05 for 5K. He opened with a 4:30 mile and didn't surrender the lead until the final half mile. He told the *Daily Illini*, "I was just pleased that I was able to hang with the leaders today as well as I did. I'm a little sore. I don't like to push myself like this when I'm not trained. After three weeks of rehabilitation, I'd say the knee is coming back. The fact that it held up on the rough ground in the field is real promising."

The *Daily Illini* also mentioned Craig's long-shot bid to make the 1988 Olympics and quoted Sandy as saying, "He's very experienced at the national level, and experience goes a long way in middle-distance running. He's also determined and stubborn. He doesn't give up easily. He comes here [to Illinois] and gets around his old friends and he wants to run more than he should."

David Hackett of the *Champaign News-Gazette* eloquently wrote: "The legs at times seem creaky as a Victorian staircase, but the ambition in Craig Virgin's eyes remains undiminished." Craig told Hackett the 1988 Olympics were "like a carrot dangling in front of me. I don't know if it's courage or stubborn pride—probably the latter—that drives me. But I'm going to give it a shot."

Craig opened his 1988 schedule in the Charlotte Observer 10K on January 2. A long hill in the fifth mile dropped his pace dramatically as he went on to finish ninth in 30:12, almost a minute behind the winner. In late January, he clocked an encouraging 29:33 for sixth in the Princess Bahamas 10K despite rolling his ankle while warming up. He lost contact with the leaders after passing two miles in 9:05. His staying power was better that night while gambling at a casino where he made his $100 in race winnings last two hours. "My deal with myself was if I doubled or tripled it, I would stop," he recalled. "Otherwise, I would just keep playing until I lost it all." In some respects he was managing his running career the same way, and his wealth of talent was running out.

Craig's roller-coaster results dipped in the February 6 Red Lobster 10K at Orlando, where he battled a 28-degree wind chill and rain to clock 30:15 for 39th, almost two minutes behind the winner. The more he'd pushed, the worse his hamstrings felt, a frustrating combination. He'd hoped to crack the top 15 and 29:00, but the results reflected how much energy he'd poured into organizing the race.

Craig would later write to a friend: "Everybody should organize a race once just to see what it entails. All of the runners would have a great deal more empathy for the race director and officials if they had to do it once themselves." Craig wrote another race director: "It just is not possible to have a significant management role and race with the 'big boys' in the same event. I was exhausted mentally and physically."

In a prerace *Orlando Sentinel* story, *Sports Illustrated* writer Kenny Moore offered his take on Craig's 1988 Olympic dream: "He's got an uphill struggle, but he's certainly got a chance. He's as tenacious as a human being can be. It makes no difference whether he has a great chance, or a one-in-a-thousand chance. He's doing the right thing by making the effort." Craig's viewpoint was that of a man seeking control of his fate. "The temptation was there to quit when things weren't going well," he told the *Sentinel*, "but I just don't want to leave on that note."

Craig hoped a positive note would come the next week in the US Cross Country Trials in Dallas. Eight spots for the nine-man team were available because Porter had already qualified by winning the 1987 TAC title. A prerace story in the *Dallas Morning News* portrayed Craig as the lion in winter. There was no denying he was a strong man whose power was being eroded by time. He preferred the metaphor of the aging gunfighter repelling youngsters seeking to prove themselves at his expense. "I know I can't necessarily outdraw them," he told freelance writer Robert Vernon, who also organized the Trials. "I can only hope that I'm a better shot."

Loving the Sport

"If I can make my 10th team, I will consider that one of the greatest achievements of my career," said Craig, whose career had lasted long enough to see the Trials finally offer $1,000 to each qualifier. "It's great to have prize money, and for many of these younger runners it will mean a great deal, but when I started out running, there was no money. I ran because I loved the sport. That's what keeps me in it. I don't have a shoe or apparel contract now, so I don't get the money, but I still love to run and I still love to compete. I love the feeling of running fast. That, more than anything else, is what I want to feel again. Then, if I decide to retire in November, I will have ended my career with that feeling and that memory."

Race day for the Trials included 20-mph winds. The 12K course at Trinity Park featured nine trips up a nasty, 30-foot ascent of a levee. "This course is extremely difficult without the wind, but with the wind, it's a monster," Craig told the *Dallas Morning News*. "It looked like we were going slow, and we were, but it's not because we weren't trying to run fast."

Craig began the race conservatively, passing the first mile in 33rd, but climbed into the top 20 by two miles. He was in the top 10 by three miles and was sixth with two to go. He clung to sixth through a 38:47 finish, 24 seconds behind surprise winner George Nicholas, a 22-year-old former University of North Carolina runner. "All those guys that were young and ahead of me that were used to 8K and 10K would fade somewhat in the last three or four kilometers and I would be moving up," Craig remembered. "I ran my guts out that day. My experience definitely helped."

That outing turned out to be Craig's final berth in the World Championships. His 10 berths were a US record later tied in 1993 by Pat Porter, who actually raced all 10 times compared to Craig's nine. Craig could've run 12 times, but he was ill in 1982 and declined to run in 1976 and 1977 despite qualifying as the top American in the NCAA cross country meets.

As Craig attempted to qualify for the 1988 Olympics, he chose William "Murray" Sanford of nearby Woodstock, Georgia, as his coach at the suggestion of Dr. David Martin of Georgia State. Sanford had helped Dr. Martin perform scientific testing on athletes such as two-time Olympic 1,500 gold medalist Sebastian Coe. Sanford once saw Nick Rose run a sub-4:00 mile on a treadmill.

As far as Sanford was concerned, Craig would always be one of the best US distance runners. "The only thing that is missing out of his accomplishments is an Olympic medal," Sanford said. "I have no doubt between the 5,000 and the 10,000, he would have gotten a medal if he'd have gone to Moscow, but it didn't happen."

By the time Sanford and Craig began collaborating, Craig was attempting to recover from one injury after another. "I was trying to fine-tune a worn-out, old body," said Sanford, who studied Craig's training logs and saw too much over-distance. "You don't need to do all these ultra-long runs. You don't need to compete against yourself in a practice run."

The Craig of Old

Sanford focused on building Craig's speed through fartlek work-outs. Such training fit Sanford's racing strategies for Craig, who was told to use tactical racing and abandon his front-running style. "That's as good a strategy as any," Sanford said in a heavy Southern drawl, "but after a while you can't do that no more. Everybody saw Craig [was] not as good as he was, but they still [wanted] to beat him just so they could say 'I beat Craig Virgin.'" When Craig let others lead, it blew their minds because he still had the "Craig Virgin mystique." They were never certain they were racing the Craig of old or the old, worn-out Craig.

Craig thanked Sanford for his services by paying his way to New Zealand for the World Cross Country Championships, a trip Sandy also made. When asked if he was surprised a two-time world champion wanted him as a coach, Sanford said, "In a way, it was an oddity."

When the long flight to Auckland ended, Craig's knee was still inflamed and his hips and lower back were stiff. He was scared, too. On the eve of the race, he wrote in his diary about his 81st-place finish of 1986: "Hopefully, this time will be better." On race day, his optimism had yet to succumb to his injuries when he wrote: "Hope to crack top 25 today." He finished 102nd on the 12K course in 37:40, 3:08 behind winner John Ngugi of Kenya. "I remember being very depressed after that race," said Craig, who was the eighth man on a seventh-place team.

Over three days after returning from New Zealand, Craig and Sandy had several arguments. "That's when she came to my office and asked for a divorce," he remembered. "That was a very low time for me. It was one depressing thing after another." Before divorcing, they tried counseling and a trial separation.

At the end of May, Craig closed the Front Runner office and moved back to his parents' farm to focus on qualifying for the Olympic Trials. He held out hope that the restorative powers of St. Clair County roads could work their magic one last time. "I was simply going to take a leave of absence from the marriage and a leave of absence from the job and just go back home and focus on whatever I could save in the last three months [before the Olympic Trials]," said Craig, who bought a used Winnebago, packed it with everything he needed and left Marietta.

Unfortunately, Craig's attempts to post Olympic Trials qualifying times of 13:49.15 in the 5K and 28:43.15 in the 10K were in vain. He dropped out of a 5K in May at Knoxville, Tennessee, and finished a June 10K in Abbotsford, British Columbia, in only 29:27.

Craig's elite running career was over, but he wouldn't officially retire until January of 1992 at age 36. He gave up racing on the national circuit and focused on regional events. He cut his mileage to 70 a week hoping to rejuvenate his knees, but nothing worked. At least one friend, Larry Gnapp, who'd raced Craig in high school, thought Craig should've retired sooner. "He kept on trying to come back and be one of the top runners in the country long past his time," Gnapp said. "He had difficulty giving up. Maybe it was the limelight. I'm not exactly sure what it was that kept him going after it. I used to think to myself, Craig, at some point you've got to say, 'That's it. It's over. I can't do it anymore.' He refused to let that go."

In September of 1988, Craig reached out to Sandy hoping to save their marriage, but it was too late. "It was a marriage that could have worked and maybe even should have worked," he said. "We both made some critical mistakes at critical times. At one point in time she was interested in saving the marriage and I was keeping things at arm's length because I wanted to focus on making the Olympic team. Once the Olympic team was over and I wanted to see if we could save it, she wasn't interested." Their divorce became final in November of 1989. She remarried in December.

Photo Finish

Craig had lost his petite Cheryl Tiegs. They'd honeymooned at the World Cross Country Championships. Their jet-setting marriage had thrived as they lived in separate states. She had a ringside seat as he fought to make the 1984 Olympic team. She had arrived too late for his fast times, but not the hard times. He'd later admit an athlete struggling with injuries and defeats isn't easy to be around. "She knew what she needed to do to pick me up and keep me on an even keel. I will always be grateful," said Craig, whose home in 2016 still had a frame of small photos from the 1984 Olympic Trials on the wall. The one photo with Sandy remained where it always had.

Athletically, Craig continued his loyal participation in the Alumni All-Comers cross country races, placing second in 1988 (15:18 for 5K), first in 1989 (14:37 for 5K) and first in 1990 (23:47 at 8K). That 1990 result ahead of Villanova star Terrance Mahon kept Craig's unbeaten status at Savoy intact and encouraged him to enter the US Cross Country Trials in February of 1991. In one of the best races of his final three years, he placed 17th at Tallahassee, Florida, clocking 36:03 for 12K. He was 76 seconds behind the winner and 35 behind the last qualifier. It was the last time he ran the Trials.

The worst part of shutting down Front Runner in 1988 for Craig was letting assistant Kay Ritchey go. He gave her severance pay and helped her look for another job. "My business with Front Runner was definitely suffering because people weren't knocking on my door and my opportunities were diminishing," he recalled. "No matter how well I did or how hard I worked for them in the past, they just wanted to pay me prize money and that was it." With no shoe contract, Craig paid his own way to races. "I was going through a lot of my savings," he said. "Financially, it was getting less feasible to stick with it."

Craig left Georgia for good late in 1990 and moved to Lebanon, where he married former classmate Donna Jeanne Schneider in July of 1991, a year after becoming reacquainted. Craig and Donna had attended grade school together for several years when her father was stationed at Scott Air Force Base. At that time Donna lived near Craig's grandparents. Sometimes Craig would walk from school with Donna to his grandparents' home. As a military officer's daughter, Donna moved several times growing up, but of all the towns she lived in she regarded Lebanon as her hometown.

She and Craig had met again at a Lebanon High School class reunion in 1983. Donna, then a flight attendant for Braniff International Airways, struck up a conversation with Sandy to compare notes about their shared profession. Craig and Donna met again in July of 1990 at the Firemen's Picnic in Lebanon where the Texas-based Donna was visiting a classmate. Donna was then a legal assistant with two children.

A year later, Craig and Donna married and lived in a house on Belleville Street near Lebanon's Locust Hills Golf Course. She was trying to quit smoking and walked for exercise. Taking on the expense of an instant family had a "sobering impact" on Craig. Within six weeks, he knew the marriage was probably a mistake. His subsequent failed campaign to join the Illinois State Senate created financial stress for the couple, but their incompatibility was the primary reason they amicably divorced in January of 1994.

Chapter 27: "Will I Walk Again?"

"Success is not accidental."

— Craig Virgin

A few heartbeats after impact, Craig smelled flammable liquids leaking from the broken engine of his 1989 Nissan 240 SX sport coupe. Being nothing if not proactive, he struggled out of the seatbelts that had saved his life during a head-on collision. His door wouldn't open, but the crash had conveniently knocked out the side windows. He grabbed the roof and pulled himself out backward and headfirst like a stock-car driver. As he attempted to stand on broken ankles, hands grabbed him from behind, carried him off the road and covered him in a blanket to protect him from the 26-degree chill. It was 6:20 p.m. on January 29, 1997. He had sidestepped death — again.

That crash on Interstate 64 at the top of a long ascent feeding into the 25th Street exit in East St. Louis, Illinois, like many disasters, warped time. Some segments happened in slow motion while others ended in an instant. The part where Craig realized another vehicle, a 1989 Toyota Camry, was facing the wrong direction in his lane was over in seconds. The part where his left front headlight exploded upon contact happened in slow motion, as did the sight of his car hood folding back toward him in a wave.

The ear-splitting noise of the impact was followed by god-awful silence. The next moments should've been filled with white-hot panic, but Craig was calm. He saw his predicament as a management operation. Considered judgment would see him through. He couldn't afford to focus on his injuries until he was out of harm's way.

Panic arrived at Memorial Hospital in Belleville not long after Craig. He could feel himself gradually losing control. That's what happens when you ask yourself the questions he did. "Will I ever be able to walk again? Am I going to lose a limb?" The emergency room doctor had different questions. "Why was his heart skipping every third beat? Did he have heart disease?" No, the heart that had won world titles was not diseased, but it was badly bruised. It had been traveling 70 miles per hour when it slammed against his sternum as his car met the Camry, which was traveling about 45 miles per hour in the opposite direction.

Space inside Craig's 1989 Nissan 240 SX sport coupe was at a minimum following his accident on January 29, 1997. *(Photo by Eileen Alexander)*

In the emergency room, where so many deals with God are brokered, Craig was counting his blessings. "I told God, 'I'm not in the morgue nor am I in the spinal care unit and for that, I'm grateful. I don't have to pass this cup. I can handle this someway, somehow.'" That is how you talk when God has asked you to carry heavy burdens before — and somehow you did.

In 1995, Craig had hoped to find running success in masters' competition for those 40 and over. His right kidney — 10 times larger than a normal kidney — had been removed on Good Friday of 1994 so the left kidney had to do all the filtering of lactic acid that running pumped into his blood. Nevertheless, he'd whittled his 10K times to almost 31 minutes. "It was kind of fun to get serious about it again," he remembered. "It just didn't last very long. I was going to do a farewell tour. That car accident robbed me of that."

Besides a bruised heart and broken ankles, Craig had a broken nose, a gash on his forehead and a shattered pinky finger on his right hand. Much later it was discovered he had torn rotator cuffs in both shoulders and damaged knees. His ankles were broken as the front of his car was pushed into the driver's compartment. The area once reserved for the brake, clutch and accelerator pedals now included a left front tire, which had split the compartment open like a ripe orange.

Servicemen from Scott Air Force Base traveling by bus to Lambert Airport had seen Craig's accident unfold. They were the ones who carried him off the highway and laid him on the shoulder of the road. He never got their names.

His Motorola cellular flip phone was retrieved from his car and he called his parents. "I didn't want them to hear about it from the state police," he told Bill Coats of the *St. Louis Post-Dispatch*. "My mom would've had a heart attack."

Craig's mother had been preparing a special fried rabbit supper for him when she answered the phone. She became suspicious when he asked to speak to his father. Craig informed Vernon he'd been in an accident and the ambulance drivers were taking him to Belleville's Memorial Hospital. Vernon took Lorna Lee there not knowing how serious the accident was. They were shocked to see Craig's face covered in blood. "The bloody face, when it was cleaned up, wasn't that bad at all," Lorna Lee recalled. "But it's kind of scary when you see your kid covered with blood." Doctors didn't voice their concerns about Craig's heart to his parents. "It was 24 hours later when we found out he could have died right on the spot," Vernon said. "Ignorance in some cases helps protect you."

That first night in the hospital, Craig was afraid if he slept, he might not awaken. The next morning, his media friendly reputation reached new heights when he agreed to be interviewed by a KSDK-TV reporter. Over the next two days, his heart improved enough that doctors abandoned plans for surgery. His lower legs, however, "were swollen beyond description."

After a week in the hospital, Craig was sent home on crutches with his legs in knee-high splints. There'd be 15 surgeries over the next 13 years involving his finger, left ankle, both shoulders and both knees. The left ankle alone had 23 bone fragments that had to be removed. Each surgery was followed by six to 12 months of physical therapy.

Dr. Richard Lehman, a St. Louis orthopedic surgeon, wasn't concerned about helping Craig return to running. "I didn't know that he was going to be able to walk," Lehman told the *Chicago Tribune*. In time, Lehman saw Craig wasn't a typical patient. "I work with a lot of professional athletes," Lehman said, "but I don't know that I have ever seen anybody work harder than he did."

The day Craig left the hospital, his father and brother took him to his wrecked car to retrieve personal effects. "When I saw it in daylight that afternoon, that's when it was very traumatic for me," recalled Craig, who was lifted into the driver's seat by his father and brother. "Only then did I realize how little space I survived in."

Wrong Place, Wrong Time

Craig's accident occurred on a highway with narrow shoulders and walls on either side. As he crested the overpass he realized a car was coming at him. There was enough time for him to take his foot off the accelerator, but not enough to put it on the brake. His initial thought was he was approaching a wreck that had already happened and a car had spun to shine its lights at him. State police would later explain Lauretta M. Arnold, 42, of St. Louis, had come up the 25th Street exit ramp heading east onto the westbound lanes of Interstate 64. At the same spot within the next two years, there'd be two more accidents with fatalities.

"I looked to the left and there was not enough shoulder room for me to go all the way to the left and get by her," recalled Craig, who was in the far left lane. There were two lanes to his right, but they carried traffic. At the instant before contact, he veered right. The rear of Arnold's car swung toward the wall while Craig's swung into traffic.

As Craig's rear wheels left the ground, the engine over-revved at the sudden loss of resistance. His forehead and the bridge of his nose struck the top of the padded steering wheel. Thirty days earlier, he'd replaced his seatbelts after a recall by Nissan. The lap belt in combination with the shoulder belt had probably saved his life.

Arnold suffered scratches and bruises, but had no serious injuries nor a valid driver's license nor insurance to cover Craig's medical expenses. Thankfully, his own insurance covered the costs. The servicemen who pulled Craig off the road, later carried him to Arnold's car so he could ask, "Ma'am, what happened? Ma'am, are you okay?" With her hands on her knees, Arnold sat in her car, mumbling incoherently. The *Chicago Tribune* later reported Arnold was a paranoid schizophrenic and court documents described her as bipolar. After the accident, she threw a punch at a nurse and identified herself to police using three different names.

While Craig was in the emergency room, his blood pressure fluctuating dangerously, a state trooper handed him a speeding ticket after a witness stated Craig had passed on I-64 at a high rate of speed. The ticket was later dismissed in court while Arnold admitted to driving on the wrong side of the highway, for which she was fined $100 and placed on six months of court supervision. The speed limit at the accident site was 65 mph. Craig confessed to driving between 70 and 75 mph on that stretch. He'd driven the previous 10 miles at less than 50 mph because of traffic. When he got a chance to make up time, he took it, but he didn't see Arnold until she was less than 200 yards away.

Within three months of the accident, Craig was doing 2½-hour physical therapy sessions. "I look at this like any athletic challenge I took on," Craig told Bill Coats. "I try to be aggressive within reason. To me, a certain amount of pain is OK. That's what I did in training."

By April of 1997, a mere four months after his accident, Craig resumed jogging. In July, he stopped twice during a five-mile race in Anchorage, Alaska, but finished. By August, he could race at a 5:50-per-mile pace. "I've told people the last seven months were tougher than any campaign to make the Olympics," he told the *Times-Courier* of Charleston, Illinois. "When you can't even walk across the room in the hospital to the bathroom, you're starting from ground zero."

The accident reminded Craig how his life had mirrored Prefontaine's, except now their paths diverged. Craig was the Prefontaine who lived.

Moving On

In the years following the 1997 accident, Craig's life resembled his collection of training routes, going in all directions. He worked with the Illinois State Police on a program to promote seatbelt usage at Clinton County high schools. He ran for the St. Clair County Board as a Democrat. (He'd lose that election as well as another county board race two years later.) In 2000 he met Janet Meek while both were receiving physical therapy. Theirs was an unconventional courtship. They dated for a short time before wedding. Their union resulted in the greatest joy of Craig's life, his daughter and only child, Annie Virgin-Meek. "Annie is more important to me than any trophy I ever won or record I ever set," he said.

With his daughter, Annie, living four hours away in Indianapolis, Craig has gone the extra mile to remain in her life. *(Photo courtesy of Craig Virgin)*

Craig cheered his daughter, Annie, at her conference track meet when she was an eighth grader in 2015. *(Photo courtesy of Craig Virgin)*

Unfortunately, Craig and Janet's marriage was rocky from the start and ended in divorce after three years. Several months later Janet got court permission to relocate with a then–4-year-old Annie to Indianapolis, a four-hour drive from Lebanon. Thus began Craig's career as a long-distance dad. Living so far from his daughter has been more tragic to him than the 1980 Olympic boycott.

During the 2016-17 school year, Annie was a sophomore in high school posting good grades and playing volleyball. She gave track a try in junior high, contesting the sprints and hurdles because she didn't want to be compared to her famous father. She also sings in a prestigious Episcopalian church choir, which occasionally travels abroad.

The other long-distance love of Craig's life in 2017 was fiancée Karen Fox, whom he met while both were spectators at the 2008 US Olympic Trials in Eugene. A former Southern Illinois University hurdler, she resides in Crystal Lake, Illinois, almost a five-hour drive from Lebanon. "She understands track and field and what it takes to be good at this business more than somebody who has no background in it," Craig said. "She can appreciate what my life before was like, and she can also appreciate what it is now." As kismet would have it, she was in the crowd in 1973 when Craig broke Prefontaine's national high school two-mile record.

Colleagues: In Memoriam

After sidestepping death a couple times, Craig outlived several with whom he shared the world of running. Bill McChesney died at age 33 after rolling his truck near Newport, Oregon, on October 29, 1992. Bob Emig committed suicide at age 51 on March 6, 2001. Paul Cummings drowned in a fishing accident on September 17, 2001, on Utah's Strawberry Reservoir. T. L. Simmons died of a heart attack at age 62 on February 5, 2007. Larry Gnapp passed away suddenly at home in Chicago at age 56 on April 6, 2010. Grete Waitz died after a six-year battle with cancer at age 57 on April 19, 2011. Cancer also killed Geoff Hollister at age 66 on February 6, 2012. Pat Porter died in an airplane crash near Sedona, Arizona, at age 53 on July 26, 2012. A day after complaining of stomach pain, Samson Kimobwa died at age 57 in a Nairobi hospital on January 16, 2013. Bonnie Robinson died from Alzheimer's disease complications at age 67 on August 7, 2014. Sam Bell died at age 88 on June 27, 2016. Miruts Yifter died from respiratory problems at age 72 on December 22, 2016.

Nearly a decade removed from serious running, honors continued to come Craig's way. He was nominated for the US Distance Running Hall of Fame in 2000, but wasn't elected until 2001 in a class that included Bill Dellinger, Fred Lebow and 1992 Olympic 10K bronze medalist Lynn Jennings. "I was happy to be in that hall of fame and be there with guys who had been great sources of inspiration to me," said Craig, referring to Billy Mills, Steve Prefontaine and Frank Shorter. In February of 2017, Craig was among 28 honorees in the University of Illinois' inaugural Athletics Hall of Fame class, which included Harold "Red" Grange and Dick Butkus.

All told, Craig is in six halls of fame. He entered his first, the Road Runners Club of America Hall of Fame, in 1984 as part of a six-member class that included Joan Benoit Samuelson, Kathrine Switzer, Bob Schul, Jacqueline Hansen and Clive Davies.

In 2011, Craig was inducted into the USA Track and Field Hall of Fame and the St. Louis Sports Hall of Fame. He was actually voted into the USATF Hall in 2010 when the induction ceremony was at Virginia Beach, Virginia, but he deferred his induction until 2011 when the ceremony was in St. Louis so his family and friends could conveniently attend. A video tribute recounting Craig's career highlights called him a "conundrum" because he could be described in one breath as being first and last, a reference to being the first and last American to win the World Cross Country Championship. The piece ended with Craig saying, "Whether I achieved the most that I had in me, the greatest potential, I'll never know. Maybe I could have done things a little bit differently. Looking back now, I think I accomplished more than most and less than a very few, and I guess I can live with that."

In a speech after the video, Craig thanked his parents and recognized his then–10-year-old daughter and his coaches, all of whom were in attendance. Also on hand were more than a dozen college teammates including two-time Olympian Mike Durkin. Craig concluded by telling the audience, "It's been a long time since I was with the front line of track and field like this. You all inspire me. Thank you for a few minutes in the sun again. I appreciate it."

Impacting Others

Like George Bailey in the movie *It's a Wonderful Life*, Craig was initially unaware of the impact he had on others. Every year a few of those influenced by his successes let him know how much he meant to them. That interaction between Craig and his fans increased thanks to Facebook. One fan e-mailed Craig in 2009, "Even when we were teenagers, you made me want to utilize my talents to the best of my ability. That still holds true today."

The 2011 July/August issue of *Running Times* included a story about Rudy Chapa, Carey Pinkowski and Tim Keough, the first high school teammates to break nine minutes for two miles in the same year. They accomplished the feat in 1975 at Hammond, Indiana. They cited Craig as their inspiration. Keough told writer Jim Ferstle, "It wasn't Prefontaine or Shorter or any of those guys that were as much of an influence. Virgin was one of us. He was our age. He was from the Midwest. Somebody we could relate to."

As decades blinked by, Craig reconnected with fellow runners such as Henry Rono on Facebook. Craig continued to follow national news about professional, collegiate and high school track from his home near Lebanon, where as of 2017 he'd lived for 56 of his first 61 years. He worked as a freelance television broadcaster, a professional speaker and a consultant to those seeking custom coaching.

Craig's a frequent spectator at the Olympic Trials and other major meets including Illinois' annual state high school cross country meet at Peoria's Detweiller Park. Since 1972, the state's best boys have ventured to the tree-lined park on the banks of the Illinois River. America's first and last World Cross Country Champion, a man whose optimism went the distance, made a mark there that stood the test of time.

Acknowledgments

*"After talent is analyzed to the nth degree,
some mystery remains."*

— Randy Sharer

The seed for this book was planted in 1973. My eighth-grade social studies teacher at Lyndon (Illinois) Junior High School, Tom Rentschler, a man who also served as a high school assistant track coach, returned from the Illinois state track meet raving about the great Craig Virgin, who'd nearly broken Steve Prefontaine's national high school two-mile record. That seed lay dormant until 2001 when I interviewed Craig after a road race near Hudson, Illinois, in my capacity as a sportswriter for the Bloomington (Illinois) *Pantagraph* newspaper. Near the end of our conversation, I asked if he'd met Prefontaine. Craig told the story of his one and only encounter with the legendary University of Oregon runner after the 1973 NCAA cross country meet in a pool hall in Spokane, Washington. That anecdote made me want to know more about Craig's long career among America's distance-running elite.

I didn't act on my curiosity until the winter of 2008, when I started to formulate a plan to pitch a book idea to Craig. The first step was learning, to my surprise, that such a book hadn't already been written. I pulled the trigger a year later and he agreed to what became more than 100 hours of interviews. Most of our discussions were done on cell phones as he was driving.

I owe much gratitude to the hundreds of newspaper and magazine writers who chronicled Craig's career. I am lucky track received greater coverage in Craig's heyday than it does now. He was fortunate in high school to be covered by the late Bob Emig of the now-defunct *Metro-East Journal* based in East St. Louis. Emig's writing leaves no doubt he appreciated Craig's rare talent. Emig kept close tabs on Craig's career and made frequent calls to *Track & Field News* to put Craig's exploits into a national perspective in the days before the Internet. Emig was fortunate to have two quote machines to deal with in Craig and Lebanon High School coach Hank Feldt.

No one covered Craig's high school career more extensively than the late Bob Emig, who wrote for the now-defunct *Metro-East Journal*.

Craig was blessed again in college to have track enthusiast David Woods on the sports staff of the *Champaign News-Gazette*. A sportswriter for the *Indianapolis Star* in 2017, Woods brings perspective, heart and soul to the mountain of statistics that is track and field. If—heaven forbid—I'd died prior to this book's completion, Woods would've been asked to finish this venture. He once told me, "I think I was always interested in doing a Craig Virgin biography, but just never really had the time."

Like other "big-name" stars of track, Craig owes part of his fame to the journalists who covered his career. Few wrote more insightfully about Craig than David Woods.

Among the greatest joys in writing this book were the 52 interviews I did with Craig's teammates, rivals, coaches, parents and siblings and others familiar with his career. Feldt and former University of Illinois coach Gary Wieneke were eager to discuss their greatest athlete. Legends such as Bill Rodgers, Rod Dixon, Nick Rose, Herb Lindsay, Greg Meyer, Matt Centrowitz, Robbie Perkins and George Malley were among many who were generous with their time. Almost every interviewee ended our conversation with the request I call again if I had more questions.

Although there wasn't room for all their stories, I am grateful to the following people: George Hirsch, Ollan Cassell, Mike Durkin, Dave Walters, Jeff Cox, Gary Mumaw, Mark Avery, Dave Brooks, Rich Brooks, Bill Fritz, Mike Bridges, Jeff Jirele, Les Myers, Rob Mango, Jim Eicken, Rich Youngs, Al Carius, Joe Newton, Murray Sanford, Joe Douglas, Dick Conley, Dr. David Martin, Dr. Jim Rehberger, Dave Merrick, Tom Graves, Stephen Pifer, Brent McLain, Lucian Rosa, Don Kopriva, Loren Tate, June Wieneke, Rod Cardinal, Vernon Virgin, Lorna Lee Virgin, Brent Virgin and Vicki (Virgin) Glodo.

Among those I owe special thanks to is my wife, Marie Bosché, whose attention to detail is world class. Her career cataloguing music at Illinois State University's Milner Library made her a marvel at sifting through mountains of minutiae and then making sense of it. Her lifetime of book reading, especially murder mysteries, surely contributed to her editing skills. This book would've never left the launching pad without the encouragement of Marie and our daughter, Molly. Marie's late sister, Joanne, who was among Craig's many fans, was instrumental in this book's production.

My second-string editor, Dennis Cler, was first string in terms of the reader I thought would most enjoy this book. He loves sports. He loves books. He already knew a lot about Craig's career and could notice if something was amiss. If Dennis didn't like something I wrote, I knew a change was needed. His constructive criticism and positive energy kept this project moving when it was in danger of stalling.

Randy Sharer began work as a sports journalist
for the *Pantagraph* newspaper in Bloomington,
Illinois, in 1981. He won awards from the Illinois
Associated Press Editors Association and the Illinois
Press Association. A graduate of Illinois Wesleyan
University, he wrote "The History of the Meet: A Year
by Year Look at Every State Meet" for the Illinois
High School Association's 1994 Commemorative
Program for the 100th boys state track and field meet.
He and his wife, Marie, reside in Normal, Illinois.
(Photo by David Proeber)

Craig Virgin's race results

Date	Meet/Location	Distance	Place	Time	Margin	Record	Winner or runner-up
8-?-69	Mascoutah Dual	2.75M	1st	16:20			Roy Alexander
9-?-69	Okawville Dual	2.6M	1st	14:46			Roy Alexander
9-?-69	Okawville-Marissa Triangular	2.75M	3rd				Gary Pechenio
9-?-69	Breese Mater Dei Dual		1st	10:56			Chris Haefner
9-?-69	Highland St. Paul Dual	2.75M	1st	15:46			Mark Bellm
9-?-69	O'Fallon-St. Henry Triangular	2.75M	1st	15:36			Chris Haefner
9-?-69	New Athens-St. Henry Triangular	2.5M	1st	13:00			Chris Haefner
10-?-69	At Okawville District	2.63M	4th				Gary Pechenio
11-?-69	At Centralia Sectional	2.67M	10th				Bill Miller
4-?-70	At Mascoutah	2M	2nd	10:07	-:07.0		Brad Cochran
?-?-70	Unknown meet	2M		10:21.1			
?-?-70	Unknown meet	2M		10:01.0			
?-?-70	Unknown meet	2M		9:58.4			
5-?-70	Cahokia Conference Meet at Mascoutah	2M	1st	10:01.0		Meet Record	Nicholson
5-9-70	At Alton District	2M	4th	9:45.3			
5-23-70	State Meet at Champaign	2M	7th	9:31.9	-:33.0		David Merrick
8-29-70	Highland St. Paul Dual	2.55M	1st	13:53.1		Course Record	
9-1-70	Mascoutah Dual	2.5M	1st	12:51		Course Record	
9-?-70	Dual at Lebanon	2.72M	1st	14:29		Course Record	
9-13-70	Columbia Invitational	2.75M	1st	13:08	:12.0	Course Record	Randy Halleran
9-16-70	At Highland St. Paul Invitational	2.55M	1st	12:48		Course Record	
9-23-70	Triad Invitational	2.75M	1st	13:42		Course Record	Paul Reynolds
9-25-70	Lebanon Triangular	2.75M	1st	13:59		Course Record	Mark Grinter
9-28-70	Cahokia Conference Meet at Waterloo	2.7M	1st	14:09	:50.0	Course Record	Randy Halleran
9-29-70	St. Henry-Wesclin Triangular	2.75M	1st	14:12		Course Record	Dana Frisby
10-2-70	At Flora Invitational	2.75M	1st	12:43.6		Course Record	Randy Halleran
10-5-70	St. Clair County Meet at Mascoutah	2.6M	1st	12:17	:26.0	Course Record	Bill Norton
10-9-70	At Waterloo Invitational	2.7M	1st	13:55.4		Course Record	Bill Norton
10-12-70	Columbia Dual	2.75M	1st	13:00		Course Record	Roy Alexander
10-27-70	At Okawville District	2.6M	1st	12:39		Course Record	Bill Norton
10-31-70	At Centralia Sectional	2.75M	1st	13:49	:25.0		Charles Simpson
11-7-70	State Meet at Peoria	2.67M	6th	13:04	-:26.4		David Merrick
2-6-71	At Mattoon Road Race	10M	4th	50:11	-29.0		Oscar W. Moore Jr.
2-12-71	Indoor Meet at St. Louis Armory	DMR	3rd				
2-21-71	Central AAU Indoor at Champaign	2M	5th	9:14.5	-30.8		David Merrick
2-21-71	Central AAU Indoor at Champaign	1M	1st	4:25.0			
3-6-71	Ill. Track Club Open Indoor at Champaign	2M	3rd heat	9:05.4	-:09.0		Michael Cassady
3-6-71	Ill. Track Club Open Indoor at Champaign	1M	1st heat	4:24.0	:01.2		Shove
4-3-71	At Alton Relays	2M	1st	9:16.7	:05.0		Don Overton
4-11-71	Mineral Area Meet at Cahokia	2M	1st	9:17.9	:36.0	Meet Record	Bob Runge
4-11-71	Mineral Area Meet at Cahokia	880	6th	2:05.4	-:07.8		Wesley Wright
4-24-71	Orphan Relays at Centralia	2M	2nd	9:12.6	-:21.0	Nat. age 15	David Merrick
4-28-71	St. Clair County Meet at East St. Louis	2M	1st	9:19.8	:31.2	Meet Record	Bill Norton
4-28-71	St. Clair County Meet at East St. Louis	1M	1st	4:32.5			
5-2-71	At Cahokia Invitational	2M	1st	9:11.6	:39.4	MR, Nat. age 15	Bill Norton
5-2-71	At Cahokia Invitational	1M	1st	4:28.4	:09.7	Meet Record	Pat Cook
5-?-71	Unknown meet	1M	1st	4:21.3			
5-5-71	At Alton District	2M	1st	9:11.4		Nat. age 15	
5-5-71	At Alton District	1M	2nd	4:23.1	-:00.1		Art Andrew
5-23-71	Meet of Champions at Carbondale	2M	1st	9:02.6		MR, Nat. age 15	
5-23-71	Meet of Champions at Carbondale	1M	1st	4:26.6			Mike Bridges
5-29-71	State Meet at Champaign	2M	2nd	8:57.3	-:08.4	Nat. age 15	David Merrick
6-5-71	Midwest Classic at Mexico, MO	1M	1st	4:19.8		Personal Record	
6-5-71	Midwest Classic at Mexico, MO	2M	1st	9:18.8		Meet Record	
?-?-71	Ozark AAU at Edwardsville	10M		54:21			
9-2-71	At Okawville Dual	3M	1st	14:15			

Date	Meet/Location	Distance	Place	Time	Margin	Record	Winner or runner-up
9-7-71	At Highland with O'Fallon	2.75M	1st	13:26		Course Record	John Wertz
9-9-71	Red Bud and Trenton Wesclin at Lebanon	2.95M	1st	14:40		Course Record	John Wertz
9-11-71	At Columbia Invitational	2.9M	1st	14:43		Course Record	Charles Simpson
9-13-71	At Marissa with New Athens	3M	1st	14:58			
9-15-71	At Highland St. Paul Invitational	2.6M	1st	12:16	:45	Course Record	Charles Simpson
9-18-71	Trico Invitational at Campbell Hill	2.7M	1st	12:50		Course Record	Charles Simpson
9-20-71	At New Athens	2.9M	1st	13:36			
9-22-71	At St. Jacob Triad Invitational	2.7M	1st	12:19		Course Record	Charles Simpson
9-25-71	At Edwardsville Invitational	3M	1st	14:47	1:15	Course Record	Ed White
9-28-71	Cahokia Conference Meet at Columbia	2.9M	1st	14:19	1:57	Course Record	John Wertz
9-29-71	At St. Henry	2.5M	1st	11:30			
10-2-71	At Flora Invitational	2.9M	1st	13:14		Course Record	
10-5-71	St. Clair County at Mascoutah	2.8M	1st	14:00	1:03	Course Record	Roger Fulton
10-8-71	At Waterloo Invitational	2.8M	1st	13:32	1:13	Course Record	Ed White
10-12-71	At Centralia Triangular	3M	1st	14:47.3	1:11	Course Record	Charles Simpson
10-13-71	St. Henry and Okawville at Lebanon	2.95M	1st	14:12			
10-16-71	At Mattoon Invitational	2.8M	1st	12:41	:32		Larry Gnapp
10-19-71	At Columbia	2.9M	1st	13:54		Course Record	
10-21-71	At Red Bud	2.7M	1st	13:38		Course Record	
10-26-71	At Marissa District	2.9M	1st	13:50	1:13	Course Record	Ed White
10-30-71	At Centralia Sectional	3M	1st	15:00	:48	Course Record	Paul Reynolds
11-6-71	State Meet at Peoria	3M	1st	13:59.3	:29.3	Course Record	Lee Erickson
?-?-72?	AAU Meet at Edwardsville	4M	1st	19:17.6			Mike Wertz
2-12-72	AAU Indoor at Champaign	2M		8:55.5			
2-12-72	AAU Indoor at Champaign	1M		4:13.3			
?-?-72	At Champaign Indoor	1M		4:14.5			
?-?-72	WIU Indoor at Macomb	1M	1st	4:18			
?-?-72	EIU Indoor at Charleston	1M	1st	4:17.7			
3-4-72	At Champaign Indoor	2M	1st	8:54.1		Personal Record	
3-4-72	At Champaign Indoor	1M	3rd	4:14.6			
3-11-72	At Charleston Indoor	1M	1st	4:17.7			
3-26-72	At Oak Park Relays	1M	2nd	4:17.7	-:04.0		Larry Gnapp
4-1-72	At Alton Relays	2M	1st	9:07.6			Mark Kimball
4-9-72	Mineral Area	2M	1st	9:14.5		Meet Record	
4-9-72	Mineral Area	1M	1st	4:27.5			
4-13-72	Dupo Quad	880	1st	1:58.6			
4-13-72	Dupo Quad	440	1st				
4-22-72	At Mattoon Invitational	2M	1st	9:13.2		Meet Record	
4-22-72	At Mattoon Invitational	1M	1st	4:15.5		Meet Record	
4-25-72	St. Clair County Meet	2M	1st	9:00.4		Meet Record	Doug Sherry
4-25-72	St. Clair County Meet	1M	1st	4:18.4		Meet Record	Wesley Wright
5-1-72	At East St. Louis Relays	2M	1st	9:04.6		Meet Record	
5-1-72	At East St. Louis Relays	Relay 1M		4:17			
5-2-72	At O'Fallon Relays	2M	1st	8:55.1		Outdoor PR	
5-5-72	Orphan Relays at Centralia	2M	1st	8:56.6			
5-20-72	At Highland District	2M	1st	9:05.6		Meet Record	
5-20-72	At Highland District	1M	1st	4:16.5		Meet Record	
5-23-72	Meet of Champions at Carbondale	2M	1st	9:01.1	:41.9	Meet Record	Paul Reynolds
5-23-72	Meet of Champions at Carbondale	1M	1st	4:14.8	:00.5	Meet Record	Stan Vannier
5-25-72	State Meet at Charleston (prelims)	1M	1st	4:13.2			
5-26-72	State Meet at Charleston	2M	1st	8:51.9	:17.6	Nat. age 16	Frank Flores
5-26-72	State Meet at Charleston	1M	1st	4:09.2	:01.7		Jim Hurt
6-8-72	Top 10 Meet at Dolton	1M	1st	4:09.8	:01.9		Gary Mandehr
6-11-72	Central AAU at Chicago	3M	1st	13:49.2		MR, Nat. age 16 Junior Class	
6-24-72	National AAU Jr. Meet at Lakewood, CO	3M	2nd	14:10.8	-:02.4		Tony Sandoval
?-?-72		3M		13:44.6		Nat.age 16,Jr.Class	
7-8-72	Ozark AAU at Florissant, MO	5K	1st	14:12.3		World age 16	
7-29-72	USA USSR Dual at Sacramento	5K	3rd	14:14.6	-:01.0		Vladimir Zatonsky

Date	Meet/Location	Distance	Place	Time	Margin	Record	Winner or runner-up
8-31-72	Highland Triangular	2.55M	1st	12:00		Course Record	
9-1-72	Wesclin-Highland St. Paul Triangular	3M	1st	14:15		Course Record	
9-5-72	At O'Fallon with Highland		1st			Course Record	
9-7-72	At Edwardsville Dual	2.75M	1st	13:26		Course Record	
9-9-72	At Columbia Invitational	2.9M	1st	13:59	1:00	Course Record	Dana Hiserote
9-11-72	Marissa and New Athens at Lebanon					Course Record	
9-13-72	At Highland St. Paul Invitational					Course Record	
9-16-72	At Belleville West Invitational	2.8M	1st			Course Record	
9-18-72	At Mascoutah with Belleville East					Course Record	
9-20-72	At St. Jacob Triad Invitational	2.7M	1st	12:36	:55.0	Course Record	Stan Vannier
9-23-72	At Edwardsville Invitational		1st	13:36		Course Record	Alton Davis
9-26-72	Cahokia Conference Meet at Waterloo	2.8M	1st	13:32.6			Tom Bartsokas
9-27-72	St. Henry at Lebanon	3M	1st	14:07			
9-30-72	At Flora Invitational	3M	1st	14:03	:56	Course Record	Stan Vannier
10-3-72	St. Clair County Meet at Mascoutah	2.8M	1st	13:04		New Course	Tom Bartsokas
10-6-72	At Waterloo Invitational	2.8M	1st	13:25.7		Course Record	Tom Barisokas
10-10-72	At Columbia with Centralia	2.8M	1st	13:39		Course Record	
10-12-72	Highland Dual at Lebanon	3M	1st	16:06			John Wertz
10-14-72	At Mattoon Invitational	2.8M	1st	12:37.3	:25.6	Course Record	John Unger
10-16-72	St. Jacob Triad Dual at Lebanon		1st	14:48			
10-18-72	At Marissa Dual						
10-20-72	Red Bud and New Athens at Lebanon	3M	1st	14:15		Course Record	
10-24-72	Lebanon District	3M	1st	14:08.3	:59.7	New Course	Stan Vannier
10-28-72	At Centralia Sectional	3M	1st	14:59.1	:34.0	Course Record	Stan Vannier
11-4-72	State Meet at Peoria	3M	1st	13:50.6	:29.4	Course Record	Stan Vannier
11-?-72	Road Race at SIU Edwardsville	6M	1st				
11-25-72	National AAU Cross Country at Chicago	10K	12th	31:13	-31.0		Frank Shorter
11-?-72	At Alton Road Race	10M	4th	50:20.0			
?-?-72	At St. Jacob Triad AAU	3M	1st	14:42			Paul Reynolds
2-11-73	AAU Indoor at Champaign	2M	1st	8:50.8			
2-11-73	AAU Indoor at Champaign	1M	1st	4:12.0			
2-23-73	AAU Indoor Nationals at New York City	3M	10th	13:50.0	-:42.8		Tracy Smith
3-3-73	AAU Indoor at Champaign	2M	1st	8:45.6			
3-3-73	AAU Indoor at Champaign	1M	1st	4:07.9			Lee LeBadie
3-16-73	Sumner Relays at St. Louis	DMR 1M		4:26			
3-24-73	EIU Indoor at Charleston	1M	1st	4:18.5			
3-24-73	EIU Indoor at Charleston	880 yd.	1st	1:57.6			
3-29-73	At Dupo	880		1:59.2			
3-29-73	At Dupo	440		54.1			
3-29-73	At Dupo	440R		55.1			
3-31-73	At Oak Park Relays	1M	2nd	4:15.5	-:02.1		Bill Fritz
4-5-73	At O'Fallon with Columbia	880		1:59.1			
4-5-73	At O'Fallon with Columbia	Mile Relay		52.7			
4-7-73	At Alton Relays	2M	1st	8:50.4		Meet Record	
4-7-73	At Alton Relays	DMR 1M		4:17			
4-17-73	At O'Fallon with East St.Louis Assumption	880 yd.	1st	1:58.1			
4-17-73	At O'Fallon with East St.Louis Assumption	1M	1st	4:15.8			
4-24-73	St. Clair County at Belleville East	2M	1st	8:55.6		Meet Record	
4-24-73	St. Clair County at Belleville East	1M	1st	4:16.6		Meet Record	
4-25-73	At Highland St. Paul with Trenton Wesclin	880	1st	1:56.8		Personal Record	
4-25-73	At Highland St. Paul with Trenton Wesclin	1M	1st	4:14.5			
4-28-73	At Granite City Invitational	2M	1st	8:59.0	:44.1		Howard Bryant
4-28-73	At Granite City Invitational	1M	1st	4:15.3	:13.6		Howard Bryant
5-2-73	At O'Fallon Relays	2M	1st	9:24.1			Tom Bartsokas
5-2-73	At O'Fallon Relays	DMR 1M	1st	4:15.6		Meet Record, 7:41	
5-3-73	Cahokia Conference Meet at Waterloo	1M	1st	4:27.9			
5-3-73	Cahokia Conference Meet at Waterloo	880	1st	2:02.1			
5-5-73	Orphan Relays at Centralia	2M	1st	8:46.5	:31.8	Meet Record	Stan Vannier

Date	Meet/Location	Distance	Place	Time	Margin	Record	Winner or runner-up
5-5-73	Orphan Relays at Centralia	DMR 1M	1st	4:11.8		MR 10:22.4	
5-10-73	At Roxana Relays	Spt.Medley	1st	1:55		Meet Record	
5-10-73	At Roxana Relays	DMR 1M	1st	4:13		Meet Record	
5-15-73	At Cahokia Invitational	2M	1st	8:53.9		Meet Record	
5-15-73	At Cahokia Invitational	1M	1st	4:13.0	:07.2	Meet Record	Stan Vannier
5-18-73	At Highland District	2M	1st	8:53.6			
5-18-73	At Highland District	1M	1st	4:10.9			
5-21-73	Meet of Champions at Carbondale	2M	1st	8:48.6			
5-21-73	Meet of Champions at Carbondale	1M	1st	4:08.5			
5-25-73	State Meet at Champaign	1M prelim	1st	4:10.5	:01.8		Bill Fritz
5-26-73	State Meet at Champaign	2M	1st	8:42.6	:23.4	Meet Record	Jim Eicken
5-26-73	State Meet at Champaign	1M	2nd	4:12.2	-:00.8		Bill Fritz
6-2-73	Top Ten Meet at Dolton	1M	1st	4:05.5			
6-9-73	Int. Prep Invitational at Mount Prospect	2M	1st	8:40.9	:16.9	US Prep Record	Matt Centrowitz
6-23-73	AAU National Juniors at Gainesville, FL	3M	1st	13:36.8	:10.6	Age 17 WR	Bob Grubbs
7-4-73	Freedom Mile at Champaign	1M	5th	4:06.1	-:07.6		Rick Wohlhuter
7-7-73	At Florissant Valley Track Club Meet	1500	1st	3:50.0			
7-14-73	At Heidenheim, West Germany	3K	3rd	8:10.2	-:01.8		Hans-Jurgen Orthmann
7-20-73	At Warsaw, Poland	3K	1st	8:16.0	:04.2		Bob Grubbs
7-28-73	At Odessa, Russia	5K	1st	13:58.2	:03.2	US Age 17 Record	Enn Sellick
9-1-73	Alumni Cross Country at Savoy	4M	1st	19:44.2	:46.8		Rick Gross
9-8-73	Illinois State University Dual at Normal	5M	1st	24:47.5	:17.5	Course Record	Randy Icenogle
9-15-73	SIU Dual at Carbondale	6M	1st	29:44.6	:26.4	Course Record	Gerry Craig
9-29-73	Dual at Missouri	5M	1st	25:14.4	:11.6		Charlie McMullen
10-6-73	Iowa at Savoy	6M	1st	29:15.8	:37.2	Course Record	Mike Durkin
10-13-73	Indiana and Miami of Ohio at Savoy	6M	1st	29:08.7	:09.3	Course Record	Pat Mandera
10-27-73	Illinois Intercollegiates at Normal	5M	1st	23:49	:15.0	Course Record	Mike Durkin
11-3-73	Big Ten Meet at Savoy	6M	1st	28:30.8	:04.2	Course Record	Pat Mandera
11-10-73	NCAA District at East Lansing, MI	10K	3rd	29:22	-:13.7		Gordon Minty
11-19-73	NCAA Meet at Spokane, WA	6M	10th	28:47.8	-:33.0		Steve Prefontaine
11-24-73	AAU Nationals at Gainesville, FL	10K	DNF				Frank Shorter
1-26-74	Illinois Invitational at Champaign	2M	3rd	8:59.0	-:04.3		Dave Walters
2-1-74	Purdue Dual at West Lafayette, IN	2M	2nd	9:04.8	-:01.7		Rich Brooks
5-4-74	USTFF Classic at Champaign	6M	1st	29:20.6	:14.6		Mark Gibbons
5-11-74	Illinois Intercollegiates at Champaign	3M	2nd	13:57.8	-:08.3		Dave Hill
5-17-74	Big Ten Meet at Ann Arbor, MI	6M	2nd	28:10.7	-:09.3		Pat Mandera
5-25-74	Stagg Relays at Chicago	5K	1st	14:14.3	:21.9	Meet Record	Tom Schumacher
6-7-74	NCAA Meet at Austin, TX	6M	DNF				John Ngeno
8-?-74	At Belleville Cross Country	3M	1st	15:01			
9-7-74	Preseason Time Trial at Savoy	4M	1st	18:51	:39		Bill Fritz
9-14-74	SIU Dual at Carbondale	5M	1st	24:45.6	:40.4		Jack St. John
9-21-74	Alumni Cross Country at Savoy	4M	1st	19:05.5	:16.5		Lucian Rosa
9-28-74	Missouri at Savoy	6M	1st	29:00.6	:57.4		Mike Durkin
10-5-74	At Iowa with Drake	6M	1st	29:10	:58	Course Record	Bill Fritz
10-12-74	At Indiana with Miami of Ohio & Minn.	6M	1st	29:46.9	:16.1		Tom Schumacher
10-26-74	Illinois Intercollegiates at Macomb	5M	1st	24:04	:53	Course Record	Mike Durkin
11-2-74	Wisconsin at Savoy	6M	1st	28:35.3	1:03.7		Tom Schumacher
11-9-74	Big Ten Meet at Ann Arbor, MI	6M	1st	29:11.4	:34.4		Greg Meyer
11-16-74	NCAA District at Madison, WI	6M	1st	28:42.8	:35	Course Record	Tom Hollander
11-25-74	NCAA Meet at Bloomington, IN	6M	12th	30:15.84	-:53.84		Nick Rose
1-25-75	Illinois Invitational at Champaign	2M	1st	8:42.0	:26.4	Meet Record	Dave Walters
1-31-75	Northwestern at Champaign	1M	1st	4:07.9	:05.2		Rick Brooks
2-7-75	Illinois Intercollegiates at Champaign	DMR 1M	1st	4:08.8		Meet Record/SR	
2-8-75	Illinois Intercollegiates at Champaign	1M	1st	4:03.2	:01.5	Meet Record/PR	Rich Brooks
2-8-75	Illinois Intercollegiates at Champaign	2M	1st	8:48.6	:12.6	Meet Record	Jerry George
2-15-75	Indiana and Wisconsin at Champaign	2M	2nd	8:38.4	-:03.8	School Record	Mark Johnson
2-21-75	USTFF Classic at Champaign	2M	2nd	8:41.0	-:06.6		Nick Rose
2 22 75	USTFF Classic at Champaign	DMR 1M	1st	4:06.5		Meet Record/SR	

Date	Meet/Location	Distance	Place	Time	Margin	Record	Winner or runner-up
3-1-75	Iowa at Champaign	1M	1st	4:09.3	:00.5		Rich Brooks
3-7-75	Big Ten Meet at Bloomington, IN	1M prelim	2nd	4:11.7	-:00.1		Dan Lyndgaard
3-7-75	Big Ten Meet at Bloomington, IN	2M	4th	8:55.2	-:10.4		Herb Lindsay
3-8-75	Big Ten Meet at Bloomington, IN	1M	6th	4:10.3	-:04.8		Mike Durkin
4-25-75	Drake Relays at Des Moines, Iowa	4M Relay	6th	4:09.0			Relay's time: 16:43.8
4-26-75	Drake Relays at Des Moines, Iowa	DMR 1M	3rd	4:13.5			Relay's time: 9:48.2
5-3-75	USTFF Classic at Champaign	3M	1st	13:41.6		Meet Record	Dan Cloeter
5-9-75	Illinois Intercollegiates at Charleston	6M	1st	28:10.0		Meet Record/SR	Dave Walters
5-17-75	Big Ten Meet at Iowa City, IA	3M	1st	13:34.7	:19.5		Dean Reinke
5-31-75	USTFF at Wichita, KS	3M	3rd	13:22.6	-:05.0	School Record	John Halberstadt
6-6-75	NCAA Meet at Provo, UT	6M	3rd	28:25.36	-:04.7		John Ngeno
6-14-75	Meet of Champions at Berkeley, CA	6M	1st	27:48.8	:13.2	School Record	Ted Casteneda
6-20-75	AAU Nationals at Eugene, OR	5K	4th	13:35.02	-:06.2		Marty Liquori
8-9-75	At Belleville Cross Country	3M	1st	14:04.5	:55.5		Chuck Korte
9-13-75	SIU Dual at Savoy	5M	1st	23:47.0	:57.0	Course Rec./SR	Jim Eicken
9-20-75	Alumni Cross Country at Savoy	4M	1st	19:09	:20		Ken Popejoy
9-27-75	Missouri Dual at Columbia, MO	5M	1st	23:49.4	1:02.6	Course Record	Mark Kimball
10-4-75	Drake Dual at Savoy	6M	1st	29:21	:01.0		Rich Brooks
10-11-75	Indiana, Minn., Miami of Ohio at Savoy	6M	1st	28:00.2	1:12.8	Course Record	Dean Reinke
10-25-75	Illinois Intercollegiates at Charleston	5M	1st	23:31	:30	Course Record	John St. John
11-8-75	Big Ten Meet at Madison, WI	5M	1st	23:04.5	:30.5	Course Record	Herb Lindsay
11-15-75	NCAA District at Bloomington, IN	6M	1st	29:18.5	:47.5	Course Record	Herb Lindsay
11-23-75	NCAA Meet at University Park, PA	6M	1st	28:23.3	:05.5	Course Record	Nick Rose
1-24-76	At San Francisco Examiner Games	2M	3rd	8:42.6	-:02.2		Ewald Bonzet
1-25-76	Illinois Invitational at Champaign	1M	1st	4:05.9	:02.8		Jeff Jirele
1-30-76	Millrose Games at New York City	5K	2nd	13:54.4	-:02.8		Greg Fredericks
1-31-76	Drake and W. Kentucky at Champaign	1M	4th	4:10.3	-:03.1		Chris Ridler
2-6-76	Illinois Intercollegiates at Champaign	DMR 1M	1st	4:05.9			
2-7-76	Illinois Intercollegiates at Champaign	1M	1st	4:04.0	:00.9		Mike Larson
2-14-76	Wisconsin Dual at Madison, WI	1M	2nd	4:03.7	-:00.7		Steve Lacy
2-14-76	Wisconsin Dual at Madison, WI	2M	1st	8:39.4	:04.8		Mark Johnson
2-21-76	At Indiana with Tennessee	1M	2nd	4:04.2	-:01.1		Steve Heidenreich
2-21-76	At Indiana with Tennessee	2M	1st	8:39.2			
2-27-76	USTFF Classic at Champaign	2M	2nd	8:32.4	-:00.8	Big 10 Record/SR	Nick Rose
2-28-76	USTFF Classic at Champaign	DMR 1M	1st	4:03.2			
3-5/6-76	Big Ten Meet at Madison, WI	2M	1st	8:39.1	:06.5	Meet Record	Herb Lindsay
3-5/6-76	Big Ten Meet at Madison, WI	1M prelim	3rd	4:09.8	-:00.5		Herb Lindsay
3-5/6-76	Big Ten Meet at Madison, WI	1M	3rd	4:05.9	-:01.2		Steve Lacy
3-12/13-76	NCAA Meet at Detroit	2M	2nd	8:33.71	-:02.80		Nick Rose
4-3-76	UCTC and Notre Dame at Champaign	3M	1st	13:39.2	:20.8	Meet Record	Bruce Fischer
4-10-76	SIU Dual at Champaign	1M	1st	4:02.8	:05.7	Personal Record	Jeff Jirele
4-10-76	SIU Dual at Champaign	3M	tie 1st	13:46.8			M. Avery, D. Walters
4-15/16-76	Kansas Relays at Lawrence, KS	1,500	6th	3:48.8	-:02.6		Francisco Morera
4-15/16-76	Kansas Relays at Lawrence, KS	DMR 1M	4th	4:02.4			
4-23-76	Drake Relays at Des Moines, Iowa	4M Relay	4th	4:01.7			
4-24-76	Drake Relays at Des Moines, Iowa	DMR 1M	6th	4:01.6		Personal Record	
5-1-76	Illinois Intercollegiates at Carbondale	5K	1st	13:53.2	:33.2	Meet Record	Mike Sawyer
5-8-76	USTFF Classic at Champaign	10K	1st	28:19.8	:53.6		Bruce Fischer
5-14/15-76	Big Ten Meet at Champaign	5K	1st	13:54.4	:15.9	Stadium Record	Herb Lindsay
5-28/29-76	USTFF Championships at Wichita, KS	5K	3rd	13:51.10	-:09.1		Frank Shorter
6-3/5-76	NCAA Meet at Philadelphia	10K	2nd	28:25.52	-:02.86		John Ngeno
6-19-76	Olympic Trials at Eugene, OR	10K prelim	2nd	28:33.6	-:00.0		Frank Shorter
6-22-76	Olympic Trials at Eugene, OR	10K	2nd	27:59.43	-:03.98	College Record	Frank Shorter
6-25-76	Olympic Trials at Eugene, OR	5K prelim	2nd	13:43.10	-:01.34		Dick Buerkle
7-12-76	Pre-Olympic Meet at Montreal	1K	6th	2:26	-:07		Mike Boit
7-14-76	Pre-Olympic Meet at Montreal	5K	3rd	13:35.3	-:10.9		Miruts Yifter
7-23-76	Olympic Games at Montreal	10K prelim	6th	28:30.22	-:08.15		Marc Smet
8-4-76	Bicentennial Classic at Philadelphia	2M	6th	8:25.3	-:08.2	Personal Record	Dick Quax

Date	Meet/Location	Distance	Place	Time	Margin	Record	Winner or runner-up
8-6-76	USSR Dual at College Park, MD	10K	1st	28:35.2	:15.4		Vladimir Myerkushin
8-8-76	At Philadelphia	2M		8:48			
8-15-76	At Belleville Cross Country	3M	1st	14:45.7	:10.0		Mike Ellington
9-11-76	SIU Dual at Carbondale	4M	1st	19:56	:22.0	Course Record	Mike Sawyer
9-18-76	Alumni Cross Country at Savoy	4M	1st	19:02	:23.0		Mike Larson
9-25-76	Missouri at Savoy	6M	1st	29:16.8	:00.2		Jim Eicken
10-9-76	Triangular at Oxford, OH	6M	1st	30:12.4	:26.6		Bill Foley
10-23-76	Illinois Intercollegiates at Edwardsville	5M	1st	24:21	:21.0	Course Record	Jim Eicken
11-6-76	Big Ten Meet at Glen Ellyn	5M	1st	23:16.7	:22.0		Herb Lindsay
11-13-76	NCAA District at Savoy	10K	1st	29:04.4	:16.6	Course Record	Herb Lindsay
11-22-76	NCAA Meet at Denton, TX	10K	3rd	28:26.53	-:19.93		Henry Rono
1-15-77	Sunkist Invitational at Los Angeles	2M	2nd	8:35.6	-:00.2		Duncan MacDonald
1-21-77	At Philadelphia Classic	2M	5th	8:44.6	-:04.4		Frank Shorter
1-22-77	Illinois Invitational at Champaign	1M	2nd	4:08.0	-:03.5		Jeff Jirele
1-28-77	Millrose Games at New York City	2M	3rd	8:44.8	-:03.4		Tony Staynings
2-4-77	Illinois Intercollegiates at Champaign	DMR 1M	1st	4:05.1		Meet Record	
2-5-77	Illinois Intercollegiates at Champaign	2M	1st	8:50.3	:00.1		Jim Eicken
2-5-77	Illinois Intercollegiates at Champaign	1M	1st	4:05.8	:03.2		Mike Bisase
2-12-77	Mason-Dixon Games at Louisville, KY	DMR 1M	2nd	4:07.8			
2-19-77	Indiana Dual at Champaign	2M	1st	8:37.5	:00.9		Dan Visscher
2-25/26-77	USTFF Classic at Champaign	1M	3rd	4:04.7	-:01.6		Tom Duits
3-4/5-77	Big Ten Meet at Ann Arbor, MI	3M	1st	13:28.2	1:08.41	School Record	Bill Donakowski
3-11/12-77	NCAA Meet at Detroit	3M	3rd	13:23.0	-:02.4	School Record	Luis Hernandez
4-9-77	Michigan and WIU at Champaign	5K	1st	14:12.8	:00.1		Jim Eicken
4-16-77	SIU Dual at Carbondale	3M	1st	13:32.5	:15.3	Meet Record	Jim Eicken
4-22-77	USTFF Classic at Champaign	5K	1st	13:46.9	:12.2	Meet Record	Tom Burleson
4-29/30-77	Drake Relays at Des Moines, Iowa	4M Relay	1st	4:04.9		Big 10 Record/SR	
4-29/30-77	Drake Relays at Des Moines, Iowa	DMR .75M	3rd	2:58.6			
4-29/30-77	Drake Relays at Des Moines, Iowa	1,500	3rd	3:48.3		Personal Record	
5-6-77	Illinois Intercollegiates at Naperville	10K	1st	28:32.6	1:20.1	Meet Record	Mark Avery
5-7-77	Illinois Intercollegiates at Naperville	5K	1st	14:05.1	:01.5		Jim Eicken
5-21-77	Big Ten Meet at Bloomington, IN	5K	1st	13:55.65	:11.88		Herb Lindsay
5-28-77	USTFF at Wichita, KS	5K	1st	13:49.17	:06.62	Meet Record	Ric Rojas
6-2-77	NCAA Meet at Champaign	5K prelim	2nd	13:53.18	-:01.40		Samson Kimobwa
6-3-77	NCAA Meet at Champaign	10K	2nd	28:22.48	-:12.21		Samson Kimobwa
6-4-77	NCAA Meet at Champaign	5K	4th	13:42.06	-:03.92		Joshua Kimeto
6-15-77	AAU Nationals at Los Angeles	10K	DNF				Frank Shorter
8-16-77	At Belleville Cross Country	3M	1st	14:13.8	:37.2		Mike Sawyer
9-5-77	Pre's Trail Run at Eugene, OR	6K	1st	17:38	:43.0		Dan Callahan
9-17-77	Alumni Cross Country at Savoy	4M	1st	19:38	:21.0		Charlie White
10-1-77	Garrie Franklin Mem. CC at Eugene, OR	10K	2nd	29:27	-:05.0		Alberto Salazar
10-22-77	USTFF CC at Madison, WI	10K	1st	28:31.2	:15.8		Jim Stintzi
11-13-77	Oregon Track Club 10K at Eugene, OR	10K	1st				
11-26-77	AAU National CC at Houston	10K	2nd	30:22.8	-:08.5		Nick Rose
2-24-78	USTFF Classic at Champaign	2M	2nd	8:37.1	-:01.5		Niall O'Shaughnessy
2-26-78	At St. Louis Olympiad Memorial	10K	1st	28:35.5	:06.5	Road PR	Jeff Wells
3-12-78	Run for the Shamrocks at Eugene, OR	10K	1st	28:02.6	:24.4	Short Course	Jim Crawford
3-25-78	World Cross Country at Glasgow, Scotland	7.5M	6th	39:54	-:29		John Treacy
4-1-78	Nike 10K at Long Beach, CA	10K	1st	29:11.9	:16.1		George Malley
5-6-78	Twilight Meet at Eugene, OR	10K	1st	28:19.4	:13.1		Jim Crawford
5-14-78	Maryland Classic at College Park, MD	5K	2nd	13:44.0	-:00.5		Jeff Wells
5-20-78	Tom Black Classic at Knoxville, TN	5K	1st	13:47.08	:01.1		
5-25-78	At Corvalis, OR	3K	1st	8:03.0	:04.6		Jeff Wells
5-25-78	At Corvalis, OR	1,500	4th	3:47.6	-:01.8	Personal Record	George Malley
5-31-78	Prefontaine Classic at Eugene, OR	5K	2nd	13:40.7	-:03.0		Marty Liquori
6-10-78	AAU Nationals at Los Angeles	10K	1st	28:14.9	:20.0		Garry Bjorklund
6-15-78	At Helsinki, Finland	5K	5th	13:34.09		Personal Record	Marti Vainio
6-19-78	At Lappeenranta, Finland	3K	1st	7:57.6		Personal Record	

Date	Meet/Location	Distance	Place	Time	Margin	Record	Winner or runner-up
6-24-78	At Kurotane, Finland	1,500	2nd	3:46.1	-:00.6	Personal Record	Phil Kane
6-25-78	At Saarijarvi, Finland	5K	1st	13:36.2	:07.7		Ismo Toukonen
6-29-78	World Games at Helsinki, Finland	10K	1st	27:57.1	:00.1	Personal Record	Jos Hermens
7-4-78	DN Galen at Stockholm, Sweden	5K	7th	13:25.41	-:09.3	Personal Record	Marty Liquori
7-9-78	At Gateshead, Great Britain	3K	6th	7:54.92		Personal Record	Rod Dixon
7-12-78	At Lausanne, Switzerland	5K	5th	13:34.82	-:10.0		Dave Fitzsimons
7-25-78	At Visby, Sweden	3K SC	2nd	8:52.1		Personal Record	
7-27-78	At Turku, Finland	5K	2nd	13:31.5	-:00.7		Marti Vainio
8-1-78	At Malmo, Sweden	3000	4th	7:51.96	-:03.4	Personal Record	John Treacy
8-3-78	At Oslo, Norway	5K	2nd	13:28.8	-:00.5		John Treacy
8-9-78	At Reykjavik, Iceland	1,500	6th	4:47.0			
8-11-78	At Copenhagen, Denmark	10K	2nd	29:52.4			
8-13-78	At Warsaw, Poland	5K	13th	13:41.5	-:14.4		Fyedolkin
8-18-78	At Brussels, Belgium	5K	15th	13:49.5	-:27.7		Rod Dixon
8-20-78	At Falmouth, MA	7.1M	3rd	32:55	-:22.0		Bill Rodgers
9-10-78	At Arcola, IL	10K	1st	31:15	:33.0		Bob Gutjahr
9-17-78	At Fort Wayne, IN	10K	1st	29:53.5	:42.5		Dan Cloeter
9-23-78	Diet Pepsi AAU Nationals at Purchase, NY	10K	10th	29:44	-1:07.7		Bill Rodgers
9-30-78	Alumni Cross Country at Savoy	4M	1st	18:56.2	:30-plus		Jim Eicken
10-14-78	At Kirkwood, MO	5M	1st	23:48	1:03.0		Steve Wilson
10-21-78	USTFF Cross Country at Madison, WI	10K	1st	29:42.7	:10.3		Steve Lacy
10-28-78	Charity Race at Champaign	10K		33:03			
11-11-78	Cross Country at Louisville, KY	10K	1st	30:45	:40		Mark Finucane
11-25-78	AAU National CC at Seattle	10K	3rd	29:56.6	-:20.7		Greg Meyer
12-31-78	Runners World Inv. at Los Altos, CA	5M	2nd	22:13	:00.01		Alberto Salazar
1-14-79	At San Diego Marathon	26.2M	1st	2:14:40	3:20.0	Course Record	Ben Wilson
1-27-79	At Bermuda International	10K	1st	29:12.6	:44.4		Garry Bjorklund
2-23-79	Illini Classic at Champaign	2M	2nd	8:34.16	-:03.36		Mark Muggleton
2-25-79	At St. Louis Track Club Road Race	10K	1st	28:58	:43.0		Tim Donovan
3-18-79	At Paris Cross Country	9K	1st	29:24	:26		Euan Robertson
3-25-79	World Cross County at Limerick, Ireland	12K	13th	38:05	-:45.0		John Treacy
4-1-79	Five Mills CC at San Vittore Olono, Italy	6M-plus	3rd	30:19	-:04.0		Leon Schotts
4-22-79	At Highland Lions Club Road Race	5M	1st	23:52	1:04.0		Jim McHugh
4-26-79	Penn Relays at Philadelphia	10K	1st	27:59.0	:12.3		Robbie Perkins
4-28-79	Trevira Twosome at New York City	10M	1st	46:32.7	1:04.0		Bill Rodgers
4-29-79	Gateway Arch Run at St. Louis	10K	1st	30:28			
5-19-79	MO KIDS Race at Kirkwood, MO	10K	1st				
5-19-79	Craig Virgin Olympic Day at Lebanon	10K	1st	33:00			
5-26-79	TFA-USA Meet at Wichita, KS	5K	1st	13:31.7		Stadium Record	Herb Lindsay
6-2-79	C-U Parks Road Race at Champaign	10K	1st	29:14.3			
6-9-79	Brooks at Berkeley, CA	3K	4th	7:48.2	-:05.2	Personal Record	Sydney Maree
6-10-79	At Golden Gate Bridge Road Race	10K	1st	30:00-plus			
6-17-79	AAU Nationals at Walnut, CA	10K	1st	27:39.4	:35.8	American Record	Ric Rojas
6-30-79	Brooks at Philadelphia	5K	2nd	13:23.6	-:02.6	Personal Record	Matt Centrowitz
7-4-79	Peachtree Road Race at Atlanta, GA	10K	1st	28:30.5	:24.1	Course Record	Mike Roche
7-7-79	Local track meet	1,500		3:47.7			
7-7-79	Local track meet	800		1:53.8			
7-7-79	Local track meet	2M		8:56.0			
7-17-79	At Oslo, Norway	2M	3rd	8:22.0	-:06.8	Personal Record	Rod Dixon
7-18-79	At Oslo, Norway	1,500	4th	3:45.7		Personal Record	
7-21-79	At Rieti, Italy	5K	2nd	13:26.4			Henry Rono
7-25-79	Paavo Nurmi Games at Turku, Finland	5K	2nd	13:27.2	-:03.5		Ralph King
7-27-79	Kauhajoki Games at Kauhajoki, Finland	1,500	2nd	3:46.0	-:00.2		
7-31-79	At Malmo, Sweden	5K	1st	13:23.4	:02.3		Gerald Barrett
8-8-79	At Gothenburg, Sweden	5K	3rd	13:23.3		Personal Record	Dave Fitzsimons
8-19-79	At Falmouth, MA	7.1M	1st	32:19.7	:08.0	Course Record	Herb Lindsay
8-24-79	World Cup II at Montreal	10K	2nd	27:59.6	:06.5		Miruts Yifter
9-3-79	Clay County Advocate-Press at Flora	10K	1st	30:58		Course Record	

Date	Meet/Location	Distance	Place	Time	Margin	Record	Winner or runner-up
9-8-79	At Arcola, IL	10K	1st	29:05	:25.0		Bob Gutjahr
9-15-79	Alumni Cross Country at Savoy	5M	1st	24:05.3	:04.2		Jim Flannery
9-29-79	Pepsi Road Race at Purchase, NY	10K	4th	28:48	-:13.0		Herb Lindsay
9-30-79	Natural Light Stadium Run at St. Louis	10K	1st	30:26			
10-6-79	Lebanon Fall Festival Footrace	4M	1st	19:07			
10-13-79	At Lafayette, LA	10K	1st	28:46			
10-24-79	At Alton, IL	10M		50:11			
10-28-79	Macy's Road Race at Kansas City, MO	10K	1st	29:23	:14.0		Charlie Gray
11-3-79	At Greenville (IL) Road Race	10K	1st	30:23			
11-10-79	At LaGrange (GA) Road Race	10K	1st	29:03		Course Record	
11-18-79	At Kankakee (IL) Road Race	10K	1st	29:04	:18.0		Dean Matthews
12-2-79	At Fukuoka, Japan Marathon	26.2M	17th	2:16:59	-6:24.0		Toshihiko Seko
1-4-80	At San Francisco Examiner Games	3K	3rd	8:01	-:01.4		James Munyala
1-19-80	World CC Trials at Eugene, OR	12K	1st	36:43.7	:24.0		Dan Dillon
1-26-80	At Bermuda International	10K	1st	29:17			
1-27-80	At New Orleans	Half Mar.	1st	1:02:31	-:14.7		Stan Mavis
2-3-80	At San Blas, Puerto Rico	Half Mar.	3rd	1:04:28.98	-:32.0		Miruts Yifter
2-15-80	Missouri Invitational at Columbia, MO	5K	1st	13:45.02		Indoor PR	
3-2-80	Bran Chex Road Race at St. Louis	10K	1st	29:37.7	:01.9		Don Kardong
3-9-80	World Cross County at Paris	11.59K	1st	37:01.1	:01.2		Hans-Jurgen Orthmann
3-16-80	Crescent City Classic at New Orleans	10K	1st	28:35	:30	Road PR	Bill Rodgers
3-30-80	3WE Run at Cleveland	11K	1st	32:00-plus			
4-12-80	Natural Light at San Diego	Half Mar.	1st	1:07:25	1:56		Ed Mendoza/D.Wilson
4-19-80	Illini Classic at Champaign	5K	1st	13:43.7			
4-20-80	College-Community Fun Run at Rolla, MO	5K	1st	15:22	:47.8		Denis Baumstark
4-27-80	Trevira Twosome at New York City	10M	2nd	46:30	-:30.2		Herb Lindsay
5-3-80	Diet Pepsi at Atlanta, GA	10K	1st	29:50	:48.0		Bob Varsha
5-10-80	MO KIDS Race at St. Louis	5M	1st	23:42			
5-18-80	Bay-to-Breakers at San Francisco	7.63M	1st	35:11.8	1:02.9	Course Record	John Andrews
6-1-80	Six Flags Road Race at Eureka, MO	10K	1st	30:24			
6-14-80	TAC Nationals at Walnut, CA	5K	3rd	13:35.65	-:02.04		Matt Centrowitz
6-24-80	Olympic Trials at Eugene, OR	10K	1st	27:45.61	:17.53	Meet Record	Greg Fredericks
7-4-80	Peachtree Road Race at Atlanta, GA	10K	1st	28:39.1	:40.0		George Malley
7-12-80	At Stuttgart, West Germany	5K	2nd	13:19.62	-:00.38	Personal Record	Kip Rono
7-15-80	At Oslo, Norway	5K	5th	13:19.1	-:01.2	Personal Record	Nat Muir
7-17-80	Sport 2000 at Paris	10K	1st	27:29.16	:08.7	American Record	Fernando Mamede
8-8-80	At London	5K	11th	13:53.7	-:13.1		John Treacy
8-23-80	At Atlanta, GA Road Race	8M		49:10			
8-24-80	At Long Island, NY Road Race	5M		23:41			
9-1-80	At Baton Rouge, LA Road Race	10K	2nd	29:48	-1:03.0		Rod Dixon
9-7-80	At Cleveland Road Race	Half Mar.	1st	1:04:54	:31.0		Wally Rodriguez
9-20-80	Alumni Cross Country at Savoy	10K	1st	31:23			
9-27-80	At Lynchburg, VA Road Race	10M	6th	48:21	-1:30		Rod Dixon
10-4-80	Lebanon Fall Festival Footrace	4M	1st	19:18			
10-5-80	Natural Light Stadium Run at St. Louis	10K	3rd	30:18		Handicap Race	
11-8-80	At LaGrange, GA Road Race	10K	1st	29:28	1:17.0		Bruce Skiles
11-15-80	Wendy's Road Race at Bowling Green, KY	10K	2nd	28:27.1	-:11.3	Road PR	Nick Rose
11-22-80	NYRRCA International CC at Belmont, NY	12K	1st	35:43.9	:07.1		Dan Dillon
11-27-80	At Port Washington, NY	5M	1st	23:27.4	:18.6		John Gregorek
12-13-80	Local road race	10K		32:00			
1-4-81	At Nancy, France International CC	11.43K	1st	31:57.72	:11.95		Alex Gonzalez
1-18-81	Bran Chex at Clearwater, FL	10K	1st	29:31.6	2:39.4		Bob Doughty
1-25-81	Miller Light Super Run at New Orleans	10K	1st	28:45	:26.0		Kent McDonald
1-31-81	Sunshine Classic at Gainesville, FL	10K	1st	29:03	:20.9	Course Record	Randy Thomas
2-6-81	Millrose Games at New York City	5K	7th	13:38.3	-:18.0	Indoor PR	Suleiman Nyambui
2-22-81	At Kiawah Island (SC)	10M	1st	47:33.6			
2-28-81	Illini Classic at Champaign	2M	1st	8:30.0		Indoor PR	Hans Koeleman
3-7-81	World CC Trials at Louisville, KY	12K	1st	36:09.8	:00.2		Nick Rose

Date	Meet/Location	Distance	Place	Time	Margin	Record	Winner or runner-up
3-22-81	Bran Chex/YMCA at Phoenix	10K	1st	29:13			
3-28-81	World Cross Country at Madrid	12K	1st	35:05	:02.0		Mohammed Kedir
4-5-81	Crescent City Classic at New Orleans	10K	2nd	28:06	:11.0	American Record	Mike Musyoki
4-20-81	At Boston Marathon	26.2M	2nd	2:10:27	-:1:01.0		Toshihiko Seko
4-26-81	Trevira Twosome at New York City	10M		1:00:40	-14:32.0		Nick Rose
5-17-81	Bay-to-Breakers at San Francisco	7.63M	1st	35:07.8	:36	Course Record	John Glidewell
5-23-81	Bran Chex/YMCA at Memphis, TN	10K	1st	29:17	2:51.0		John Mohundro
5-31-81	At Chicago Orange Crush Road Race	10K					runners went off course
6-3-81	At London	3K	6th	7:56.90	-:02.79		Steve Ovett
6-7-81	At Gateshead, England	5K	8th	13:32.60	-:11.46		Barry Smith
6-20-81	USA-Mobil Nationals at Sacramento, CA	5K	2nd	13:31.64	-:02.42		Matt Centrowitz
6-24-81	Sport 2000 at Paris	5K	4th	13:24.83	-03.73		Suleiman Nyambui
6-26-81	Bislett Games at Oslo, Norway	5K	3rd	13:25.73	-:06.34		Bill McChesney
7-4-81	Peachtree Road Race at Atlanta, GA	10K	1st	28:03.4	:07.0	American Record	Rod Dixon
7-8-81	At Milan, Italy	5K	7th	14:06.69	-:39.49		Alberto Cova
7-18-81	Kids Run at Kirkwood, MO	5.5M	1st	27:25	:56.0		Steve Baker
7-27-81	National Sports Festival at Syracuse, NY	5K	1st	13:35.4	:02.8	Meet Record	Alberto Salazar
8-1-81	At Maggie Valley, NC	5M	4th	22:59.5	-:17.0		Rod Dixon
8-5-81	At Long Island, NY Road Race	4M		23:06			
8-16-81	At Falmouth, MA	7.1M	5th	32:50	-:55		Alberto Salazar
8-30-81	Diet Pepsi at Seattle	10K	1st	29:30.6		Course Record	
9-12-81	At Arcola, IL	10K	1st	30:38	1:00		Tom Condit
9-13-81	St. Jude Road Race at Peoria, IL	10K	1st	29:13	:17		John Wellerding
10-3-81	Lebanon Fall Festival Footrace	4M		26:00-plus			
10-4-81	Pepsi Challenge at Purchase, NY	10K	38th	38:00+	-9:16	(jogged)	Rob de Castella
10-31-81	At Dallas Dash	10K	1st	30:03	:18.0		Manfred Kohrs
11-21-81	At LaGrange, GA Road Race	10K	1st	30:36			
11-28-81	At Rock Island, IL	8M	2nd	38:38			Tony Sandoval
12-19-81	Bran Chex/YMCA at San Antonio, TX	10K	1st	29:35.1			
1-31-82	Bran Chex/YMCA at Clearwater, FL	10K	1st	29:06.2	1:04.9	Course Record	Chris Sly
2-6-82	Gasparilla at Tampa, FL	15K	9th	44:13	-1:05	Personal Record	Mike Musyoki
2-15-82	World Cross Country Trials at Pocatello, ID	12K	3rd	37:09.0	-16.6		Alberto Salazar
2-27-82	Illini Classic at Champaign	3M	1st	13:13.85		Armory Record	
3-6-82	Bran Chex Road Race at New Orleans	10K	1st	33:32			
4-10-82	Bran Chex Road Race at Memphis, TN	10K	tie 1st	32:19.2			
5-1-82	Bran Chex Road Race at Cleveland	10K	2nd	29:51.8	-:18.7		Ted Rupe
6-12-82	Kinney Classic at Berkeley, CA	2M	8th	8:47.6	-:24.0		Doug Padilla
6-25-82	TAC Nationals at Knoxville, TN	10K	1st	28:33.02	:00.56		Steve Ortiz
7-4-82	Peachtree Road Race at Atlanta, GA	10K	6th	28:47.9	-:31.9		Jon Sinclair
7-24/25-82	Sports Festival at Indianapolis	5K	3rd	13:35.88	-:02.47		Jim Spivey
8-7-82	At Maggie Valley, NC	5M	1st	22:46.9	:01.1		Mike Musyoki
8-15-82	At Falmouth, MA	7.1M	2nd	32:12.3	-:19.0		Alberto Salazar
8-20-82	At Berlin, West Germany	3K	3rd	7:56.10	-:10.55		Bill McChesney
8-22-82	At Cologne, West Germany	3K	7th	7:55.96	-:16.62		Thomas Wessinghage
8-27-82	At Brussels, Belgium	10K	2nd	28:07.88	-:17.06		Bill McChesney
9-11-82	Alumni Cross Country at Savoy	5K	1st	14:35.7			Mike Patton
9-26-82	At Chicago Marathon	26.2M	16th	2:17:29	-6:30.0		Greg Meyer
10-2-82	Lebanon Fall Festival Footrace	4M	1st	19:53	:49.0		Bobby Williams
11-27-82	At Gateshead, England	12K	10th	38:12	-:23		David Lewis
12-9-82	Diamond Head Duet at Honolulu, HI	4.6M	1st	21:45			
1-?-83	Bran Chex/YMCA at Clearwater, FL	10K	1st	29:31.6	2:29.4		
1-15-83	Race of the Americas at Miami	10K	10th	28:54.8	-:52.8		Alberto Salazar
1-30-83	Galtee Grange Int. CC at Fermoy, Ireland	10K	6th	33:10	-:29.0		Leon Schots
2-5-83	Gasparilla at Tampa, FL	15K	8th	43:56	-1:09	Personal Record	Rob de Castella
2-20-83	World CC Trials at Edwardsville, IL	12K	2nd	36:50	-:17.0		Alberto Salazar
3-6-83	Continental Homes at Phoenix, AZ	10K	17th	29:13	-1:12.0		Alberto Salazar
3-20-83	World Cross Country at Gateshead	11.99K	42nd	38:06	-1:14.0		Bekele Debele
3-27-83	Crescent City Classic at New Orleans	10K	8th	28:37	-:16.0		Gidamas Shahanga

Date	Meet/Location	Distance	Place	Time	Margin	Record	Winner or runner-up
5-1-83	Trevira Twosome at New York City	10M	3rd	47:36	-:29.0		Geoff Smith
5-8-83	Rock N Run at Los Angeles	10K	4th	28:14	-:06.0		Paul Cummings
5-15-83	Bay-to-Breakers at San Francisco	7.63M	3rd	35:15.0	-:13.7		Rod Dixon
5-28-83	Meet of Champions at Houston	5K	2nd	13:55.16	-:03.82		Yobes Ondieki
6-18-83	TAC Nationals at Indianapolis	10K	2nd	28:13.06	-:02.78		Alberto Salazar
7-4-83	Peachtree Road Race at Atlanta, GA	10K	6th	29:08	-:46.0		Mike Musyoki
7-22-83	All-Comers Meet at Eugene, OR	10K	DNF				
7-30-83	At Maggie Valley, NC	5M	6th	23:24	-:27.0		Mike Musyoki
9-10-83	At Arcola, IL	10K	2nd	32:24	-1:04.0		Craig Young
9-17-83	Alumni Cross Country at Savoy	4M	4th	20:54	-:17.5		Mike Patton
10-1-83	Lebanon Fall Festival Footrace	4M	22nd	24:17	-4:17.0		Mike Moore
10-2-83	Bacardi Rum Run at Miami	5M	1st	24:09	1:00.0		Bob Dugan
10-29-83	At Dallas Dash	10K	1st	29:13	:25.8		Mike Novelli
11-20-83	At East Rutherford, NJ Cross Country	12K	1st	34:46	<2:00		
12-3-83	Capital City Classic at Jefferson City, MO	10K	1st	30:18			
12-10-83	Back Bay Road Race at Los Angeles	8K	8th	22:48	-:20.0		Gidamas Shahanga
1-7-84	Red Lobster Road Race at Longwood, FL	15K	1st	44:28	1:04.0		John Tuttle
1-15-84	At New York City	6M	1st	29:16			Tim Hassal
1-29-84	Runner's Den at Phoenix, AZ	10K	3rd	28:33.5	-:01.5		Markus Ryffel
2-4-84	Orange Bowl Road Race at Miami	10K	12th	29:28.22	-:54.53		John Gregorek
2-19-84	World CC Relays at E. Rutherford, NJ	12K	3rd	35:18	-:31.0		Pat Porter
3-3-84	Continental Homes at Phoenix, AZ	10K	15th	28:53	-1:10.0		Zachariah Barie
3-25-84	World Cross Country at E. Rutherford, NJ	7.3M	17th	34:07	-:42.0		Carlos Lopes
4-1-84	Crescent City Classic at New Orleans	10K	10th	28:38	-1:15.3		Mark Nenow
4-21-84	1040K Road Race at Atlanta, GA	10K		39:20			Ran for fun
4-28-84	Mount SAC Relays at Walnut, CA	5K	23rd	13:48.0	-:17.33		Todd Harbour
5-4-84	Oregon Relays at Eugene, OR	10K	2nd	28:13.02	-:01.30		Paul McCloy
5-12-84	At Bloomington, IL Road Race	5M	1st	23:24			
5-18-84	Gatorade Classic at Knoxville, TN	5K	8th	13:40.65	-:09.45		Ray Flynn
5-26-84	Hills Family Road Race at Nashville, TN	10K	1st	29:59.1	1:38.1		Jon Barker
5-31-84	At Boston	5K	2nd	14:02	-:23.0		Bruce Bickford
6-16-84	Olympic Trials at Los Angeles	10K prelim	1st	28:19.59	:00.04		Paul Cummings
6-19-84	Olympic Trials at Los Angeles	10K	2nd	28:02.27	-:03.19		Paul Cummings
6-21-84	Olympic Trials at Los Angeles	5K 1st round	3rd	13:50.62	-:02.28		Ross Donoghue
6-22-84	Olympic Trials at Los Angeles	5K semifinal	6th	13:40.30	-:05.08		Don Clary
6-24-84	Olympic Trials at Los Angeles	5K	8th	13:41.63	-:15.29		Doug Padilla
7-4-84	Peachtree Road Race at Atlanta, GA	10K	4th	29:02	-:27.0		Filbert Bayi
7-14-84	Kinney Race at Berkeley, CA	3K	2nd	7:59.0	-:01.7		Doug Padilla
7-21-84	Prefontaine Classic at Eugene, OR	5K	7th	13:54.5			
8-3-84	Olympic Games at Los Angeles	10K prelim	9th	28:37.58	-:15.71		Fernando Mamede
8-18-84	At Maggie Valley, NC	8K	11th	23:52.7	-1:09		Nick Rose
9-8-84	Alumni Cross Country at Savoy	4M	1st	19:32	:32.0		Ty Wolf
1-12-85	Red Lobster Road Race at Orlando, FL	15K	5th	46:04	-1:35.0		John Tuttle
2-16-85	World Cross Country Trials at Waco, TX	12K	5th	37:03	-:32.0		Ed Eyestone
3-9-85	At Jacksonville, FL River Run	15K	6th	44:45	-1:28		Simeon Kigen
3-24-85	World Cross Country at Lisbon, Portugal	12.19K	19th	34:12	-:39.0		Carlos Lopes
3-31-85	Crescent City Classic at New Orleans	10K	8th	29:02	-:45.0		Carlos Lopes
4-20-85	1040K Road Race at Atlanta, GA	10K	1st	29:38	:25.0	Course Record	Arega Abraha
4-21-85	MLK Jr. Freedom Games at Atlanta, GA	5K	2nd	13:58.59	-:02.48		Jim Cooper
4-27-85	Trevira Twosome at New York City	10M	2nd	47:33	-:15.0		Dave Murphy
5-5-85	IAC City Centre Series at Glasgow	10K	8th	28:24	-:15.0		Dave Clarke
5-12-85	IAC City Centre Series at Cardiff, Wales	10K	10th	27:59	-:17.0	Personal Record	Eamann Martin
6-2-85	IAC City Centre Series at London	10K	10th	28:51			Fernando Mamede
6-15-85	TAC Nationals at Indianapolis	10K	9th	28:49.91	-:49.81		Bruce Bickford
7-4-85	Peachtree Road Race at Atlanta, GA	10K	18th	29:15.19	-1:07.19		Mike Musyoki
8-10-85	At Asbury Park, NJ	10K	46th	30:36	-1:57.0		Keith Brantly
8-24-85	At Maggie Valley, NC	8K	5th	23:03.3	-:20.2		Dave Murphy
9-7-85	Alumni Cross Country at Champaign	4M	1st	19:47	:31.0		David Halle

Date	Meet/Location	Distance	Place	Time	Margin	Record	Winner or runner-up
9-21-85	Berry College CC Inv. at Rome, GA	5M	1st	24:25.4	:29.0	Course Record	Roger Jones
10-2-85	Man. Hanover Challenge at Atlanta, GA	3.5M	1st	15:49	:38.0		John Barbour
10-6-85	Octoberfast at Itasca, IL	12K	2nd	34:28	-:06		Rob de Castella
10-12-85	Stroh's Run for Liberty at Atlanta, GA	8K	1st	23:46	>1:00		Mike Kominsky
10-19-85	Peachtree City 15K at Atlanta, GA	15K	1st	46:35.0	3:35.0	State Record	Sean Kelly
10-26-85	At Tulsa, OK Road Race	15K	2nd	43:44	-:14.0	Personal Record	Marcos Barreto
11-9-85	Wendy's Road Race at Bowling Green, KY	10K	3rd	28:41	-:12.0		Keith Brantley
11-30-85	TAC Cross Country at Raleigh, NC	10K	14th	31:44.5	-:11.4		Pat Porter
1-4-86	At Charlotte, NC Observer	10K	2nd	28:56	-:01		Jim Cooper
1-11-86	Red Lobster Road Race at Orlando, FL	15K	1st	44:05	:07.0	Course Record	John Tuttle
2-1-86	Orange Bowl Road Race at Miami	10K	10th	28:48	-:28.0		Peter Koech
2-8-86	Gasparilla at Tampa, FL	5K	1st	14:11	:56.0		Kiernan Boyle
2-15-86	World Cross Country Trials at Waco, TX	12K	5th	35:32.81	-:25.32		Pat Porter
2-23-86	At Williamsburg, VA	Half Mar.	102nd	1:23:51			
3-1-86	Set the Pace Classic at Rockledge, FL	5K	1st	14:13	:48.0		Fred Klinge
3-8-86	At Jacksonville, FL River Run	15K	8th	44:09	-:51.0		Arturo Barrios
3-16-86	Lakeside Hospital Scrub at New Orleans	5K	1st	14:05		CR; Road PR	
3-23-86	World Cross Country at Neuchatel, Switz.	12K	81st	37:26.4	-1:53.5		John Ngugi
4-5-86	Crescent City Classic at New Orleans	10K	14th	29:11	-:55.0		Arturo Barrios
4-12-86	At Ellaville, GA	5M	1st	24:41			
7-4-86	Peachtree Road Race at Atlanta, GA	10K	87th	31:29	-3:33.0		John Doherty
8-17-86	Presidential Challenge at Chicago	5K	1st	14:48	:30.0		Rolf Craven
8-23-86	At Maggie Valley, NC	8K	22nd	24:27	-2:06.0		Mike Musyoki
9-6-86	Alumni Cross Country at Champaign	5K	4th	14:51	-:10.9		Jeff Jacobs
1-31-87	Orange Bowl Road Race at Miami	10K	22nd	30:26.88	-1:27.11		Mauricio Gonzalez
4-4-87	Crescent City Classic at New Orleans	10K	25th	29:21	-1:22		John Treacy
5-9-87	Griffin Invitational at Atlanta, GA	5K	2nd	14:08.89	-:08.80		Herman Beltrand
5-22-87	Gatorade Classic at Knoxville, TN	10K	1st	29:29.05	:03.44		Chris Pryor
5-30-87	Cellular One 8K at Chattanooga, TN	8K	2nd				Ashley Johnson
6-13-87	N.England Ath. Congress at Needham, MA	5K	9th	13:49.1	:17.3		Sydney Maree
6-25-87	USA-Mobil Nationals at San Jose, CA	10K	12th	29:03.4	:28.3		Gerard Donakowski
7-4-87	Peachtree Road Race at Atlanta, GA	10K	27th	29:48	-1:14.0		Joseph Nzau
7-18-87	Buffalo, NY Suburu 4-Mile Classic	4M	1st	18:26	:10	Course Record	John Tuttle
7-26-87	U.S. Olympic Festival at Durham, NC	5K	4th	13:57.32	-:09.60		Keith Brantly
8-8-87	Dilworth Jubilee at Charlotte, NC	8K	1st	24:15	:02.0		Bill Will
9-12-87	Alumni Cross Country at Champaign	5K	3rd	15:05			Jeff Jacobs
12-5-87	Chieftains Road Race at Rome, GA	10K	1st	30:40	:29.0	Course Record	Alan Drosky
1-2-88	At Charlotte, NC Observer	10K	9th	30:12	-:57.0		Vince Draddy
1-23-88	At Freeport, Bahamas	10K	6th	29:33			
2-6-88	Red Lobster Road Race at Orlando, FL	10K	39th	30:15	-1:57.0		Paul Davies-Hale
2-13-88	World Cross Country Trials at Dallas	12K	6th	38:47	-:24.0		George Nicholas
2-28-88	At Raleigh, NC Trail Race	10K		31:11			
3-5-88	At Jacksonville (FL) River Run	15K	19th	44:58	-1:38.0		Steve Spence
3-26-88	World Cross Country at Auckland, NZ	12K	102nd	37:40	-3:08.0		John Ngugi
4-9-88	Peoplechase 5K at Rocky Mount, NC	5K	2nd	14:43	-:01.0		Bernie Prabucki
4-16-88	Crescent City Classic at New Orleans	10K	17th	29:38	-1:44.0		Matthews Motshwarateu
6-11-88	At Abbotsford, BC	10K		29:27	-:30.04		
8-?-88	Alumni Cross Country at Mahomet	5K	2nd	15:18	-:02.0		Chris Inch
8-?-89	Alumni Cross Country at Champaign	5K	1st	14:37	:03.0		Neal Gassmann
7-28-90	Run for Life at Marietta, GA	5K	2nd	14:13.19	-8.75		Tim Gargiulo
10-30-90	Alumni Cross Country at Savoy	8K	1st	23:47	:08.0		Terrance Mahon
2-2-91	World CC Trials at Tallahassee, FL	12K	17th	36:03	-1:16.0		Aaron Ramirez